CADBURY CASTLE
The Hillfort and Landscapes

CADBURY CASTLE
The Hillfort and Landscapes

Richard Tabor

Front cover photograph of Cadbury Castle from Sigwells by Jim Easthaugh

First published 2008

The History Press
The Mill, Brimscombe Port,
Stroud, Gloucestershire, GL5 2QG
www.thehistorypress.com

© Richard Tabor, 2008

The right of Richard Tabor, to be identified as the Author of this work has been asserted in accordance with the Copyrights, Designs and Patents Act 1988.

All rights reserved. No part of this book may be reprinted or reproduced or utilised in any form or by any electronic, mechanical or other means, now known or hereafter invented, including photocopying and recording, or in any information storage or retrieval system, without the permission in writing from the Publishers.

British Library Cataloguing in Publication Data.
A catalogue record for this book is available from the British Library.

ISBN 978 0 7524 4715 5

Printed in Great Britain

CONTENTS

	Acknowledgements	7
	Preface	10
1	Introduction	13
	Research into hillforts and their hinterlands	15
	Cadbury Castle's physical setting	17
	Research on and around Cadbury Castle	19
2	The South Cadbury Environs Project	23
	Objectives	26
	Sampling issues	27
	Technique selection	31
	The South Cadbury strategy	34
	The SCEP chronology	39
3	First transformations	40
	Neolithic	41
	Early Bronze Age	47
	Middle Bronze Age	54
	The quiet centuries?	69
4	A central place	73
	Dating in the first millennium BC	74
	Late Bronze Age	77
	Early Iron Age	100

	Middle Iron Age	112
	Late Iron Age	147
5	Slaughter, imperialism and resurgence	156
	AD 43 to AD 70	156
	AD 70 to AD 450	164
	AD 450 to AD 900	167
	From Ethelred to Arthur	174
6	Continuity, rupture and the future	177
	Directions for hillfort and landscape studies	180
	Appendix: Maps	183
	Glossary	185
	Further reading	186
	Index	187

ACKNOWLEDGEMENTS

The greater part of the book is concerned with the results of the survey and excavations carried out by the South Cadbury Environs Project from December 1992 until July 2007. This would not have been possible without the cooperation and, in some cases the active support, of landowners, tenant farmers and their staff. Special thanks are due to Archie, James and Elizabeth Montgomery and to Brian Green, who have tolerated prolonged and intermittent investigation of their fields for over a decade. I have been struck by the consistently helpful response of nearly all the landowners I have approached, so the project is indebted to Royston Amor, Michael Bishop, Jack Castleman, Justin Crawford, Richard Creed, Mr Good, Richard Hickman, Terry Holly, Jennifer Hunt, John Kerton, William Salomon, Jonathon Sprake, John Stretton, James Tabor and Richard Tyley.

The project would never have happened if Philip Freeman had not suggested that I should set it up during an evening of slight inebriation in 1992, but its roots and trunk were provided by Paul Johnson, who travelled from the University of Glasgow to provide free professional labour as an excavation director and geophysical survey practitioner and teacher for one to three weeks in every year from December 1992 until 1999. He had a huge influence over my choice of methodology but, above all, was a great moral support in the early days. At around the same time, Jim Eastaugh responded to my request for help by rallying the members of the South East Somerset Archaeological Society to support the survey work and to help set up the infrastructure for processing finds. It is my great regret that many of the stalwarts who provided the foundations for the fully funded project have not lived to see the results of their work.

I am grateful to Peter Leach who added a new dimension to the project by instigating the first training excavations at Sigwells in 1994, which in turn led to my enrolment as a PhD student at the University of Birmingham. Of the staff there I am particularly indebted to Vince Gaffney. The report of his work at Maddle

Farm and discussions with him led me to rethink archaeological survey methodology. Vince also suggested that Mark Corney should take an interest and he must take the greatest credit for the first successful application to the Leverhulme Trust which enabled the University of Bristol to employ me as a full-time research fellow working exclusively on the project. Mark has been a continuing support behind the scenes through the advice he has offered Giles Cooper concerning Roman pottery. Since 2001 Mark's co-applicant, Michael Costen, has been a staunch supporter, taking an interest, offering wise advice and quietly sorting out any administration problems with a minimum of fuss. Last year he was the volunteers' choice for the project's patron. Since his retirement, Josh Pollard and Naomi Baker have continued to provide support from the Department of Archaeology and Anthropology. I am also very grateful to Alistair Pike for guiding students in this direction for dissertation topics and to Stuart Prior for encouraging landscape archaeology postgraduate students to do placements at South Cadbury. They have proved a very valuable resource. Gary Lock of the Institute of Archaeology, Oxford, made the project's continuation possible by agreeing to head the successful application for a further four years' funding from the Arts and Humanities Research Council and providing quietly good-humoured support during that time. A quiet but very valuable supporter has been Steve Minnitt, curator of Somerset County Museum. He has helped greatly with storage, and has given research access to Cadbury Castle and other material.

Over the years the project has benefited from the work of many excellent students from the Universities of Glasgow, Birmingham and Bristol as well as those from placements elsewhere and it would be invidious to name any particular individuals. However, Chris Hooper overran his due placement by several months and his contribution over three years proved hugely valuable in all areas of work, including supervision. He deserves great credit for ensuring that we kept to our fieldwork schedule.

The cornerstone of the project has been its regular volunteer base. Immense gratitude is due to the many occasional volunteers over the years but it would be improper not to thank by name those who have kept coming for one or more days, week in, week out, for several years: Duncan Black, Liz Caldwell, Mary Claridge, Giles Cooper, Tony Dickinson, Pam Gait, Nigel Harvey, Derek Jackson, Clare Randall, Shirley Ryan, Neil Tinkley, Del Wiggins, Roland Williams and Peter Wright, most of whom are still involved. Over the past year Nigel has assumed responsibility for the continuity and supervision of post-excavation work and without him I would not have been free to complete this and other publications on schedule. Giles deserves a very warm special mention as the longest serving volunteer (since 1995), for taking on the documentary work for which I had no time and for assuming complete responsibility for Romano-British pottery analysis,

Acknowledgements

much to my personal relief. He also provided major input into John Davey's PhD and its subsequent published version. The choices of Liz and Clare as paid staff are measures of their value to the project, but Clare can be said to have added new dimensions through her knowledge, clarity of thought, organisational skills, ability to network and sheer energy. She has also made many thought-provoking suggestions which have informed this book. Through Clare I have also benefitted from current research by Susan Watts and Susan Jones into quern and human bone deposits respectively. Roland, Tony and Peter have also made very helpful corrections and comments although they will be relieved to know that errors and opinions ventured in the text are my own!

Important sections of this book necessarily draw on analysis and interpretation of Leslie Alcock's excavations on Cadbury Castle and due credit should go to the authors and contributors including Leslie Alcock, John Barrett, Philip Freeman, Chris Musson and Ann Woodward. In a similar vein, John Davey deserves mention for his contribution to debate respecting Cadbury's Early Mediaeval archaeology. Direct contributions in the form of artefact drawings have been provided by Colette Maxfield, Joleen O'Neill and Amanda Tabor. Mandy has also been an invaluable support in creating reconstructions of past events and landscapes, a discursive process which has shaped the written narrative. All other images are by the author excepting those individually referenced.

This book is dedicated to the memory of my mentor, Leslie Alcock, and to the great discovery of 1985 and subsequent remarkable finds of 1989, 1991 and 1997 (no, not the shield!).

PREFACE

There are brief records in Somerset's archaeological proceedings of excavations by the Revd Bennett and Harold St George Gray (of Glastonbury Lake Village fame) from the later nineteenth and early twentieth centuries at Cadbury Castle but these entries are mere footnotes compared with the data amassed from the then largest exploration in Europe of a hillfort's interior, from 1966-70. Led by Leslie Alcock, these campaigns made international news and within two years of completing the work he had published an excellent popular account of his findings, in which he stressed that a final report should follow soon. Sadly this did not happen. An important contribution to Iron Age pottery studies appeared as a paper in 1980, shaped by further excavation of an open rampart section in 1973, but the culminating English Heritage volume did not appear until 2000, when the three main authors struggled to make sense of an old and fragmentary archive. The inadequacies of this final account were rendered more acute by the exemplary publication in the same year of Professor Barry Cunliffe's work on the landscape around Danebury, Hampshire, several years after the comprehensive report on excavations of that hillfort, which had begun in 1969.

The Danebury Environs Project brought an entirely new perspective to hillfort studies. Since 1992 Cadbury has been the centre of its own landscape survey, the South Cadbury Environs Project (the acronym SCEP is used throughout the rest of this book), following on from another at Maiden Castle, Dorset, carried out in the mid 1980s. It was recognised that a massive undertaking such as a hillfort would have required substantial resources from beyond its ramparts, both during its construction and while it was settled. In the 1970s Cunliffe had postulated that there would have been a farmstead at roughly every kilometre around the perimeter but could not find the evidence for this. Instead, by 2000, he reached the conclusion that there had been no settlement within nearly a 10km (6.2 miles) radius of a highly nucleated Danebury population which would have travelled out to the

Middle Iron Age field systems serving them. A similar lack of Middle Iron Age material from the area around Maiden Castle suggested that this might be a pattern typical for the period. SCEP's findings are at odds with this view and for this reason the project's methodology is outlined.

In Chapter two I have presented an account of the evolution of SCEP from haphazard data collection in the early 1990s to a well-conceived but unfunded programme of research in the mid to late 1990s, to a period of fulfillment from 2001 to 2007, when first the Leverhulme Trust and then the Arts and Humanities Research Council provided major funding. On one level the project's development may prove an inspiration to amateur archaeologists or professionals wanting to instigate their own research. On another level the techniques eventually embraced by this project, and the reasons for that choice, offer a daunting model of labour-intensive work for rich rewards. I would argue further that what follows will demonstrate that any programme of landscape survey targeting pre-Mediaeval periods should use the South Cadbury method or something which improves upon it.

Chapters three to five present the project's findings in a period sequence extending from the Early Neolithic to the present. Prehistory receives the most attention, reflecting the project's principal research objectives. The final chapter considers future avenues for hillfort and landscape research in view of the findings of SCEP, using a very particular methodology. It also considers key themes which have proved of particular importance to the project.

The chief sources of information about Cadbury Castle are Leslie Alcock's books and papers and the book by John Barrett, Philip Freeman and Ann Woodward, all coloured by my own experiences of digging on the hill as a boy and by my subsequent work in its surrounding landscape. The information about that landscape is almost exclusively derived from the innovative work of SCEP, much of it by dedicated volunteers who have participated regularly for one or two days a week over many years, creating a warm sense of community in labour. The detailed analysis of Romano-British pottery was undertaken by Giles Cooper, and Clare Randall's analysis of the environmental data is a major plank in understanding the evolving economies over the long period treated by this book.

Finally a caveat. SCEP *sampled* its target landscape. The finds distribution maps in the period sections of Chapters three to five reflect the findings of mainly 1:10,000 samples, within roughly 20 per cent of 11 sqkm of the surface area, within a 64 sqkm study area! I cannot claim that our findings represent more than a small portion of the evidence which remains in the soil, although they give great insight into its character and extent. Readers should refer to two maps at the back of the book showing the locations of the project's test pits (*99*) and geophysical survey (*100*) to be aware of the inherent spatial bias. The second map shows key place and fieldnames used in the text. There are other inherent problems in using these maps for interpretation: they depict patterns of artefact loss and subsequent movement over variable lengths of time, sometimes several centuries, often during periods where 'settlement sites' may have been fairly ephemeral. Let the reader beware!

I

INTRODUCTION

Do hillforts exist? The question may seem absurd in the face of the massive physical presences of the largest and most frequently surviving prehistoric phenomena in northern Europe, but in recent decades it has been asked. Before addressing the issue it will be helpful to narrow the frame of reference. There are univallate (single bank and ditch) enclosures from the Middle Bronze Age through to the Early Iron Age which are simply too large to have been defensible by the population in or, more likely, around them. It may well have been that they served as seasonal places of meeting for several communities, where craft production took place, goods and animals were exchanged and marriage alliances were made. If we go back to the Early Neolithic, although scale is not a problem, it is probably reasonable to remove the category of causewayed enclosure from the debate, despite unambiguous evidence from one of three at Hambledon Hill, Dorset, that it was the scene of a violent episode. The ditches inside the bank would have been more of an obstacle to defenders than putative attackers.

This still leaves a substantial number of smaller univallate and, in particular, multivallate hilltop enclosures, of which Cadbury Castle is one. Some prehistorians prefer to view the latter as symbols of status and power in the landscape, not forts at all. Others, myself included, see their foremost role as the provision of security for particular groups of people, sometimes over two or more centuries. The distinction has crucial implications: if defence was the purpose, each of these massive undertakings would necessarily have been conceived and executed in a fairly short span of time, perhaps two or three years. This in turn would imply the availability of a substantial labour force. Alternatively, if symbolic authority was the issue, a much longer period of construction, such as the decades taken by some Mediaeval cathedrals, might even add to the prestige of the project, providing a monument to institutional or dynastic continuity. In either case the sheer number of hillforts (*1*) raises many issues about population and social organisation in the Middle Iron Age.

Cadbury Castle: The Hillfort and Landscapes

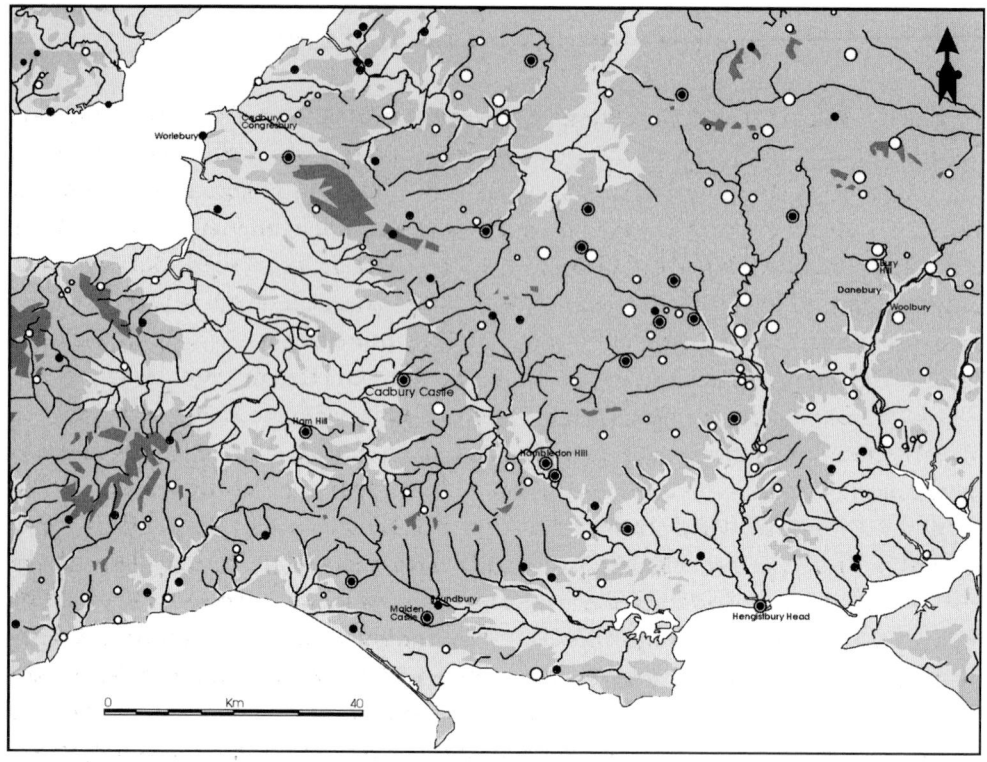

1 Hilltop enclosures in central southern Britain

Standing on a hillfort you can feel insulated from the surrounding landscape by the massive defences. This would have seemed the more so in the Middle Iron Age when, even on the highest point, a person's view was restricted by houses and fences, whilst in the lee of the inner ramparts it would have been impossible to see outside at all. There would have been an illusion of self-sufficiency: dwelling space, animals in pens, areas for textile manufacture and metalworking, and an abundance of grain stored above and below ground. Yet the moment our Iron Age subject mounted the platform on top of the rampart and walked its circuit, the view would have been of the landscape which produced the animals and grain, and the nearer settlements of those who worked it. He or she might then contemplate the origins of more exotic materials and goods. Conversely, while many hillforts stand proud of a lower surrounding landscape, Cadbury is overlooked from the south and east, and afforded a stage for the drama of its interior life to an approaching visitor. In fact the very physique of hillforts is the most substantial proof of the flux of ideas not only overland but also across the sea. Although central southern Britain is the area with the greatest density of hillforts, particularly the multivallate or developed variety, they also occur in a variety of forms in northern Europe, sometimes corresponding well with their British counterparts.

Introduction

RESEARCH INTO HILLFORTS AND THEIR HINTERLANDS

Cadbury Castle has been something of a barometer of academic interest in hillforts for four and a half centuries. Its dramatic ramparts and ditches, as well as its seemingly inexhaustible capacity to enrich the local population with Roman coinage, were first mentioned in 1542 by John Leland, a man who assumed for himself the status of King's Antiquary to Henry VIII. It was visited and described in succeeding centuries by several important antiquaries, all of whom accepted the then prevailing view that hillforts were far too impressive to have been built by anyone other than the Romans, until in the late nineteenth century, when the Revd J.A. Bennett, a former vicar of South Cadbury, dug a trench through the inner rampart and recovered pottery produced by a 'rude race'. His observations were commensurate with a sea change in hillfort studies which had begun when, starting in 1851, the Revd Francis Warre used volunteer help to dig a remarkable total of 93 Iron Age pits at Worlebury, near Weston-super-Mare. Col. Augustus Lane Fox (better known as one of the founders of scientific archaeology, General Pitt Rivers, the name he took to accede to the family estate on Cranborne Chase, Dorset) was most notable among those informed by Warre's findings. As a man who had made a study of the historical development of firearms, with a view to improving the weaponry of the British army, and with a deep interest in ethnography, he was particularly susceptible to the 'Three Age' archaeology (Stone, Bronze and Iron Ages) first proposed by the Dane, Christian Thompsen. By the late 1860s he was willing to express the view that hillforts were more probably the natural result of pre-civilised (in other words, pre-Roman) inter-tribal hostility. A decade later, the material recovered from campaigns on hillforts in Sussex and Kent led him to the opinion that whilst most hillforts were at least occupied during the Iron Age there were examples of both earlier and later foundations.

On assuming his inheritance, Pitt Rivers increasingly turned his attention to the earlier archaeology on his new estate, leaving hillforts to less rigorous amateurs. Maud Cunnington was the first of several enthusiastic part-time archaeologists to dig and record trenches through the ramparts of a growing number of Wessex hillforts in the early decades of the twentieth century. The prolific activity amassed a wealth of diverse data out of which emerged an overarching pattern when a member of staff at the British Museum, Christopher Hawkes, compared it with material from northern Europe, some of which displayed analogous form and decoration. He conceived of waves of invasions from the continent during the sixth to the earlier first centuries BC, giving rise to distinct material cultural phases which he named as Iron Age A, B and C. This model dominated British Iron Age studies until the mid 1960s and was the general paradigm which Sir Mortimer Wheeler brought to his unprecedented scale of investigation into the interior of Maiden

Castle, Dorset, from 1934-7, finding unequivocal evidence that it had been a centre of dense and continuous settlement for several hundred years. During this period he turned his attention firstly to other nearby Dorset hillforts and then to France, his work eventually overtaken by the outbreak of the Second World War.

Hawkes' model began to whither in the early 1960s when Roy (F.R.) Hodson made well-founded assertions that Iron Age Britain's material culture was best explained in terms of largely indigenous evolution. Wheeler's legacy of large-scale, well-executed investigations of hillfort interiors and defences still informed the technical approach of a decade-long series of excavations along the Welsh Borders by Stan Stanford, but the rethinking of the problems to be addressed revealed consistent patterns of spatial organisation and material culture demonstrating a complex system of interaction, including exchange between hillfort communities. Leslie Alcock's work at Cadbury Castle played its part in this period of change which will be discussed in the following section, but it is Barry Cunliffe's modelling and testing of hypotheses which revolutionised the discipline through his own 20-year programme of excavations at Danebury, his reassessment of earlier excavations in the region by Hawkes and others, and the subsequent Danebury Environs Project.

In 1971, two years after the excavations at Danebury had started, Cunliffe produced a paper exploring hillfort catchment areas, giving consideration to the conditions which might have brought them into being. He identified five possible pre-hillfort categories: 1) settlement sites, 2) religious foci, 3) focal position in relation to ranch boundaries, 4) pastoral enclosures, and 5) plateau enclosures used as tribal or religious meeting places or for seasonal large-scale herding. He then explored the conditions under which these already significant hills and others might be transformed into hillforts. He envisaged a situation in which agriculture had become more productive, stimulating a growth in population. This led to more competition for favourable land resources and the centralisation of coercive power. The latter would lead in turn to the redistribution of land, as loosely affiliated groups merged into single tribal identities, with more strongly defined territories represented by the limits of their grazing areas. The resulting tensions between territorial groups would have led to warfare and the need for more secure defences, eventually realised in univallate and ultimately 'developed', multivallate, hillforts.

It had always been Cunliffe's intention to understand Danebury within its wider landscape and the essential foundation for that was Rog Palmer's seminal interpretation of an extensive aerial photographic archive collated from military flights in the early twentieth century (many by the technique's great pioneer, O.G.S. Crawford) right up to the 1970s. Palmer created maps of the monuments of the Neolithic, Bronze Age, Iron Age and Romano-British landscapes, necessarily crude but of enormous value for the way in which they showed how long linear (coaxial) ditches became the basis for extensive field systems in the Iron Age. The hypothetical maps enabled Cunliffe to identify key points in the structure of the prehistoric landscape for investigation through a combination of geophysical survey and excavation from 1989-96. More discussion of the Danebury approach will be included in the rationale for SCEP strategy below.

The results from 28 years of fieldwork on and around Danebury form the benchmark against which modern developments in Iron Age studies must be measured. Cunliffe felt able to make assertions about land use and internal social interaction and production, short- and long-range trade, territory and tension. Specifically, he identified the apportionment of the landscape within linear boundaries, the development of fields around them, and the early enclosure of hilltops during the latter second and early first millennia BC, giving way to the construction of the developed hillforts in the third quarter of the first millennium BC, when Danebury itself becomes pre-eminent in its region. He asserts that during its Middle Iron Age zenith habitative settlement appears to have been exclusive to Danebury within a nearly 10km (6 miles) radius around it. He notes that at around the time of Danebury's decline in the earlier first century BC, a new defensively restructured hillfort may have housed an elite which eventually gained ascendancy over its neighbour, 6km (4 miles) to the south.

Research since 1996 includes the exclusively geophysical investigation of 20 hillforts by English Heritage's Wessex Hillforts Survey Project, and Chris Gosden's and Gary Lock's Hillforts of the Ridgeway Project, using geophysical survey and excavation to explore three hillforts and their landscapes. The survey conducted around Maiden Castle in 1985 will be discussed below.

CADBURY CASTLE'S PHYSICAL SETTING

The particular fortune of Cadbury Castle was to be at the intersection of two faults, creating a weakness in the surrounding geology which brought about its sharp separation from a ridge to its south and east. A multivallate hillfort in the neck of Britain's south west peninsula (*2*), the most spectacular views of it are to be had from Sigwells, the top of the escarpment overlooking it from the south-east (*colour plate 1*). The tonsured plateau forms a dome above a late eighteenth-century plantation of mixed woodland, covering much of the earthworks rising above sharply defined Mediaeval contour lynchets. The hilltop is surrounded by four massive ramparts and ditches, all breached by passages through the defences from the north-east, east and south-west, with an inner bank length of around 1.2km (three quarters of a mile) enclosing approximately 8ha (20 acres). The interior comprises a small high plateau of 153m ASL (502ft), dipping moderately towards

Cadbury Castle: The Hillfort and Landscapes

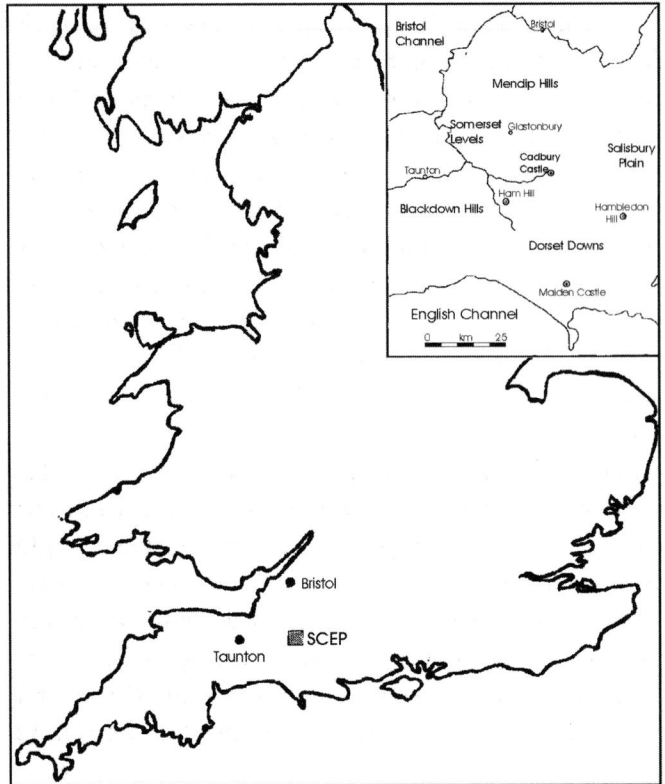

2 Location of The South Cadbury Environs Project

the north and east, but falling steeply to the north-west, west and south, the latter in part due to quarrying, to a height of approximately 130m ASL (426ft) immediately inside the inner bank. The east gate opens into a steep-sided half-dish with a radius of approximately 40m. The dish is deep enough to obscure entirely the view of the plateau from the gate. The other gates offer more expansive, but still restricted, views of the hilltop.

Two sources of water within the ramparts probably have prehistoric origins. The stone-walled, brick-headed King Arthur's Well lies immediately south of the passage to the north-east gate, low on the side of the second bank. Queen Anne's Well is a year-round muddy spring, lost in the trample of cattle hooves.

Twenty-three kilometers (14.3 miles) north of the hillfort, the south slopes of the Mendip Hills form a backdrop which stretches westwards until it terminates in the narrow peninsula of Brean Down, 50km (31.1 miles) to the west-north-west. Brean, itself the site of a Romano-British shrine and a long sequence of Bronze Age activity, is only visible on very clear days; exceptionally the Welsh Black Hills can be seen across the Bristol Channel. Glastonbury Tor is a famous landmark midway between Brean and Cadbury which marks the east edge of the Somerset levels, a flat, low-lying area of marine clays below deep peat deposits, formerly prone to inundation and still subject to flooding. Five kilometres (3 miles) in from the coast Brent Knoll emerges dramatically from the levels as the most distant hillfort intervisible with Cadbury. From the hillfort's plateau, the viewshed takes in a second hillfort, Ham Hill, 18km (11 miles) to the south-west and Lamyatt Beacon, the site of a Romano-British shrine at a similar distance to the north-east. A slightly nearer hillfort to the west, Dundon Hill, is concealed from Cadbury by the ridge from which it is an outlier. The horizons to the east and south are brought to within 2km (1.2 miles) by the steep scarps of a sandstone ridge, in places capped by Upper Inferior Oolitic limestone, obscuring the succession of ridges which eventually rise as the westernmost Wessex chalk at Mere, Wiltshire, 19km (12 miles) to the east and at Melbury Bubb, Dorset, to the south-south-east.

The combination of topography and geology in the study area's 64 sqkm has generated light, very tractable soils on Jurassic limestone ridges to the south and east which are much reduced by millennia of ploughing, creating fertile, light colluvial soils on the valley sides and bottoms. Much heavier soils cover the low-lying lias rocks and clays and the rhaetic ridge to the west of the hillfort. Springs issuing from the lower slopes drain westwards, eventually converging as the Rivers Cam and Yeo, tributaries of the River Parrett, which empties into the Bridgwater Bay. In general there is a ready supply of water on the low ground, but the plateau areas are very dry.

Fifty years ago apple orchards were a significant feature of the low-lying landscape, dominated by grazing dairy cattle, with sheep on the hills. Cereals formed only a small part of agricultural production. Subsequently the cider orchards have been grubbed and the number of dairy herds greatly reduced, whilst arable agriculture is now far more widespread. There are fewer individual farmers, but those still engaged in the industry own or rent much more land. From 1970 until the mid 1980s there was a marked trend to remove hedges to create large arable units but in the current climate of subsidy, field boundaries are being reinstated and there is a growing number of woodland plantations. The rapid changes reflect the underlying versatility of the available resources as well as the use of much heavy machinery.

RESEARCH ON AND AROUND CADBURY CASTLE

As noted above, Cadbury Castle has frequently attracted the attention of those interested in what are now called hillforts. The very particular reason for this lies in its traditional association with the legendary King Arthur. John Leland was working within this ideological framework in 1542. He would have been aware that one way in which to enhance his prestige in the eyes of the Tudor monarch would have been to stress the importance of Arthur, the figure through which that dynasty legitimised its accession to the throne (it was no coincidence that Henry VII so named his first son). Research by David Morgan Evans suggests that Leland was on friendly terms with the Hastings family, at that time the owners of the North Cadbury estate which included Cadbury Castle. Doubtless they were conscious of possible preferment at court through their association with the hill, which Leland unblushingly called 'Camallate'. As well as giving a description of the hillfort's topography, Leland noted that an abundance of Roman coins had been found on it. In his *Britannia* (1586) William Camden was clearly aware of the linking of Cadbury to Arthur but he had no doubts that these and similar earthworks elsewhere were Roman.

Camden's view of hillforts prevailed until the nineteenth century and was repeated by several antiquarian visitors to Cadbury. Most notable was William Stukely, who in 1723 stayed long enough to give us the first surviving drawing of the then largely unwooded ramparts and lynchets, viewed from the north. Perhaps the most significant fact we garner from both Leland and Stukely is that the plateau was under plough. It remained so until the 1960s. The first formal plans of Cadbury were made in the nineteenth century, the best by C.W. Dymond, although his written account did little to add to the antiquarian version. The Revd Bennett's identification of a 'rude race' of builders gives him the credit for the first formal acknowledgement of Cadbury's pre-Roman foundation.

Over a week in June 1913, Pitt Rivers, former archaeological foreman, and Harold St George Gray, opened five trenches, one on the hill's summit, three around the south-west gate and one through the defences near the gate. The man who remains famous in Iron Age studies as Arthur Bulleid's partner in the long-running excavations of the Glastonbury and Meare Lake Villages concluded that the defences were 'Late Celtic' in origin but that there had also been some Neolithic and a great deal of Roman activity on the hill. Like Alcock, 60 years later, he was struck by the absence of Bronze Age material.

In 1955 Ralegh Radford and James Stevens Cox published a summary of what was known of Cadbury, including the germ from which the 1960s campaigns were to grow. In the 1930s Radford excavated extensive Early Mediaeval deposits at Tintagel, Cornwall, and had no difficulty in identifying imported Mediterranean pottery of the fifth to sixth centuries AD amongst the material recovered from Cadbury. In 1955 a local amateur, Mary Harfield, persuaded the Fleet Air Arm (now the Royal Naval Air Service) commander at nearby Yeovilton to have cropmarks in a field of oats photographed from the air. The prints showed two well-defined holloways leading to the plateau from the north-east gate, as well as an abundance of probable pits. Finds from her regular fieldwalking forays from

1954 to 1962 confirmed the broad span of activity on the hillfort, and included more of the imported Early Mediaeval pottery.

This set the scene for the foundation of the Camelot Research Committee in 1965, chaired by Radford. Mortimer Wheeler added lustre as president, whilst the Arthurian scholar, Geoffrey Ashe, was secretary. Leslie Alcock, then a lecturer at the University of Cardiff, was appointed director of the reconnaissance excavation which took place the following year. Undoubtedly his spell in the late 1940s working as Wheeler's deputy in the Indus Valley helped him gain the post, but his qualifications included important excavations at Dinas Powys, near Cardiff, in the 1950s, another Iron Age settlement with significant Early Mediaeval deposits.

Although the excavations carried out under the direction of Leslie Alcock from 1966-70 and in 1973 were at the instigation of the Camelot Research Committee, the stated aim was to explore all periods of activity in an even-handed manner. In the first season trenches were opened through the north inner bank, on the slope between the plateau and the north-east gate, and towards the west of the summit. No less important for archaeological science, Alcock encouraged the use of a variety of geophysical techniques on the plateau, where the Howell Soil Conductivity Meter (nicknamed 'banjo' by archaeologists and the press due to its appearance) and Proton Magnetometer met with outstanding success, which enabled the targeting of work on the summit in the following season. By 1970 a total of four different instruments had been used across the whole of the interior, but the success of the early results was not repeated, almost certainly due largely to the increased soil depth off the plateau. Nonetheless this was a ground-breaking survey, the first to cover the whole of a hillfort's interior and the largest absolute area of archaeological geophysical survey, a suitable complement to the largest absolute area of excavation within a hillfort interior (7 per cent of the 8ha (20 acres) (3)).

Prior to the formation of SCEP there had been extremely limited archaeological research within the limits of the study area. In 1876 Prof Rolleston and Lane Fox dug trenches into the three surviving round barrows on Sigwells, and exactly a century later members of the Wincanton and District Archaeological Group fieldwalked the same field, finding a Romano-British stone altar and a scatter of pottery and flint. C.E. Bean, a keen Dorset amateur, collected worked flint from several fields in the south of the area but made no systematic catalogue of the material. In 1992 a watching brief over a pipeline found evidence for an Iron Age ditch at Sparkford, a small Romano-British settlement south of Queen Camel, and a scatter of a few sherds from the same period in North Cadbury, plus two undated ditches or trenches.

By a strange coincidence the year in which Alcock started excavating, 1966, proved to be a particularly good one for accidental finds. In January, workmen building a reservoir on Hicknoll Slait, a hill overlooking Cadbury from the east,

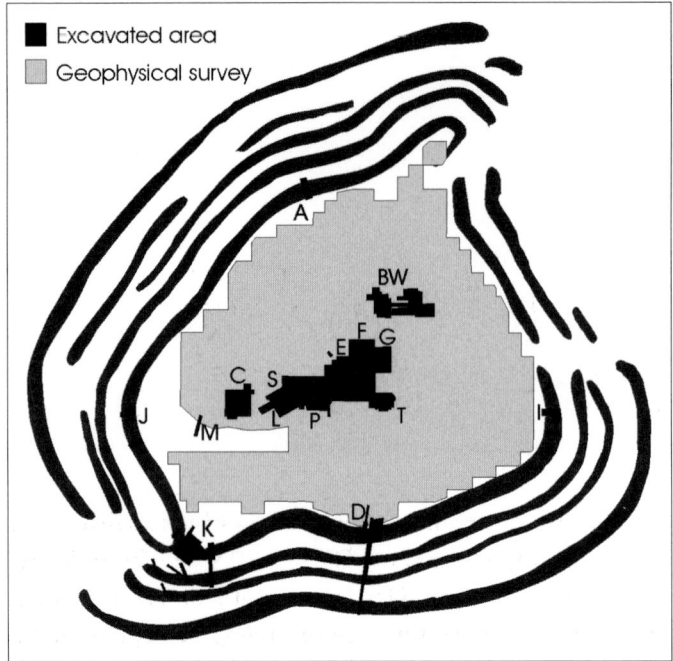

3 Leslie Alcock's work on Cadbury Castle, 1966-70

discovered a Saxon cemetery and at Bratton Seymour, less than 1km (0.6 miles) north-east of the study area, a farmer's plough cut into a tessellated pavement, leading eventually to the identification of several Romano-British buildings. Then a retired headmaster found a considerable amount of Romano-British pottery between the church and the hillfort, when he demolished a dilapidated cottage in South Cadbury to build a retirement bungalow. His wife had recently started archaeology evening classes and she and some of her fellow students started their own dig which was resumed the following year, with some support from Alcock's team. They found features dated by first- to fourth-century AD pottery.

Since this *floruit* of archaeological good fortune, the local fields have been left to the furtive activities of metal detectorists. Roman coins and brooches are known to have been found at Sigwells, and Mediaeval objects at North Cadbury and Woolston.

2

THE SOUTH CADBURY ENVIRONS PROJECT

The South Cadbury Environs Project was prompted by the imminent publication of the final reports of Leslie Alcock's excavations on Cadbury Castle. The task was facilitated through the University of Glasgow's Department of Archaeology, with Dr Phil Freeman assuming the main administrative responsibility. In 1991 he led a topographic and geophysical survey of the interior. None of his team had been present during the excavations so he was intrigued to hear of a local man, Richard Tabor, who had worked through all five main seasons as a boy. This led to several evening meetings in a local pub and at the end of a particularly refreshing night Phil suggested that the author set up a project to explore the area around the hillfort. In Autumn 1992 I instigated an opportunistic programme of fieldwalking at Sigwells, an 18ha (45 acre) field overlooking the hillfort from 1.5 km (1 mile) south-east of it, assisted by members of the South East Somerset Archaeological and Historical Society (SESAS). The turning point for the project came that December when Paul Johnson, who was in charge of Glasgow's geophysical survey, introduced the local amateurs to resistivity and, most significantly, magnetometry (*4*). Over subsequent years he spent several weeks of his own time expanding the geophysical survey and leading small teams of his students in excavations.

The excellent results from Sigwells encouraged postgraduate students from the University of Birmingham to extend the fieldwalking in February 1994 and this became the foundation for training excavations in 1994 and 1995, directed by Peter Leach. The excavations were as opportunistic as the orignal fieldwork and all concerned felt that fieldwork should be conducted within a formal research framework. A committee was formed comprising members of SESAS, the County Museums Service and University-based professional archaeologists, Paul Johnson (Glasgow) and Peter Leach (Birmingham). Subsequently Yeovil Archaeology and Local History Society was also represented. The author, who had started a PhD at Birmingham, investigating the efficacy of a wide range of archaeological survey

4 Geoscan gradiometer: Paul Johnson on Sigwells

strategies applied in various environments, drew up a sampling strategy covering an 8 x 8km area (5) centred on the hillfort (see below). Preliminary reviews of the aerial photographic and other documentary evidence demonstrated the lack of research in the area, previous fieldwork amounting to watching briefs over a pipeline and the construction of a dual carriageway 500m north of the hillfort. However, a programme of survey at Shapwick, Somerset, had demonstrated the value of regressive map analysis and the use of fieldnames as archaeological indicators. A SESAS member, Giles Cooper, collected all the names of fields recorded on the nineteenth-century Tithe Maps, a considerable labour given that the study area impinges upon 19 different parishes.

Within the formal scheme, the work at Sigwells cohered into a pilot study which the author and Johnson aimed to publish as supporting material for funding applications to enable the project to develop on a professional footing. In February 1998, the magnetometry at Sigwells was supplemented by shovel and test pitting, the first implementation of a triad of techniques which was to become the foundation of all the project's survey work until 2003. In 1999, the University of Bristol became the project's sponsoring institution and in 2000 an application to the Leverhulme Trust was successful, enabling the university to employ the author

The South Cadbury Environs Project

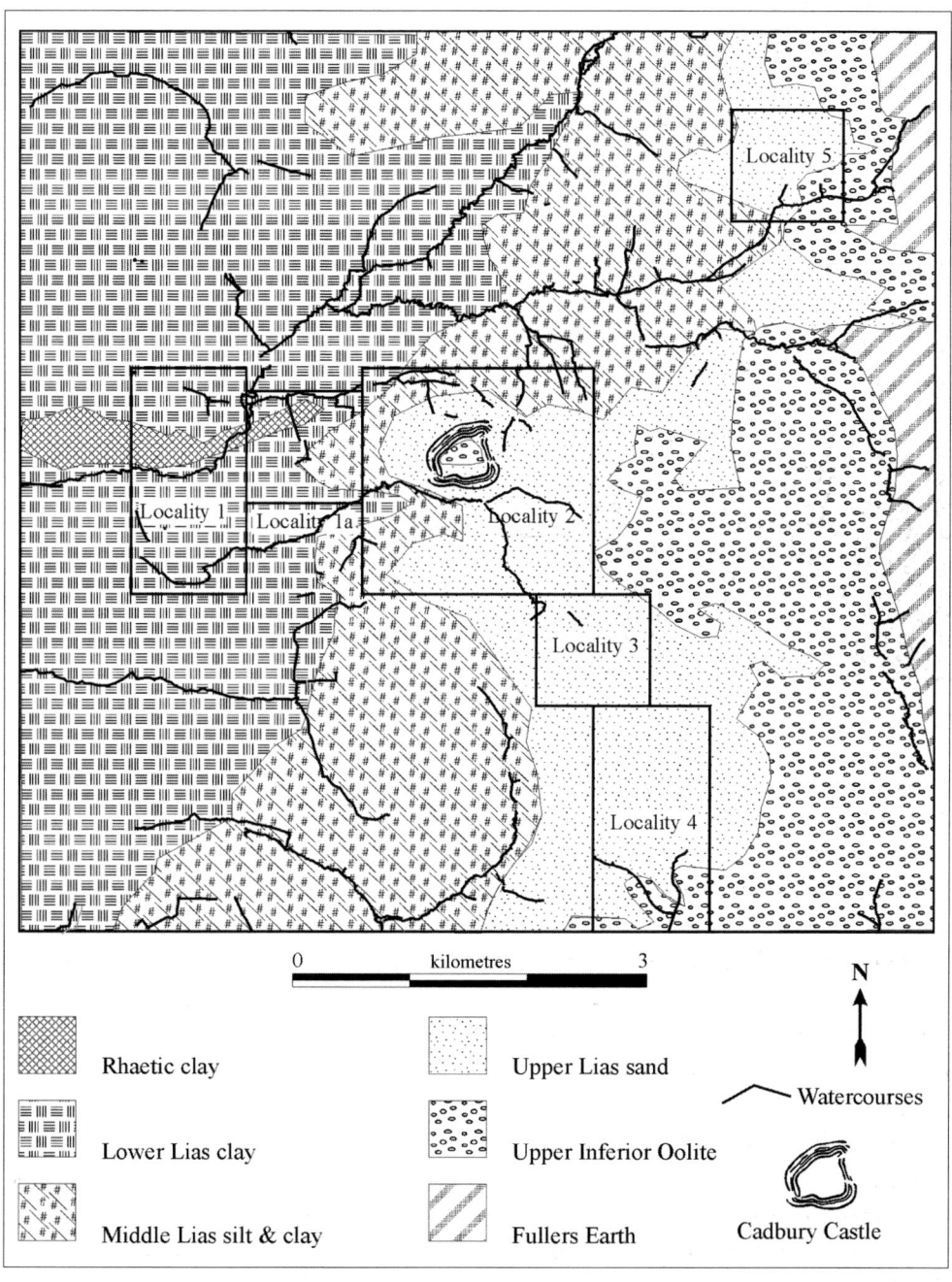

5 Sampling localities superimposed on the study area geology

as a full-time researcher for the project from April 2001. The project remained dependent on a volunteer base with individuals each working one or two days per week throughout the year, a typical field season lasting from early April until late November, when post-excavation work was done under cover. Over the years, the volunteers have become skilled not just in the use of geophysical equipment, excavation and drawing, but in flotation, finds-washing and pottery-recording. At the same time, the project sought undergraduate and postgraduate students to do dissertations relating to particular emerging themes. In 2001 John Davey began a PhD investigating the Late Roman to Mediaeval transition in an area expanded to include Sherborne in Dorset, and Ilchester in Somerset.

From April 2004 to March 2008 the project was sponsored jointly by the Universities of Oxford and Bristol, thanks to a grant from the Arts and Humanities Research Council which funded a full-time researcher, a part-time technician and a temporary part-time research assistant. In 2006 the assistant, Clare Randall, began a PhD at the University of Bournemouth incorporating SCEP's faunal remains and other environmental data with that from the hillfort excavations and placing them in a regional context.

OBJECTIVES

The project had two classes of stories which it aimed to address through particularised narrative objectives. The first class was based on a sequence of synchronic (the spatial dimension in a slice of time) or system maps derived from the geophysical survey and concerns, it included: 1) the fluctuation of Cadbury Castle's status as a central place within the wider landscape from the Neolithic to Late Saxon periods, 2) the changing patterns of access and movement in the landscape, reflecting shifts in central place, and 3) the changing patterns of access which may reveal the prioritising of resource zones, defined by topography and ancient soil types.

The second class of narrative objective was set within a diachronic (chronologically sequential) framework and explored: 1) the apparent increase in settlement nucleation in the Late Bronze Age and Early Iron Age, 2) the manner and extent of the Late Bronze Age pre-hillforts' influence over the division of the surrounding landscape, and 3) the local social and productive conditions in the Iron Age enabling the high-input construction and maintenance of a hillfort, as reflected in more intensive subdivision of the landscape. Our work in the core localities (5) also investigated the rapidity and impact of the Roman occupation on the Cadbury Castle landscape, its population and the processes of change identifiable in the local landscape of the late fourth to sixth centuries AD which brought about reinvestment in the hillfort.

To meet these narrative objectives the project: 1) endeavoured to refine the local ceramic form and fabric chronology or phasing using samples from Cadbury Castle and the project's excavations to enhance the diagnostic resolution of ploughzone and test pit data, 2) created a sequence of base maps representing each phase or land division system detected, comprising geophysical anomalies of a particular alignment or morphological group (i.e. type of form), 3) endeavoured to generate chronologically highly resolved ploughzone and test pit artefact distribution maps, 4) created maps of ploughzone soil variation, 5) created a Geographical Information Systems resource (a computer-based method of displaying and analysing data on a map whose scale can be varied according to need; distribution figures in this book were created in a programme called ArcView), and 6) assessed the results, devising an evaluation programme to test the validity of the geophysical interpretations.

All work by the project has attempted to establish the extent and quality of the archaeological resource in the survey area and to provide a resource which may be used to inform decisions concerning how it may best be managed.

SAMPLING ISSUES

Despite the unsettling lack of stability inherent in the idea, archaeology's legitimacy is based upon the assumption that it *reconstrues* the past, and does so inductively. Yet as well as the malleability of the data, which can so easily protect us from accountability, the paradigmatic frameworks within which we gather and process information constantly change, as indeed they do in other areas of science. A major cultural shift within archaeology is that from research concerned with a particular feature, the *site*, to the landscape, sometimes treated as the backdrop for a particular feature or monument, and sometimes chosen as an arbitrary example of a particular geological or ecological range. Within this shift are regional studies ranging from those borne of empiricist traditions to those which seek to provide a mental or phenomenological landscape.

Empirically based archaeological story telling is hierarchical. Raw data inform, even if only rarely can they be said to necessitate, an interpretation which, placed alongside other interpretations, forms the platform for the next layer of analysis. Thus, from surface collection, a given number of artefacts will be assigned the label *site*; other sites matching the criteria come to indicate settlement patterns; population growth and distribution is assessed, and with it the efficacy of a particular productive mode within the constraints of a landscape, inferred from environmental data. Thereafter settlement or other activity distributions may be clothed in economics, politics and ideology, in effect an analysis layered according to the remoteness of an explanation or interpretation from the raw data which can be classified in stages (*6*).

	Social	**Ideological**
Class G	Political (G1)	Belief system (G2)
Class F	Economic (F1)	Ritual practice (F2)
Class E	Distribution behaviour	
Class D	Artefact-determined behaviour	
Class C	Artefact chronology	
Class B	Artefact/Ecofact type	
Class A	Artefact/Ecofact	

6 Classified narrative sequence

This scheme does not pertain specifically to regional survey, but to archaeology more generally. The basis of narrative structure should not necessarily differ, whether applied to a single excavation or to a region, although certain narrative classes, notably D, have an especially prominent role in regional survey. Frequently, in practice, there has been a different treatment of artefactual data, with much greater investment of resources in the analysis of excavated data rather than in that derived from surface collection.

The division of classes under *social* and *ideological* (*6*), while not entirely arbitrary, is by no means clear cut. *Social* refers to classes of indirectly perceived activity which are generally held to take place, and to be accountable, within the living human sphere; they structure authority and determine the character of agency for individuals and groups.

Ideological refers to classes of indirectly perceived activity, revealing phenomena which invest all spheres of life with authority, including the political and economic. The source of its authority may sometimes reside in something perceived as beyond the living human, for instance in tradition or religion. The word is used here to indicate those moments of behaviour and individual or group self-perception where the authoritative rationale is made explicit. Thus, when an English monarch addresses the House of Lords, he/she is acting within the social sphere; but a public view that he/she acts within a 'god-given' role to invest parliament with his or her authority is ideological. This, as John Barrett might point out, 'is not a 'false consciousness' but a dominant discursive reading of key cultural values'.

In the field, an archaeologist will frequently make experience-based judgements concerning classes B to D and less frequently F (*6*). In short, the narrative structure includes feedback loops so that, for instance, class D information obtained earlier and, frequently, elsewhere may inform class B inferences in the field. This compression of explicit narrative structure is almost inevitable yet, as will be shown below, it can have dramatic consequences for the day-to-day operation of a project when, for instance, a scatter of variously dated pottery within a limited area may be used to diagnose a settlement site. Even Class A should be seen as integrated into the narrative process, not simply precipitating it. An object may not be collected or counted (i.e. regarded as an artefact) because either an inexperienced fieldworker fails to recognise it as an unconformity, or an experienced fieldworker regards it as a class of data without value to the particular project. In the worst cases the material will be collected, but then discarded without record.

A researcher must decide which classes of data will enable the optimum reconstruction of the past and what strategy is most likely to succeed in collecting that data. It remains true that most British landscapes surveys still treat fieldwalking as the fundamental technique. Simply stated, the participants walk across an exposed soil (normally a surface which has been weathered after ploughing) collecting or recording finds with varying degrees of precision to build distribution maps for a range of target periods. At the time of the project's inception it seemed merely a matter of deciding which variety of fieldwalking to use. This had become a hot issue in the 1980s. On the one hand there was a school of thought associated with several large-scale Mediterranean projects which regarded archaeological survey as a matter of finding *sites*, typically areas of habitative settlement; on the other there was a view that if we aspired to recovering a wider range of activity we needed to account for *off-site* archaeology, treating the distribution of artefacts as continuous but varying in density. The problem is just as compelling in the case of upstanding earthworks. Does a single Bronze Age barrow (burial mound) constitute a site? Or should the boundary system within which it is integrated, or the hill with which it was intervisible, also be included? *Site* merely describes an arbitrarily designated area for investigation or conservation and has nothing to do with the mental framework of our ancestors.

Most surveys explicitly recognise that they can cover only a proportion of their study areas and a wide variety of sampling strategies have been tried. The objective of rigorous sampling procedures in regional or landscape archaeology is to produce a consistent body of data which will reflect the varying intensity of horizontally distributed residues of past human activity. If consistency is achieved, an appropriate range of variables may enable the making of probability statements about the distribution of residues across the wider study area.

There has long been an appreciation that purely random sampling can distort results so the notion of stratified sampling has been introduced. Most commonly, environmental characteristics which may have influenced patterns of human behaviour (and hence distribution of its residues) are identified and the percentage, of the area they cover, calculated. Each characteristic represents a *stratum*. A simple set of strata might comprise 'plateau', 'valley side', 'valley bottom', 'plain' etc. In some notable cases, where it has been possible to reconstruct the environment of the target period, classes of vegetation cover have been used as variables. The total area to be sampled is then allotted proportionally to each stratum. This may be carried out entirely randomly, according to a predetermined pattern, or by judgement based on assessment of existing archaeological information in particular zones. The latter practice is frequently frowned upon because inevitably it undermines the statistical integrity of subsequent analysis.

Some researchers have eschewed simple random and stratified sampling, deliberately introducing weighting towards certain areas or features. A survey aiming to understand a villa economy at Maddle Farm, Berkshire, employed transects across the geological grain, centred around a more heavily sampled core area, in an attempt to reconstruct a Romano-British villa's economy. Whilst it may be argued that such an approach introduces a judgemental bias by overvaluing a particular locality, the underlying assumption remains that artefact distribution exists in a continuum. The concept of *site* was dissolved in favour of an interpretation based on general patterns which generated a coherent narrative for a specific agricultural economy. This strategy presumed a villa system and duly characterised it, arguing for wider relationships based on received information.

For pre- and post-Roman periods, knowledge of that kind is poorly established; one systemic unit cannot be investigated discretely then related to a known overarching social structure. For these periods only a narrow range and number of artefacts survive in the ploughsoil, and we have a limited understanding of the activities they signify. Consequently, researchers are not yet in a position where the routine application of either a uniform or a unilocal ploughzone sampling will characterise a particular activity area, or place it in a wider scheme. In a large region, with limited time and labour, it may be more effective to work intensively in several localities.

As well as the essentially spatial, there are diachronic or chronological issues. In 1991, A.J. Schofield felt able to state that regional survey should be concerned with patterns 'of continuity and accumulation' rather than 'specific moments in time' without expectation of challenge. Yet in the same year John Cherry thought legitimate the endeavour to recognise 'relatively ephemeral economic and social transformations', an aspiration still rarely achieved. In either case, a project's strategy should be governed by the requirements of its chronological range and by the quality of the comparative database for each period studied. Higher chronological and functional resolution can only be achieved by targeting intensive work, typically excavation, in areas with a high density of stratified data, or by reviewing an existing rich database, such as the one from and around Danebury.

Such a variety of sampling strategies has been employed that it is often difficult to compare the results of one study with another. There are three principal

The South Cadbury Environs Project

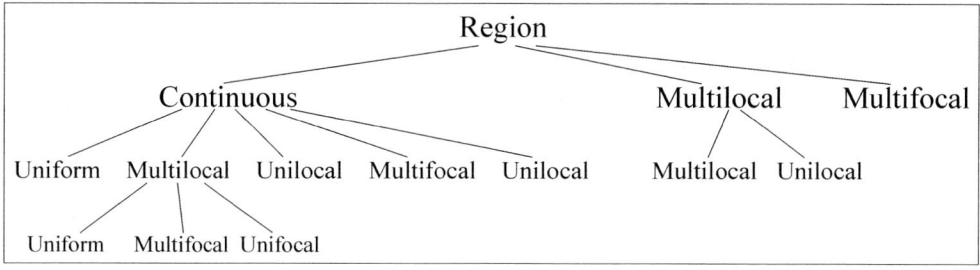

7 Resource distribution tree

parameters to be established when comparing databases: the conceptual scheme by which a programme distributes its available resources across a region; the resolution of the collection and mapping of data (i.e. sampling interval), and the chronological resolution determined by the character of targeted artefacts or landscape features. A 'syntactic' tree of resource distribution illustrates the range of approaches at that level (7). The issue of sampling has become even more acute as different survey techniques have developed.

TECHNIQUE SELECTION

Fieldwalking is cheap to run, typically carried out by students or volunteers, and usually it will demonstrate rapidly that there has been past activity in a study area, but it has inherent weaknesses. Studies at Shapwick, Somerset, and elsewhere demonstrated varying perceptual skills in team members, whilst ground and light conditions also affected the visibility of finds. There is scope for some statistical mitigation and with a little extra work researchers can record local topography, soil types, drainage and much else besides, at a micro level, as they collect artefacts. It can work well in arid areas, where the soil is severely depleted by wind and targeted artefacts are durable enough to survive the processes of erosion without significant horizontal movement.

The instigator of the Stonehenge Environs Project, Julian Richards, suggests that all fieldwalking should be done by professional archaeologists, believing that only those with skills commensurate with his own will be able to identify finds effectively. Going further, he has asserted that surface finds should be recorded but not collected. In this way the same quality of recorded database would be created, whilst obviating the need for large-scale storage (temporary for a project; long-term for overcrowded museum warehouses) and maintaining the integrity of the archaeological landscape (by leaving finds where they were lost or deposited). Sometimes called scanning, variations of this method have been used extensively for several decades in countries fringing the Mediterranean. There are major problems with it. Firstly, even if a particular archaeologist has the knowledge to classify adequately all the material encountered (this is without taking into account that the artefacts are usually dirty when found), archaeology is a developing science in which objects are subjected to re- or sub-classification. Secondly, the integrity of the landscape is better maintained by the collection of the finds rather than by leaving them. It has long been recognised that ploughing breaks up pottery and exposes it to weather which in a few seasons destroys prehistoric ceramics completely. SCEP's work has shown that increasingly even the flint is damaged beyond the point where it can be analysed usefully.

In any event, all forms of fieldwalking are an extremely unreliable way to construct an overarching narrative in an environment where there have been periods of rapid soil movement, such as the one we are living through. In the early 1980s, a team of experienced archaeologists re-walked a field at Maddle Farm over three successive years. The plotted flint distributions revealed marked differences from year to year. They also carried out a limited sub-surface survey to examine the correlation between the volume of Romano-British pottery collected from the ploughed surface and from lower strata. On the whole there was a close correspondence between the two although, perhaps counter-intuitively, there were occasions when the surface finds far exceeded those from the lower strata. A few years earlier, Martin Bell excavated long, deep trenches across the bottom of valleys in Sussex, then dug one side of each by hand. He demonstrated conclusively that these valleys were filled by a sequence of hillwashes, not least the deep deposits laid down in modern times. He was able to show the existence of archaeological remains completely sealed by the overburden and entirely safe from the plough, hence inaccessible to fieldwalking. It is a lesson most researchers choose to ignore as the implications are daunting (*8*).

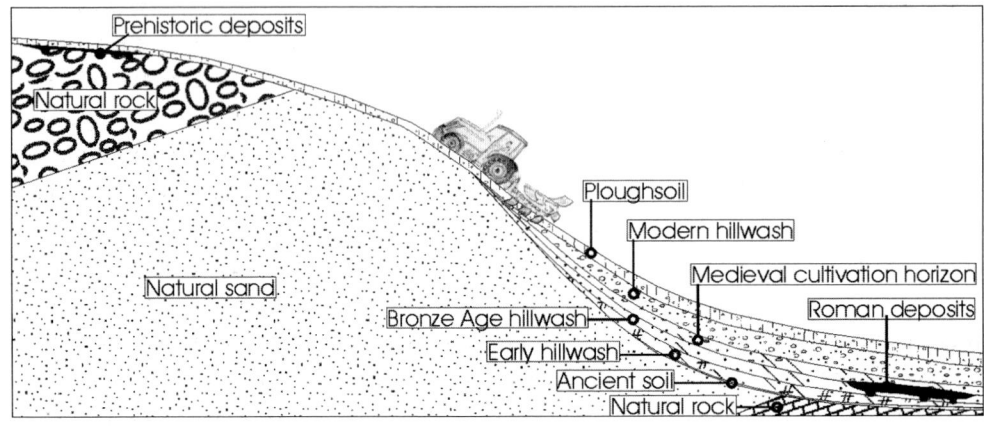

8 The soil movement problem

The South Cadbury Environs Project

The methodology used around Maiden Castle in 1985 derived from earlier completed surveys, particularly the one applied in the Stonehenge environs. Fieldwalking was the principal technique in an area where up to 90 per cent of the surrounding land was ploughed in rotation. Seven small trenches were spread over two river valleys to collect environmental samples. The fieldwalking identified marked concentrations of different categories of worked flint, but only one where hardy black burnished pottery suggested Late Iron Age or Romano-British activity, coinciding with an area rich in aerial photographic linear and enclosure features. The complete lack of pottery from the Neolithic to Middle Iron Age periods suggests a methodological problem: whereas flint was the key target artefact at Stonehenge, the dating of contemporary activity around the Iron Age hillfort depended on pottery, most of it very friable, so that although a desire for direct comparability was laudable it was not appropriate.

The Danebury Environs Programme attempted to deal with the landscape itself as a modified artefact by identifying successive boundary systems from aerial photographs, then carrying out intensive work, including geophysical survey in advance of excavation. It targeted different types of Iron Age enclosure as well as major linear boundaries and successfully expanded knowledge of the date and range of landscape features. It showed that ditches were frequently multiphased through re-cutting, extending or shortening, and that major boundaries originating in the Bronze Age continued to have significance in ordering Iron Age landscapes. Ultimately the study presented hypotheses concerning shifts in power and influence through the Iron Age, concluding that during Danebury's zenith there were few or no settlement sites within a 10km radius of the hillfort. The programme did not attempt to characterise the density or range of activity for the targeted periods within the survey area, deliberately eschewing ploughzone collection techniques. The landscape was analysed through the multifocal exploration of cut features: a site-based method, but within a wider scheme.

Where a multifocal survey does not treat human activity and its residues as a continuum interacting with and developing landscapes, it is bound to restrict the spatial range of socio-economic narrative. By looking at a smaller area, a parish on the Somerset Levels, the Shapwick Project was able to superimpose carpets of multiperiod artefactual data, derived from fieldwalking, over maps derived from regressive analysis refined by earthworks and geophysical surveys. In some areas they used shovel pitting, the sieving of a given volume of topsoil through a specified mesh at regular intervals. Although very labour intensive, it has the virtue of vastly reducing perceptual error and enabling the coverage of uncultivated areas. These refinements also underpinned interpretations of soil chemistry distributions, adding another dimension to a functional narrative. However, they do not deal with the deep soil problem.

SCEP developed a new approach. In 1996, the magnetic survey with a Geoscan FM 18 gradiometer was completed in the 18ha (44.5 acres) field at Sigwells,

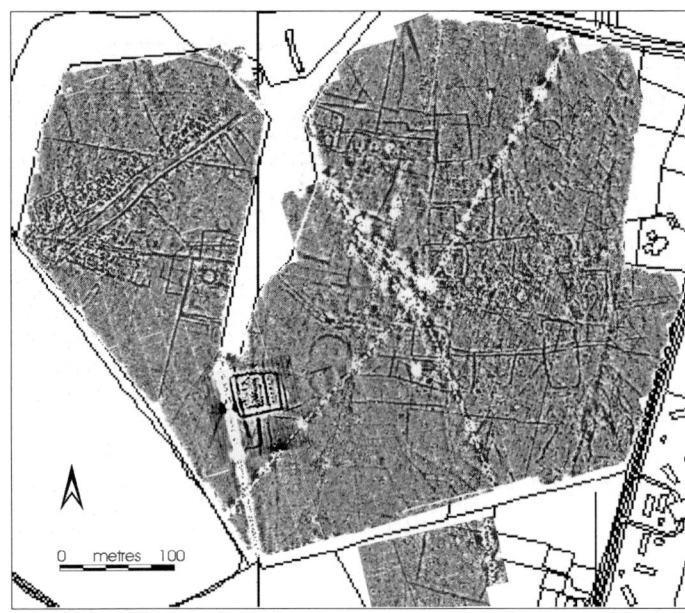

9 Sigwells: plot of the gradiometer survey

Charlton Horethorne, providing a base map for the plotting of finds recovered from several episodes of gridded fieldwalking. Despite a very coarse sampling interval of one reading per metre, the results were so impressive (*9*) that although progress had been slow (depending entirely on the availability of volunteers) it was decided that if the project gained funding for a full-time researcher, the technique would be employed over the entirety of sampled areas. In February 1998, a pilot study was carried out in the field to see if techniques other than fieldwalking would better enhance the geophysical data. For shovel pitting two level buckets full of ploughsoil were sieved through a 1cm mesh (0.5 inch) at every 20m along corridors set 20m apart. The relationship between the ploughsoil finds and those from lower down was explored by digging a 1m² test pit into the geological surface at regular intervals in every 1ha (2.5 acres) of the field. The results provoked a radical departure from other surveys: in future the whole of each sampled area would be subjected to geophysical survey, shovel pits would largely replace fieldwalking and we would continue to dig 1m² test pits in every 1ha.

THE SOUTH CADBURY STRATEGY

Since 1995 the fieldwork objectives and detailed documentary studies of the project have been set within the 8 x 8 sqkm box described above (*5*). Documentary information (textual, cartographic and aerial photographic) was drawn from the

The South Cadbury Environs Project

10 'Corridor' fieldwalking: one person scans the surface between two 20m ropes while a second records information about conditions

whole study area, but the project's fieldwork resources dictated the need for sampling, not total coverage.

A two-tiered field strategy was planned. A string of five contiguous and a sixth outlying *localities*, ranging from 1 sqkm (0.4 sq miles) to 4 sqkm (1.6 sq miles), were chosen to represent the range of geology and topography within the study area, totalling 11 sqkm. A second phase was planned to comprise fieldwork across transects made up of 500 x 250m segments in a contiguous 50 per cent offset pattern. The intention was to sample 20 per cent of the surface area within each locality and segment with the chosen techniques, but ultimately the coverage of large blocks of land proved so advantageous for interpretation of the geophysical survey that localities 4 and 5 were expanded and the transects discarded.

Fieldwalking continued to be used sporadically in 1m-wide, 20m-long strips, marked by ropes which were moved forward 20m after the completion of the strip, eventually forming a continuous south to north corridor across a targeted area at 20m intervals, giving a 5 per cent coverage of the surface area (*10*). However, as much of the study area was ploughed only rarely, fieldwalking was substituted increasingly by shovel pitting. Samples were collected at every 20m along similar corridors, but with the volume of soil double that of the pilot study at approximately 60 litres (13.2 gals) to improve the chances of gaining a representative range and volume of finds (*11*). Similar record forms were completed for both fieldwalking and shovel pitting (*12*). The radical departure from other surveys was the introduction

Cadbury Castle: The Hillfort and Landscapes

11 Shovel pitting (Milsoms Corner)

of geophysical survey over the whole sample area and the digging of 1m² test pits to the geological surface in every 1ha (2.5 acres).

Throughout the project there have been modifications of preference and necessity. By 1999, access to the Geoscan Research FM 36 gradiometer, with double the memory capacity of the FM 18, allowed readings to be taken at 0.5m intervals along traverses set 1m apart. A lunchtime download enabled completion of up to 30 20m² grids in a day. Three years later, the dual system Bartington Grad 601-2 collected readings at every 25cms (10in) and more than doubled the number of grids we covered in a day (*13*). Both systems record ditches, stone structures, pits, hearths, postholes and, if they are filled with burnt material, small gullies and concentrations of decayed organics, the Geoscan equipment to a specified depth of 1m (our own data suggested this was a conservative estimate which might be increased by at least 50 per cent), the Bartington to over 3m. The technique's efficacy as a landscape tool varies according to the target periods, depending upon the forms of boundary employed (ditches usually show well; fences or hedgerows often not at all) and the local soil character and depth.

Once we had moved off the Sigwells plateau there was a marked impoverishment in the rate of finds from shovel pits when compared with test pits. Dry weather and heavier soils rendered shovel pitting impracticable in the summer and early autumn of 2003, provoking a crisis which led to the technique's replacement with additional test pits, targeting key geophysical anomalies. These proved hugely

The South Cadbury Environs Project

Right: 12 An example of a fieldwalking record sheet

Below: 13 Bartington gradiometer: Liz Caldwell on Sigwells

Cadbury Castle: The Hillfort and Landscapes

14 Processing soil samples in a flotation tank

effective as a means for dating boundary systems and have almost entirely replaced all forms of topsoil sampling.

There have also been unexpected bonuses. For a postgraduate dissertation at the University of Bristol, a long-term volunteer, Duncan Black, decided to introduce magnetic susceptibility testing, a technique usually employed as a coarse substitute for gradiometry. He quickly identified that it could be used to much greater advantage in the vertical plane, diagnosing layers which were the likely sources of gradiometer anomalies. His soil samples have been retained as potential samples for further chemical analysis, which may yet give us a more detailed view of animal husbandry and other activities.

In every year since 1994, environmental data (bone, molluscs, carbonised material) have been collected from excavations and test pits, from contexts dated by diagnostic finds within a wide area and from a range of periods, adding important detail about early local economies or subsistence patterns unexplored in surface-based surveys. Apart from doing the bulk of the fieldwork, volunteers have been responsible for most of the finds washing, for extracting carbonised residues by flotation (*14*) and for pottery and flint recording. There remain problems with finding the means to analyse some of the data. The appointment of Clare Randall as a research assistant, a then aspiring animal bone specialist who has since moved on to a doctorate including the project's material, has dealt with one particular problem but we have had to depend on undergraduate dissertations to process only a very small percentage of the carbonised remains.

Although centred on Cadbury Castle, the programme aimed to understand a changing landscape rather than a castle or other site. Our perspective treats the term 'site' as an arbitrary construct which inhibits rather than encourages a full understanding of the range of past human activity, and the data collection strategy has been devised accordingly. Within the framework outlined above, SCEP is a regional, continuous, multilocal survey (7).

THE SCEP CHRONOLOGY

The principal dating tool for this project has been pottery. We had the considerable starting advantage of a sequence for Cadbury Castle's first millennium BC, elaborated by Leslie Alcock in 1980, which in 1995 he supplemented with the final publication of the post-Roman and Late Saxon remains. By 1997, our own excavations below the west and east of the hillfort — the former including Early Neolithic and Early to Late Bronze Age pottery, the latter Early to Late Romano-British — had established a 20 phase sequence from the Early Neolithic to the modern period which could be amplified where appropriate. It was assumed that this comparative database would enable us to date most of the pottery from the study area. Whilst this has proved largely true, very significant Middle and Late Bronze Age assemblages forced some revisions.

Although test pitting has greatly enhanced the pottery's diagnostic potential there will always be some frustratingly small formless sherds. Sometimes a rough date can be assigned based on sherds' fabrics or finish, but huge overlaps in fabric chronology render the approach fraught with pitfalls. What follows is an outline of Cadbury Castle and its surrounding landscape which should be read with this warning in mind!

3

FIRST TRANSFORMATIONS

The vegetational landscape confronting small groups of hunter-gatherers who began to exploit the area around Cadbury Castle in the Mesolithic, was very different from today's and would have changed gradually from one generation to the next. In the latter stages of the last Ice Age (Late Pleistocene) such cover as there was comprised subarctic grasses and shrubs such as dwarf birch and juniper. Permafrost had penetrated and fractured natural rock so that as the climate warmed, subterranean water caused the subsidence and movement of material, particularly where past tectonic movement had induced heavy east to west and south to north faulting. Gravelly head deposits were laid down in the valleys and in occasional broad bands across the lias clays to the west. From around 7500 BC to 4000 BC, the sea level rose by approximately 30m, with extensive marine incursion occurring in the late sixth to early fifth millennium.

By around 8000 BC, and over the following 1500 years, the climate warmed enough to allow the spread of birch, willow and pine, as well as smaller plants which attracted larger mammals, including wild cattle indigenous to northern Europe, deer and pigs. Aveline's Hole in the Mendip Hills, north Somerset, has provided the most direct evidence of human activity during the earliest part of this period. The bodies of more than 100 people were laid deliberately in a cave over a few generations, although flintwork of the period is better represented in the centre of the Somerset Levels.

The earliest evidence for human activity around South Cadbury is mainly from high ground, or the slopes below it, and comprises rare Late Mesolithic (6500-4000 BC) microliths and a handaxe. Similar material was collected from the ridge to its south-east by C.E. Bean and forms part of an eponymous archive held in Dorset County Museum. By this time the woodland had become denser and more varied, including oak, hazel and lime.

First transformations

Hazelnuts were harvested and roasted each autumn, and there is evidence of tubers being eaten but the diet was very high in meat and low in carbohydrate. A large shell midden at Culverwell, Portland, Dorset, revealed that oysters and muscles were sometimes part of the diet but the nutritional value of one deer, pig or auroch was far greater than several hundred crustacea. A particular hunting strategy may have been responsible for an enhanced background of fine charcoal in soils of the Late Mesolithic. An area of scrub close to water was burned, creating an open space in which new shoots would rapidly appear, attracting large mammals who would then be easy prey without cover. Natural fires may have been part of the cause, also, as the period during which the charcoal most increased was dry.

The known rare examples of structures are small, stake-built, some with a hearth and presumably covered with skins. Two stakeholes cutting an ancient soil found in a regular test pit at the bottom of a valley on the south side of Sheep Slait, Poyntington Down (Locality 4), were next to an ashy deposit including carbonised hazel shells, and may have been supports for such a shelter. However, there are examples of substantial stone-slabbed floors from Scotland, Ireland and England, the closest to South Cadbury, and most substantial, constructed over and around the Portland shell midden.

We can say little about social organisation and belief but there are important environmental changes in the Late Mesolithic which persist into the Neolithic. It has been suggested that the decline in elm is a symptom of more intensive human activity; disease is just as probable but not necessarily unassociated. At the same time, millennia of vegetation growth and decay had increased the acidity of the soils.

NEOLITHIC (15)

The Neolithic is generally held to be the period during which cultivation was introduced and with it a more sedentary way of life. The ultimate artefactual expression of the change is pottery, a product which is at once cumbersome and fragile, and hence not particularly portable. There are conflicting explanations for the arrival of these changes in north-west Europe at the beginning of the fourth millennium BC, more than 1000 years after a similar stage had been reached in southern Europe. They range from population movement to indigenous development. There are equally divergent views about how rapidly the new pattern of subsistence replaced the old. On the one hand, recent data from Scotland suggests an absolutely clear-cut change from a marine to a terrestial-based diet at precisely the time when cultivated cereals first appear, soon after 4000 BC. On the other hand, a site in Berkshire, England, has all the material attributes of a Late Mesolithic culture but

Cadbury Castle: The Hillfort and Landscapes

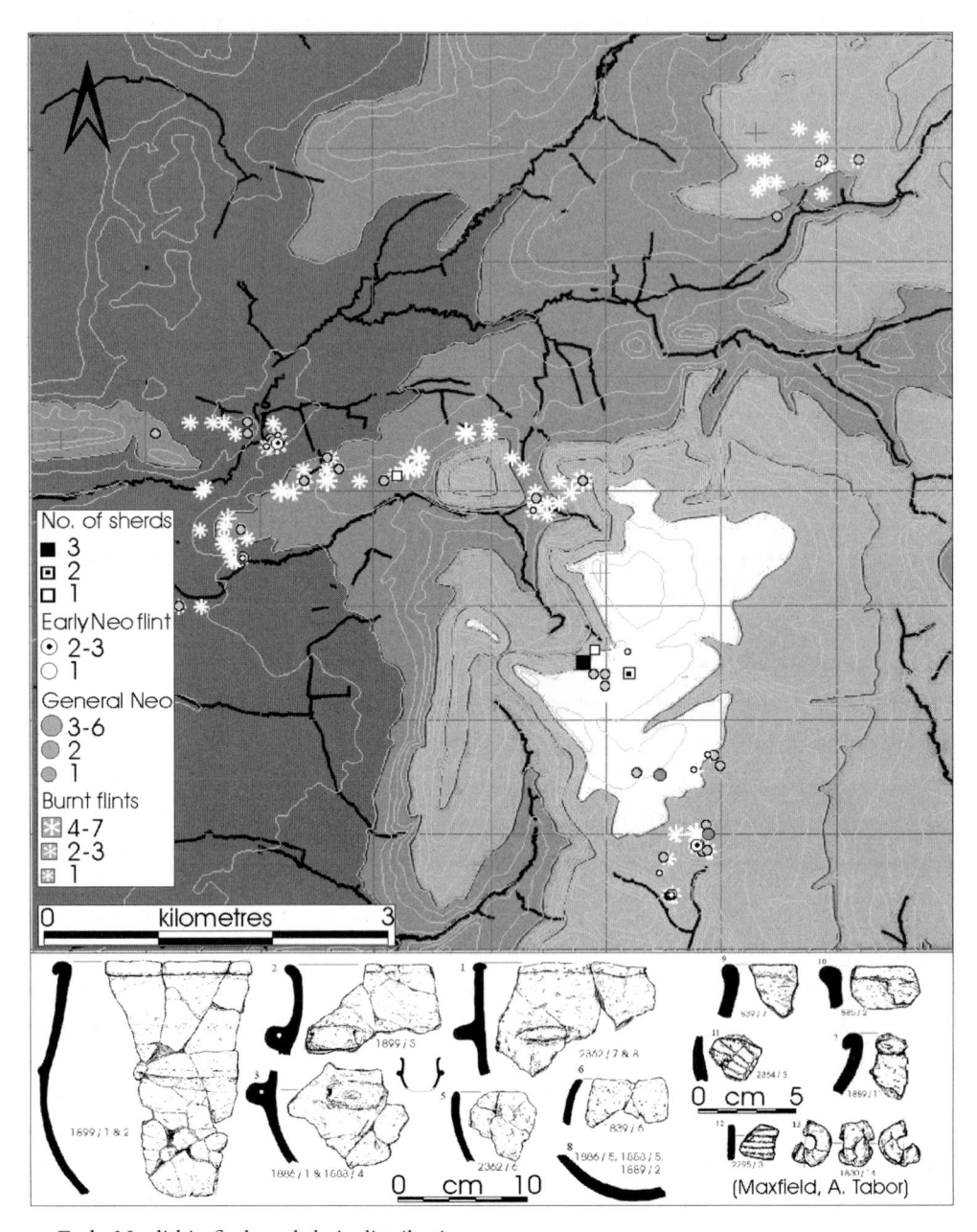

15 Early Neolithic finds and their distribution

is dated to around 3300 BC, a century later than a long barrow at nearby Lambourne.

The period is poorly represented in south-east Somerset and north Dorset, excepting Alcock's discoveries, yet it is surrounded by significant sites from further afield. Six kilometres (3.7 miles) west of Glastonbury there is the remarkable wood Sweet Track, dated to 3806 BC by dendrochronology, and to the south and east there are the causewayed enclosures at Maiden Castle, Hambledon Hill (no less than three) and Whitesheet Hill. Peter Woodward identified six settlement sites in his survey of the South Dorset Ridgeway. More tracks on the Somerset Levels, concentric pits and the stone circle of Stanton Drew in the north, various long barrows, Maiden Castle bank barrow and the Dorset Cursus on Cranborne Chase, offer a tangible Late Neolithic. In south Dorset, Peter Woodward has ventured territorial units.

The South Cadbury area has yet to produce any monumental structures and change was at a variable rate. However, traces of human activity are perceptible. Pits, postholes and ditches were dug, there was a clear conception of giving shape to the landscape and there is some evidence for substantial settlement on Cadbury Castle. Nonetheless, for at least some of the time people continued to gather and probably hunt.

Paths through the woods

The people who made pots and took the trouble to bring heavy saddle querns (grinding stones) from the Mendip Hills to this area were probably following paths which had been well-established by their ancestors, varying mainly according to the moisture in the ground and vegetation cover. Cadbury's free-draining plateau and those forming an arc around it from the north-east to south, would have been covered with thin grasses, sparse small trees and shrubs. The water-retaining soils of the North Cadbury and Weston Bampfylde ridges, to its north and west respectively, would have had much heavier growth of oak, with willow following the watercourses at their bases, mixed with reeds and marsh grasses. Springs still issuing from the lower slopes of many of the hills would ensure that these areas were richly vegetated.

Flints from the lower deposits in test pits provide the best evidence for the general distribution of activity during the period (*15*), a stark contrast to the results from ploughsoil collection which produced very little Early Neolithic evidence. Gradiometry is less effective as there appears to be a lack of larger-scale boundary systems or characteristic landscape features of the period, such as causewayed enclosures. Otherwise it is unsurprising that the rare structural evidence encountered has been a valuable by-product of other research agendas. Alcock found several Early, and a few Late, Neolithic features during his campaigns. SCEP's excavations on the spur overlooking the hill's west approach revealed a pit alignment and occupation area. There are also plenty of isolated and grouped pits in the study area, the bulk of which are probably Iron Age and which will remain unexcavated and amongst which there may be Neolithic examples.

The most striking distributional aspect of substantial Early Neolithic cut features is their proximity to Cadbury Castle, all occurring within 100m of it or on it. A pit alignment at Milsoms Corner appears to have marked the west approach to the hill where the widespread distribution and number of Early Neolithic features, even though some are unlikely to have been exactly contemporary, suggest that much or all of the hilltop was cleared of woodland during some part of the fourth millennium BC. Gullies with integral post settings showed that there were substantial rectangular buildings on the south-west of the lower hilltop, associated with a terrace, and another group of posts 140m further east suggested that some of the hilltop was fenced. Perhaps the largest building, with a similar foundation to that in the south-west, was on the highest, most exposed part of the plateau, where it may have had a particular association with a group of pits, one of which included burnt hazelnut shells which gave a carbon date centred on the mid fourth millennium BC. It is tempting to argue that the structures on the sheltered south side of the plateau were permanent dwellings and that the features on the plateau were associated with ritual and belief. In 1993 Paul Johnson's geophysical survey of the hilltop identified a holloway emerging from under the west inner bank and clearly pre-dating it. Its orientation suggests a continuation from the lower west passage through the Iron Age ramparts. This early route to and within the hilltop leads towards the Iron Age east gate which is likely also to have a Neolithic origin. It faces due east towards Hicknoll Slait, a striking dome-shaped hill which provides the best view of Cadbury's interior (*colour plate 2*).

The three, possibly four, pits along the spine of the Milsoms Corner spur formed part of a line which marked the route to the hilltop. Large fragments of pottery, much of it in the elegant style associated with the south west peninsula sites of Hembury, Devon, and Carn Brea, Cornwall (*15*), were deposited with flint flakes, many of them burnt, a Cornish polished axe, a rubber stone and quern fragments from the Mendip Hills, extremely fragmentary burnt bone, an abundance of charcoal, much of it hazel shell, and large amounts of half-baked clay (*colour plate 3*). The pits ranged from being roughly 1m diameter basins, to 2 x 1m and lozenge-shaped. In the latter, a group of flint flakes/blades appeared to be the remains of a hafted tool. A complete saddle quern had been placed face down in a smaller pit containing few other finds other than an abundance of charcoal (*16*). Most tantalising of all was a floor which had been hollowed into the north side of the spur. The layers sealing it were rich in pieces of struck flint but the floor itself was clean apart from a thin layer of ash spreading from a central, basin-shaped hearth

First transformations

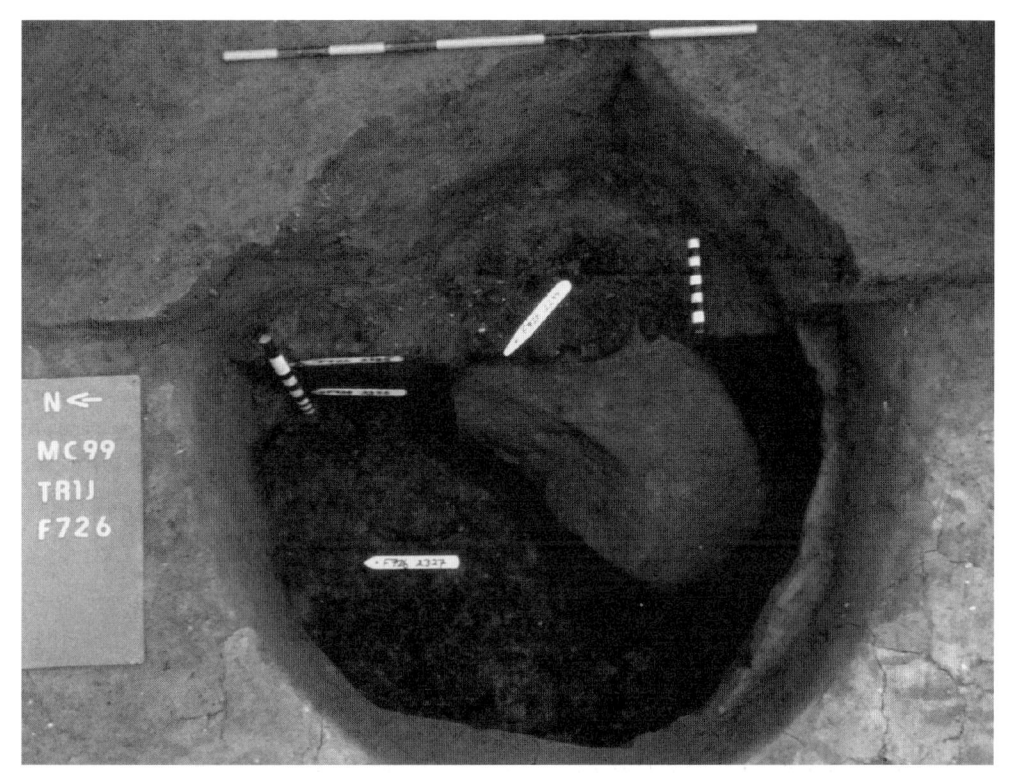

16 Milsoms Corner: saddle quern in an Early Neolithic pit

which included a single flint bladelet. Several stakeholes and a possible narrow timber slot provided clear evidence that the hollow had been covered.

Although the pits marked the route to the hill they did not do so as pits. They were dug and filled with specially significant deposits in the space of a few weeks since there is minimal natural silting in them. They are the earliest sign of people imposing a structure on the landscape but the material in them indicates a range of activities wider than sign-posting. It seems likely that the events took place during the autumn. Hazelnuts were dried and some ground into flour using millstones carried over at least 24km (15 miles), providing a base for food cooked in large bowls, in clay ovens (*17*). During their stay, members of the group felled trees and cleared scrub to provide an open, highly visible path to the hilltop. When they had finished, many of their tools – their temporary means of subsistence – were returned to the earth, buried in pits marked by a means which has left no trace.

Despite the presence of what are usually taken to be the accoutrements of a more sedentary life, the people marking the route appear to have owed much to a mobile, Mesolithic way of life. If they co-existed with, or were even the same group as, the people on the hilltop they lived at the very beginning of the building

Cadbury Castle: The Hillfort and Landscapes

17 Marking the route to Cadbury. Amanda Tabor

of permanent houses there, such as those below the plateau's south side. A lynchet shows that soil formed behind a boundary due to cultivation, and it may well be that Cadbury was able to meet most or all of the cereal needs for a small population still used to hunting and gathering. The structures on the exposed hilltop may have been for storage, but there is none of the carbonised cereal grain found in abundance in a longhouse of the period in Scotland and it may be that they represented the first ritual buildings in a sequence which was to continue intermittently until the tenth century AD.

Over the following millennium there was a decrease in human activity in the local landscape. The considerable amount of flint attributable to the period is a consequence of the material's durability rather than the intensity of its use. It is difficult to distinguish Late Neolithic lithic technologies from those of the Early Bronze Age but on Cadbury a layer of hillwash sealed a soil with diagnostic Late Neolithic pottery and was not itself sealed until a ploughsoil formed, dated by Late Bronze Age pottery. A roughly circular enclosure with a diameter exceeding 50m, close to the head of a valley cutting Seven Wells Down in the north of Locality 4, was identified in an aerial photograph and located by geophysical survey. It produced a few non-diagnostic flints from a test pit and might be of the period. Otherwise many of the comparatively rare cleared areas were lost to regenerating woodland and scrub and with them many of the marked and unmarked paths through the woods disappeared. With only a small population, cultivation, such as it was, would have been of low intensity, with cleared areas cropped for perhaps two or three years before being left fallow for as long as two decades, giving the soil ample time to recover. It is likely that animal husbandry played at least as important a role in the pattern of subsistence. There are no signs of widespread enclosure systems and on the whole herds of cattle and pigs and flocks of sheep are likely to have been followed by those who tended them and only brought into enclosed settlement areas, such as that at Cadbury, to be wintered.

EARLY BRONZE AGE (18)

If the Neolithic was when tracks between clearings and settlements were given physical definition in a ritualised process, the Bronze Age was when marking of much larger cleared spaces came to dominate. During the earlier period, members of communities recognised their particular space or home range in terms of natural and man-made landmarks. Over the course of the Bronze Age the *definition* of a community's space becomes the issue. Increasingly, the Bronze Age is represented as the period when the tension between ritual authority invested in the ancestors was played out against secular power emerging within an increasingly atomised society, where people with specialised skills were needed, yet undermined the existing structures. We see this in the individualised marking of the dead in Early Bronze Age round barrows, some of which play a part for the living in their relationships with later linear boundaries.

In his recent survey of Bronze Age field systems in southern England, David Yates is sceptical of claims made for Late Neolithic field systems, but is more receptive to the identification of a few examples of small Early Bronze Age farm plots in south-east England, most notably along the Thames Valley. He is prepared to accept a similar date for discontinuous or interrupted ditches found in that area, but has more reservations about some similar features in Dorset, highlighting the problem of dating extensive systems on very slight evidence. The same problem applies to the famous Dartmoor Reeves.

Evidence on Cadbury hill is limited to a single flanged axe. In such splendid isolation, it seems either to have been a ritual deposit disturbed and relocated by later activity or, perhaps, an heirloom curated over generations. This perspective ought now to be reviewed in the light of discoveries from the surrounding landscape.

Cadbury Castle: The Hillfort and Landscapes

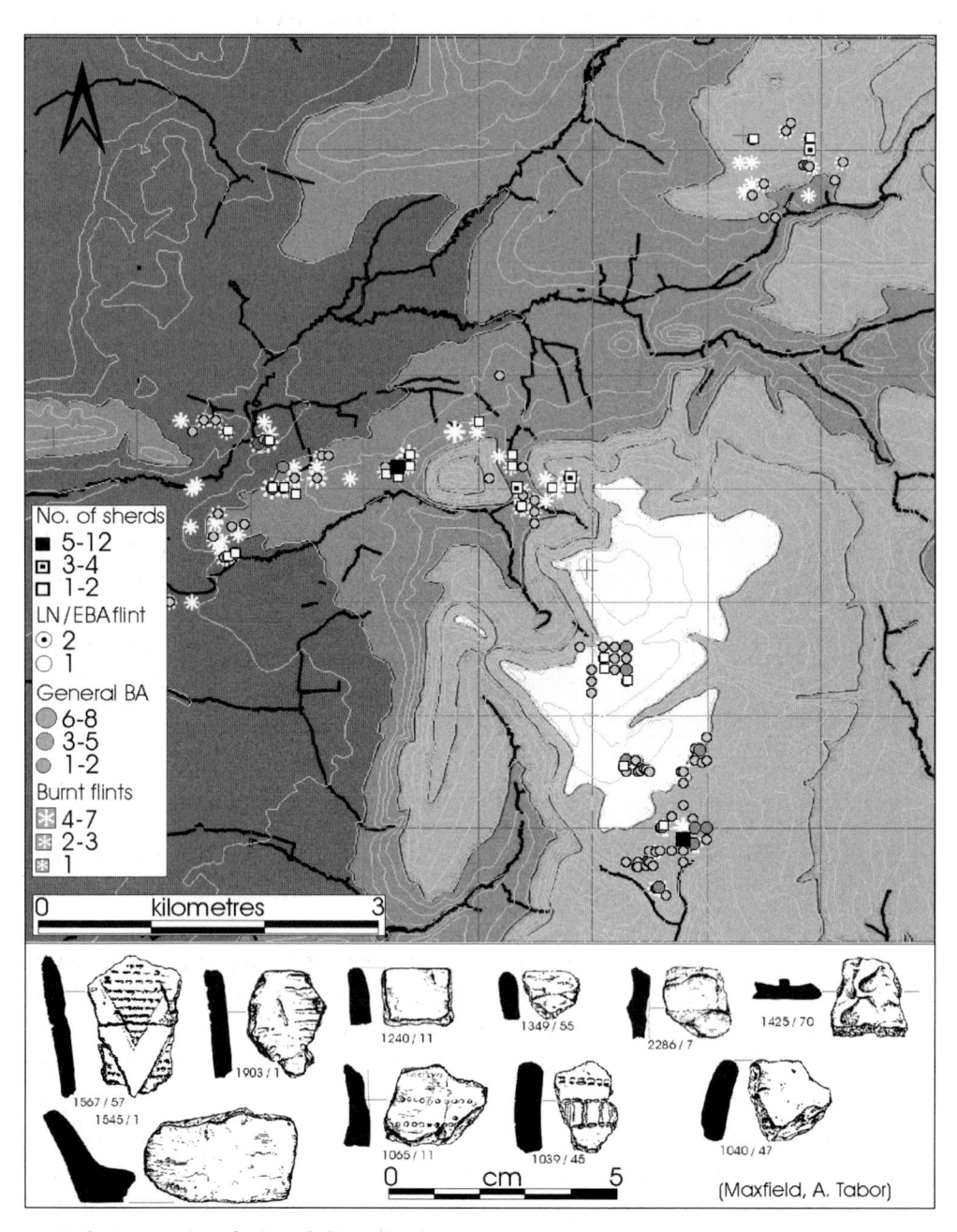

18 Early Bronze Age finds and their distribution

Territory and movement

One of the most frustrating aspects of working around Cadbury Castle is the general lack of upstanding earthworks earlier than from the Middle Iron Age. Until recently it had been assumed that for whatever reason, the causewayed enclosures, long barrows and henges of the Neolithic were simply never built in this region. Although SCEP has yet to find an example of one of those particular features, geophysical survey has demonstrated that some very substantial prehistoric landmarks have been obliterated. The earliest exceptions throughout the study area are three Early Bronze Age round barrows, two forming an overlapping 'twin', which Lane Fox and Rolleston excavated at Sigwells in 1876.

The relationship between the Sigwells north barrow and one of three, or possibly four, west-north-west to east-south-east long linear ditches, provides the first unambiguous evidence of large-scale clearance in Cadbury's environs (*19*). The linear ditch was cut by the barrow ring ditch, hence pre-dating a known Early Bronze Age feature. Relationships between barrows and linear features, usually ditches or lynchets, have been noted elsewhere, some in neighbouring counties. It has been assumed, and sometimes demonstrated, that the boundaries were later than the barrows, making the Sigwells discovery exceptionally early. The geophysical survey revealed a distinctive form of access from the north to south side of one boundary. For around 20m it became two overlapping ditches around 2m apart, the north one in discontinuous segments, the south continuous, in effect creating a double-ditched passage from one side to the other. The passage was long enough and wide enough to sort sheep marshalled by hurdles. The digging of segments may well pre-date the continuous ditch (although they are unlikely to be contemporary with a leaf-shaped arrowhead found in the upper fills of one) but they appear to have remained in use until backfilled by rubble upcast from a Middle Bronze Age enclosure ditch (see below, *30*).

The Victorian excavations of the barrows produced few diagnostic finds, with the notable exception of a 15cm (6ins) long three-rivetted bronze dagger and a two-piece 'bark coffin' housing a cremated youth from the south twin barrow. This secondary cremation (the burnt remains had been placed in the coffin *after* cremation) contrasted with the primary cremation identified in the single northernmost barrow but no form of burial was found in the other half of the twin. However, it has some features in common with an inhumation at Milsoms Corner. Both were set in large graves and in both cases preservation conditions allowed the mineralised survival of two-piece 'coffins' far bigger than required for the dead individual. At Milsoms Corner a 2.6m (8ft 7in) 'coffin' was made from a single layer of long narrow slat, fixed at either end to cross pieces, close to where small dowel-like pieces of wood penetrated its inner surface (*20*). The fully

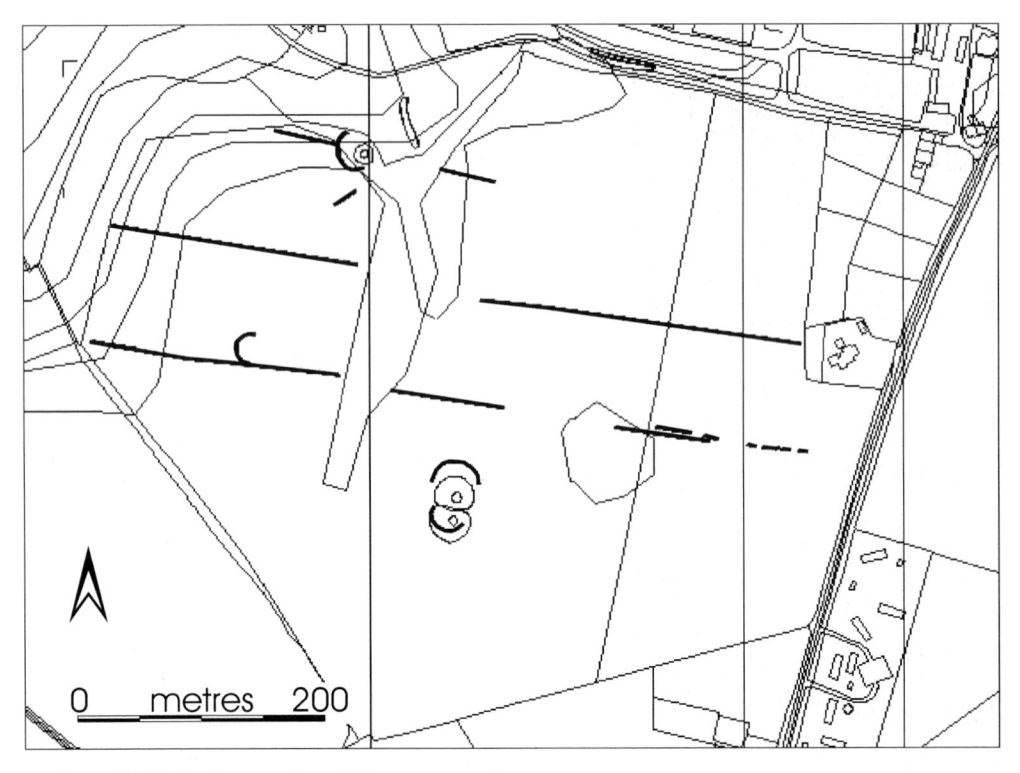

19 Sigwells: Early Bronze Age field system and barrows

articulated, flexed, body extended over 1.2m (4ft) in the middle of what Paul Johnson has described as a blunt-ended, boat-like, vessel aligned on Glastonbury Tor, some 19km (12 miles) north-west. The Sigwells grave was recorded as having a north to south alignment but it is tempting to speculate that it, too, might have been oriented towards the Tor.

If the Milsoms Corner burial ever had a covering mound it did not survive into the Late Bronze Age. In contrast, despite continuing modern ploughing, the Sigwells twin barrow still provides a fine platform. From its base a person can only see the plateau around him or her, but from the top the view takes in Glastonbury Tor, 22km (14 miles) north-west, the Mendip Hills behind it, the isolated hillfort of Brent Knoll rising from the Somerset Levels, 43km (27 miles) and, on a clear day, Brean Down, 50km (31 miles), both west-north-west. At Brean a deeply stratified sequence begins in the Early Bronze Age on a sea cliff projecting into the Bristol Channel, the west tail of the Mendip Hills. Thirty kilometres (19 miles) to the south-east, Hambledon Hill is the most prominent feature with three Neolithic causewayed enclosures and surely still a significant landmark to the communities of the Early Bronze Age.

First transformations

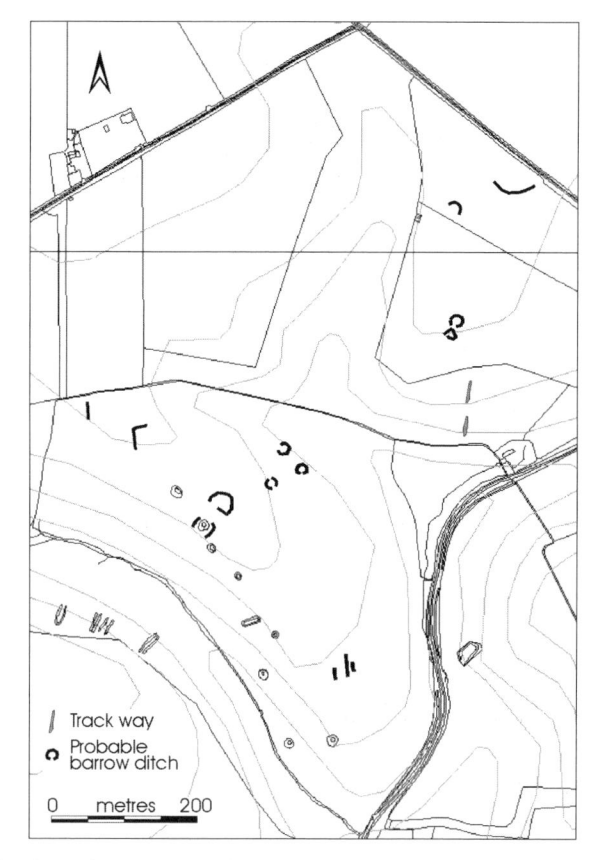

Left: 20 Milsoms Corner: Beaker burial. Glastonbury Tor is a hazy outline on the horizon

Right: 21 Seven Wells and Poyntington Downs: barrows

There is a widely held view that whilst barrows were set on high ground, typically just below the crest of a hill, settlement was on the valley sides and bottoms, and at some distance from the burial mounds. The thin but widespread distribution of pottery of the period, often diagnosed by the very distinctive thin-walled decorated Beaker sherds, may be regarded as further evidence for a similar pattern in the study area. There appears to have been a preference for valley sides and, in particular, low rises on valley bottoms and open lowland. There was also a pronounced clustering around Cadbury Castle (*18*). Traces of long linear north-west to south-east boundaries at Sparkford and Weston Bampfylde may be contemporary. A linear passed immediately to the west of a barrow ring ditch at Worthy, Weston Bampfylde. The barrow was probably destroyed during or before the Iron Age but the linear boundary has survived, with modification, up to the present.

Beaker vessels are associated more often with space reserved for the dead than the living, exemplified by the hot spot at Down Close, Seven Wells Down (*21*), where a

Cadbury Castle: The Hillfort and Landscapes

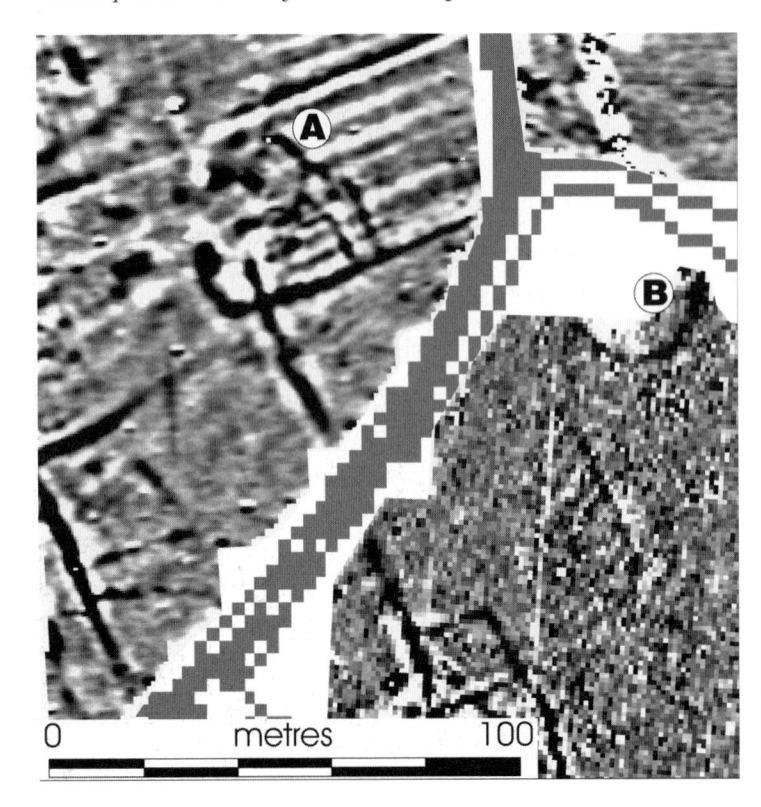

22 Crissells Green and The Moor: gradiometer plot showing ring ditches

regular test pit happened to bisect the ditch of a previously unknown barrow situated, typically, on a false crest. On the opposite side of the valley at Sheep Slait, Poyntington Down, geophysics has identified three more barrows and reports of beaker pottery found during the levelling of 'pillow' mounds (man-made rabbit warrens) on the south side of the same field suggest that at least some of these were also barrows. The dispersed sherds at Sigwells are unlikely to have a direct association with a barrow, but a group on the east of Woolston Manor Farm have been moved down a valley side in modern times and may well derive from a ploughed-out example. Much or all of the remaining pottery is likely to be associated with the living.

Less than 400m east of Cadbury, situated between the east gate and Hicknoll Slait (the hill offering the most expansive view of Cadbury's interior, *colour plate 2*), a 25m diameter ring ditch at Crissells Green included a small amount of Early Bronze Age pottery. The lack of a mound beneath deep hillwash suggests that it ringed a pond or disc barrow. A small portion of the ditch was excavated in 2002. Its steep sided U-profile was cut through thin ancient soil and gravels. As at Sigwells, it sliced through an earlier ditch but this one could not be traced reliably on the geophysical plot. After a short phase of silting, small localised deposits of charred wood and cattle long bones were laid at intervals along the ditch. One of the

First transformations

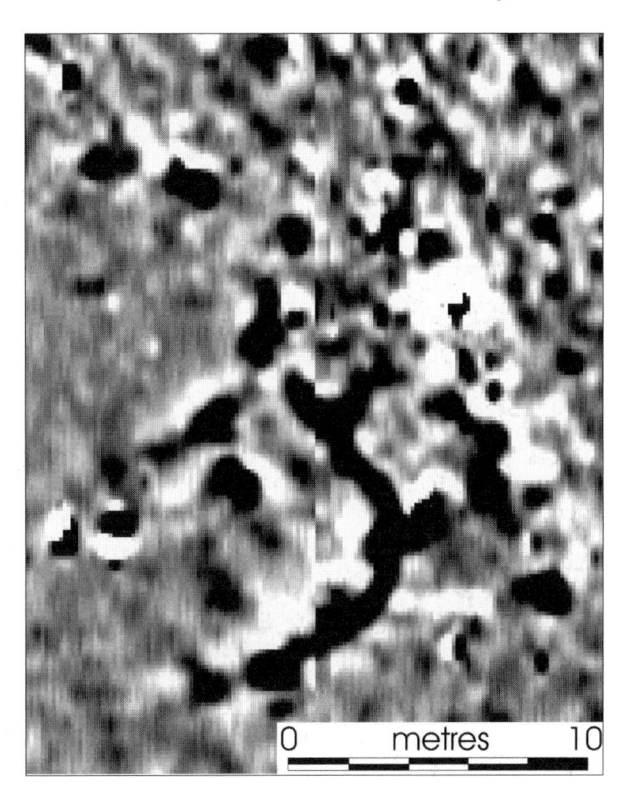

23 Card's Piece, Woolston: Early Bronze Age structure

deposits included a young man's lower jaw. Another circular geophysical anomaly, 100m further north in The Moor, remained elusive (*22*). A small excavation in 2005 encountered several Iron Age and Romano-British features but the circle remained safe under deep hillwash deposits and a raised water table in a valley choked by sediments washed down from the valley sides.

The clearest evidence for dwelling space is in areas east and, particularly, west of Cadbury Castle, a point of special interest because Alcock recovered remarkably little material of the period and concluded that the hilltop was largely unoccupied from the late third to the late second millennium BC. The west area, all within 500m of the hilltop, appears to centre on a low knoll, badly degraded by the plough in the later twentieth century but retaining the faintest trace of a broken 30m-diameter circular ditch on its east side. It may be contemporary with a semi-circular feature 240m further west, and with a 12m² enclosure and its annex in between the two. The latter seems likely to be associated with habitation and is strikingly similar in scale and form to a 15 x 15m sub square ditch with annex (*23*) and a possible associated boundary system on a plateau overlooking Cadbury from the north-east at Card's Piece, Woolston. Two targeted test pits across the ditch produced sparse non-diagnostic flint and rare, but exclusively, beaker pottery.

Some of the numerous linear magnetic features discovered during the gradiometer survey belong to a land management system similar to that on Sigwells. In the valleys immediately south-east of Cadbury a substantial holloway, with a long prehistoric life, already extended from the upper south-facing slopes of Littleton Hill and across Crissells Green to the stream in the valley bottom by the first half of the second millennium BC. Several boundary systems pre-date an Iron Age and Roman system within the valley in the 1000m dividing it from Cadbury Castle.

Pottery find-spots at North Field and Middle Mead, Weston Bampfylde, are in areas now clogged with alluvium and probably relate to special activities associated with watercourses, but the former was on a gentle slope which would have been well above the water level, while the latter was on a low gravel terrace. There is no reason why both should not have been close to settlement. In contrast, test pits between this low-lying land and Milsoms Corner produced no prehistoric pottery on a ridge of particularly intractable clays which would have remained wooded.

The marked variation in pottery distribution suggests that the methodology has successfully characterised foci of activity and that negative evidence, quite simply where finds of the period have not been found, genuinely reflects preferences in the pattern of land use. After excluding the barrow at Down Close, preference for south through to west-facing slopes, steep and gentle, or locations immediately above them, is discernible at Weston Bampfylde, Milsoms Corner, Littleton Hill and Woolston. North facing locations at North Field and Homeground appear to be associated with a river and a spring respectively (*18*). Other findspots are on nearly flat low or high ground. In a landscape where the population was well below its holding capacity, south-facing settlement is predictable. These topographic preferences on their own are not enough to indicate widespread arable agriculture nor are the long linear boundary systems which are more consistent with the management of livestock. More compelling is the marked preference for lighter, more tractable soils, and the avoidance of heavy soils around Sparkford, the Weston Bampfylde ridge and Scourlands, and north-facing slopes generally. On the sides and in the bottoms of several valleys from Seven Wells, Littleton and Woolston Manor Farm, small sherds of Early Bronze Age pottery and sparse flints from test pits are associated with charcoal-flecked hillwashes of up to 60cm (24in) in depth. These soils, some sealed by as much as 2m of overburden, constitute the first major phase of anthropogenic erosion.

MIDDLE BRONZE AGE (*24*)

Prior to the last two decades, much of the information about non-funerary aspects of Bronze Age life relied on excavations of very few enclosures and thousands of

First transformations

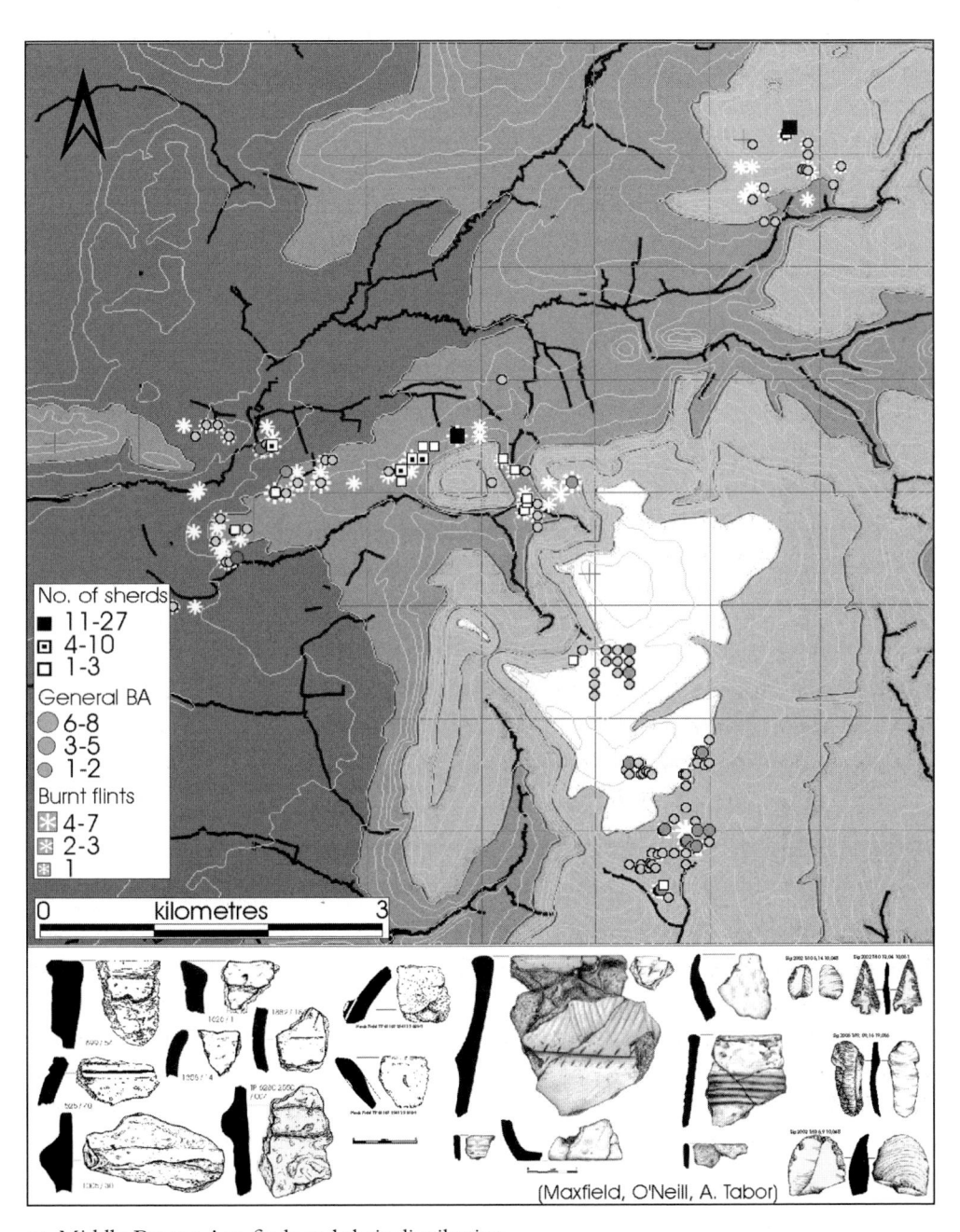

24 Middle Bronze Age finds and their distribution

metalwork deposits in wetlands and along watercourses, most found accidentally. The subsequent explosion of development-led archaeology not only identified new forms of site but revealed several hundred Middle to Late Bronze Age field systems, where previously fewer than a dozen were known.

Linear boundaries had an earlier inception in the Cadbury area but during the middle and later second millennium a new approach to claiming the landscape took shape. Where the regular strips on Sigwells were integral to a developing barrow cemetery (whilst other small enclosures and barrows used or accentuated the existing topography) there was a new assertiveness over not only the natural topography, but ancestral modifications of it. Difficult soils were still avoided, although the linear system around Sparkford and Weston Bampfylde represents a significant transgression, and wholesale alteration of existing system orientations showed a willingness to disregard, rather than modify, what went before.

Leslie Alcock held the view that for much of the second millennium BC Cadbury was dormant, an assumption repeated by subsequent writers. Certainly it is true that the excavations produced no more than a smattering of Middle Bronze Age pottery and fragments from a spearhead and blade, but the proliferation of material recovered from the immediate hinterland seems at odds with the hypothesis.

The landscape redefined

Important Middle Bronze Age structural remains are well-known from neighbouring counties, especially in south Dorset, yet in spite of the comparatively slight investigation of sites of the period, Somerset has produced a large number of very distinctive, highly wrought, bronze weapons and tools, contributing a distinctive Taunton phase to what has been termed the Ornament Horizon. Where once it was assumed that these beautiful bronzes were imported or derived from central European originals (largely on the assumption that Britain was a net importer of ideas from the continent) their proliferation around Taunton and the Levels suggests that trade in artefacts or ideas was sometimes in the opposite direction. Prior to SCEP, two sickles and a chisel recorded and accessioned to the County Museum by the redoubtable Revd Bennett in 1856 (*25*), were the only evidence for activity in the Cadbury area.

Since at least the Early Bronze Age there had been a trend towards the focusing of habitative settlement around Cadbury. This became more pronounced during the mid second millennium BC. The earliest pottery of the phase was from regular test pits at Milsoms Corner (some neighbouring an irregular rhomboid geophysical anomaly enclosing roughly 600m^2 on the west-facing side of the Milsoms Corner knoll). One pit was in the adjoining Homeground and another was a waterlogged alluvium-targeted test pit on the south side of the River Cam between Sparkford and Weston Bampfylde. In one of the Milsoms Corner test pits, a hollow surrounded

First transformations

25 The Sparkford Hoard

by stakeholes was dated by pottery. The Homeground pit produced a remarkable 27 sherds associated with large lumps of soft baked red clay. The magnetic responses in the west of the field suggest that there may be up to 30 similar features over an area of roughly 40 x 60m (*24*), constituting a form of burnt mound. These may comprise burnt stone, as is typical of these structures. There is strong evidence that they were linked to cooking, possibly metalworking and, more exotically, saunas. It is probably unhelpful to identify a single activity as they occur in various shapes and sizes.

Sporadic traces of long linear ditches to the west in the Weston Bampfylde and Sparkford areas, and perhaps at Woolston in the north-east, were oriented roughly north-west to south-east or approximately at a right angle and may have been constructed in the Early or Middle Bronze Age. In either case it can be demonstrated that at Sigwells at least one of the Early Bronze Age long linears survived to influence the layout of an otherwise north to south oriented enclosure and this may be true elsewhere. Reference to earlier landmarks was exemplified also by the digging of shallow scoops into the uppermost fills of the Sigwells north barrow ring ditch. Two were found in a 2m-wide trench, each including a cylindrical loomweight set in an ashy fill. 'Loomweight' is widely considered to be a misnomer as recent analysis of these perforated clay objects (also available in triangular and cuboid shapes) shows an association with heat-related activities. The prevailing view is that they were

Cadbury Castle: The Hillfort and Landscapes

bricks to allow air circulation in an oven or furnace. These deposits may represent a more widespread practice of integrating the residues of the living into the monuments of the long dead. Fire, whether of the furnace or the oven, was at the heart of the living as they sought to legitimate or newly assert rights over land.

The dense activity north and west of Cadbury is particularly striking. Seven of 14 regular test pits within a 300m arc around this side of the hill produced pottery, two bisecting features and two cutting into occupation soils of the Middle Bronze Age. Bearing in mind that this is a sampling rate of 1:10,000 over a 14ha area, it can be stated with some confidence that significant occupation lasted for several centuries. As time elapsed, a long linear, doubling as a track and boundary, was dug at the bottom of the lowest slopes of the Milsoms Corner spur, continuing north along the west side of the knoll, and stamped across an earlier north-west to south-east orientation. Several shorter lengths of ditch were parallel or perpendicular to it, some forming enclosures, incomplete where either the boundary form was not susceptible to magnetometry or it had been destroyed subsequently (*26*).

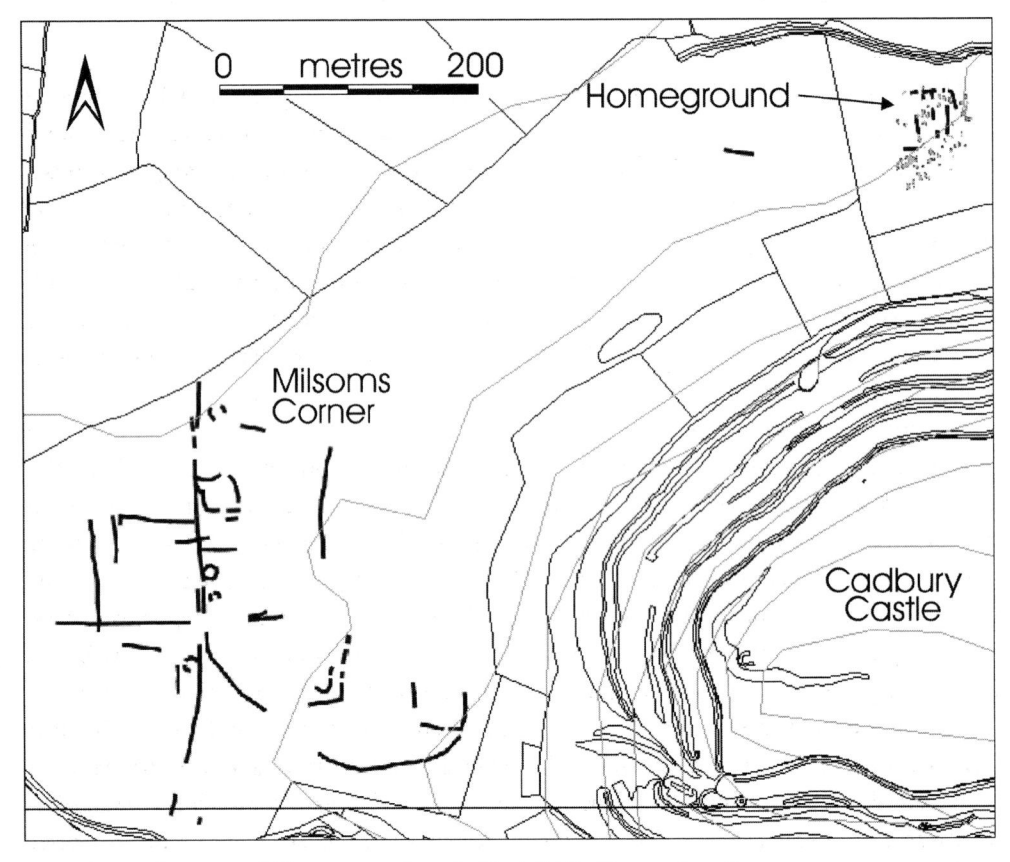

26 Milsoms Corner and Homeground: probable Middle Bronze Age features

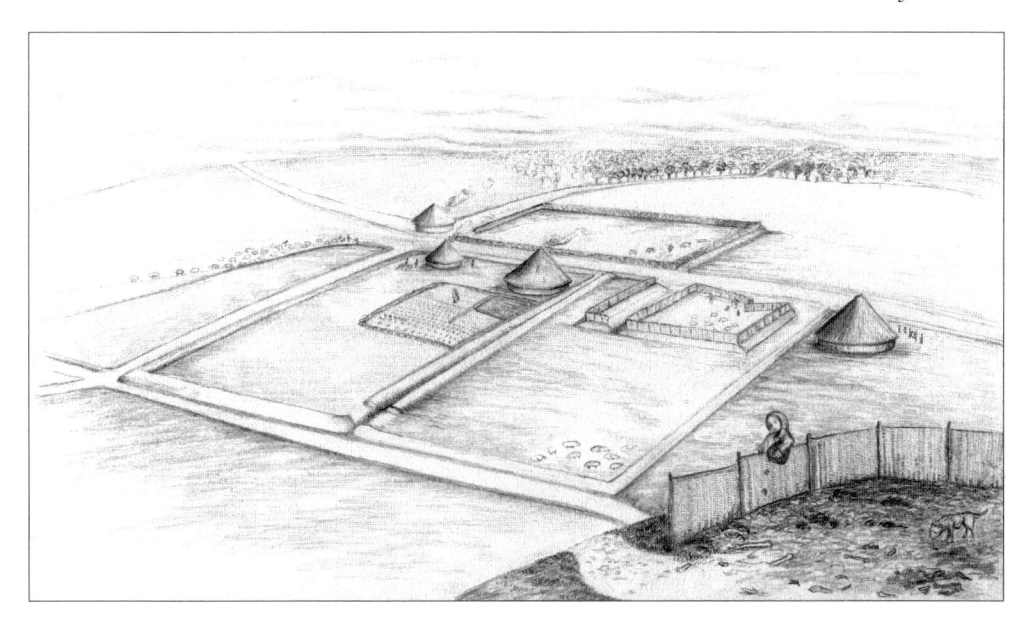

27 Milsoms Corner: view west from spur in the Middle Bronze Age. Amanda Tabor

The relationship of the boundary to Cadbury was analogous to a later Bronze Age ditch which determined the orientation of the man-made landscape around Danebury. Here, too, it determined the layout of enclosures and, arguably, plots. Two roundhouses to the east of the linear and one on the west, detected by the gradiometer, each set within ring ditches with diameters of around 10m, were bounded in a manner suggesting apportionment of land in family plots, but with ready access between plots implying a wider sense of community (*27*). One of the houses had a much smaller, possible ancillary, structure immediately to its south of a sort sometimes thought to shelter a few animals over winter.

A similarly oriented discrete rectangular ditch on the spur, partly lost to a combination of intense subsequent prehistoric activity to its north and to the modern plough along its west side, also enclosed a substantial structure discovered during excavations. Its floor was identified as a hollow gradually filled with a richly organic soil following its abandonment. The paucity of finds from within both the enclosure and the structure suggest that neither served a domestic purpose. Two metres from its south-east corner, the east ditch cut through the lower legs bones of an Early Bronze Age grave, causing Beaker sherds to be scattered amongst its initial silts. Whilst the slighting of the body may have been accidental, it is clear that the subsequent intention was to incorporate the possible ancestor, probably as a means for legitimising the claims of the ditch diggers to the land extending westwards, and to the hill rising behind it. As we shall see, at least one of the lower leg bones was retained and cared for over a long period. Radiocarbon dating gave

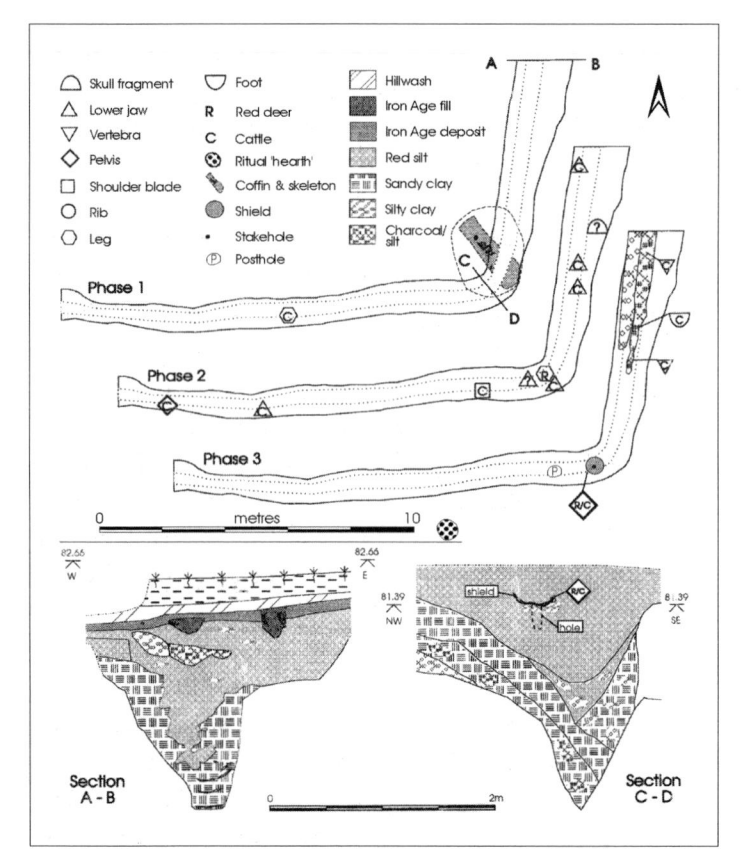

28 Milsoms Corner: section and schematic plans of the Bronze Age enclosure ditch

a date of 1380 to 1210 BC for a cow jaw from the upper middle ditch fills, and pottery included sherds related to the Middle Bronze Age style named after Trevisker in Cornwall, several centuries later than the burial. The individual within it, or what the community chose to make him represent, was considered significant enough for at least one of his leg bones to be kept with care for several more centuries (see *Milsoms Corner shield*, p.84).

Towards the east, the truncated V-profiled ditch has survived to its full depth of up to 1.2m. On the south side, traces of an internal upcast bank were found, slumping into it over slowly formed primary silts, already up to 30cm deep, after which it appears to have stabilised, probably due to turf formation. Subsequently there were one or more episodes of deliberate infilling, starting with a small dump of hearth material on the west side of the east ditch. Later fills included individual animal bones, usually cattle and, typically, their lower jaws. After further natural silting, the ditch stabilised again as a slight depression with a commensurately slight, and probably intermittent, residual bank (*28*). The pattern of cattle jaw deposition

First transformations

turned out to be a feature elsewhere at this time and was to continue as a distinctive preferred rite in the area until at least the Late Romano-British period, surely indicative of resilient local beliefs and the long-term continuity of a particular population.

A roughly 16m² ditch on a plateau at Lady Field, Woolston, enclosed a floor area which was dated by exclusively Middle Bronze Age pottery from a targeted test pit. It is the only probable domestic dwelling space of this period excavated by the project. Its contrast with several areas of specialised activity suggests methodology-induced bias.

The new south to north orientation of land division appears to have been specific to an area within approximately 1000m of Cadbury Castle, west and east of the hill. Elsewhere broadly north-west to south-east boundaries either originated in the Early Bronze Age or are expansions of the earlier system. A track extended south from the steep Littleton Hill, a step below Hicknoll Slait, across Crissells Green to the stream, but although it would appear to have been a prime site for cultivation there is no evidence for a field system there.

Craft fairs at Sigwells

One of the most intriguing features revealed by the geophysical survey was a 30 x 60m enclosure (*9, 29*) at Sigwells, rectangular but for its north boundary which respected one of the Early Bronze Age linear ditches (*30*). The data suggests that it had a south entrance with complex related external features and a less elaborate entrance towards the north end of the west boundary. When exploratory trenches targeted its north-west corner and south entrance in 2000, the long linear was expected to prove Late Roman and the enclosure Early Mediaeval. However, the relatively few sherds recovered were thought to be later Bronze Age and the lack of later finds demonstrated that it was most unlikely to be Roman. In 2002, a larger trench along the west side uncovered not only the enclosure ditch but the first substantial contemporary feature within it, a trough-shaped pit (*colour plates 4 & 5*) with a rapid fill including many large sherds of globular urn type, Middle Bronze Age, pottery. It was not until a 20 by 35m trench was opened in 2005 along the north, central and east areas of the enclosure that its significance became clear.

Sections across the east ditch showed three phases. In the first, it had silted up slowly before being re-cut. In its second phase, the ditch had not been open long enough for any silt to accumulate on its bottom before a rubble fill was thrown in from the inside. Had the ditch been open for a winter, or even during a single heavy rain storm, some basal silt would have been present. After backfilling, shallow cylindrical pits were dug at approximately 2m intervals in a line along at least 20m of the inside edge of the ditch (*31*). This side of the enclosure displays the sequence

Cadbury Castle: The Hillfort and Landscapes

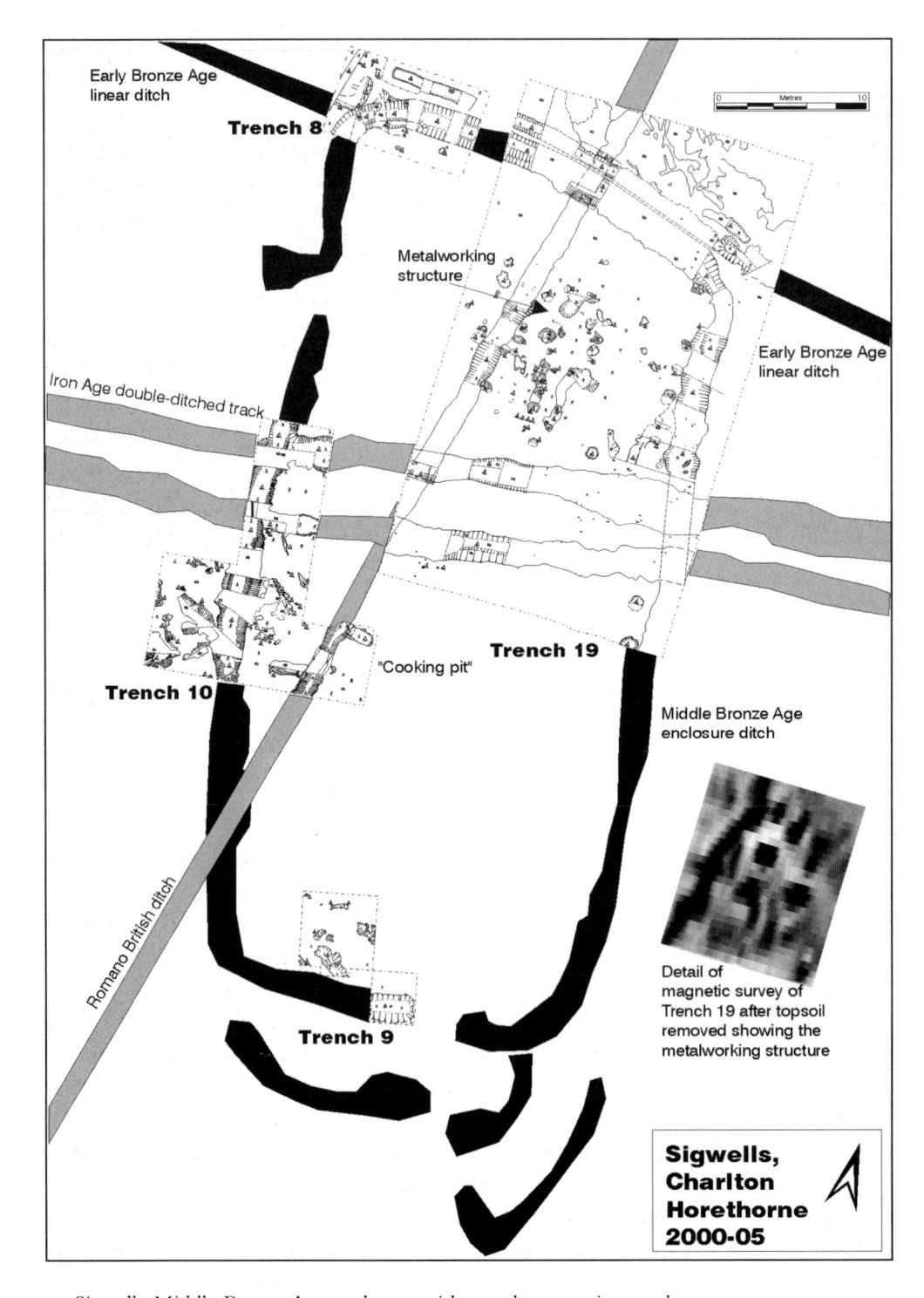

29 Sigwells: Middle Bronze Age enclosure with trenches superimposed

30 Sigwells: enclosure's north ditch showing its relationship to the smaller Early Bronze Age long linear ditch

most clearly, although some sections on the west side show traces of a slow-filling phase before the rapid rubble fill cut. The rubble fill was re-cut on the west side over a 12m length, revealing natural rock which was exposed long enough to weather while the re-cut filled slowly. The terminus at the south entrance showed only one phase, a rapid rubble fill. The siting of the enclosure's north ditch was determined by and incorporated the passage between the north and south sides of the Early Bronze Age linear. In its first form the enclosure appears to have used the existing linear, but later a ditch specific to it was dug and part rapidly backfilled with rubble, with its upper portion left open, effectively assuming the function of the old boundary, and possibly associated with the cylindrical pits.

Although magnetometry suggested that the north end was the site of the most intensive activity, our first objective as a landscape project was to establish the enclosure's date and its relationship with features playing a significant part in the wider landscape. The presence of a small number of casting mould fragments in the earlier trenches raised the tantalising possibility that the busy north end had been the site of metalworking so the final large trench was targeted there. After the topsoil had been removed by machine and the surface cleaned down to natural rock by hand, cut features began to appear, but a new magnetic survey over the cleared area suggested the presence of further features which had been merely indistinct 'possibles' (*29*).

31 Sigwells: enclosure's east ditch rubble fill, cut by Pit F034

A 2.5m-long area of intermittently scorched natural rock was all that remained of a hearth or furnace where copper alloy was heated for casting on the west side of a circular building with a diameter of just under 6m. Although a Romano-British ditch (F004) had removed a nearly 2m-wide swathe from the west of the building, we can determine something of its layout. Centred on a 40cm (16in) diameter packed post (F043), access was gained to the east side of the slightly oval structure via a 4m-long, 1m-wide corridor from the south (*32*). The gloomy interior was divided by a screen or partition wall, supported by much less substantial posts extending from south to north in a continuation of the line of the corridor's west side. The scoops in the lee (F011, F013) of the building were filled with burnt stone, mainly of a bluish grey colour, implying that the fire had been enclosed, with a few fine sandy clay casting mould fragments (*colour plate 6*) mixed in, among 600 from the four trenches. A single droplet of bronze casting waste was found in a scoop and another in the upper fill of the east ditch and small pieces of slag were found during the processing of environmental soil samples. There were also whetstones and hammerstones within and close to the building which would have had a role in finishing cast objects (*33*). Some fragments of quern may have had secondary roles as anvils. Most, if not all, of the cut features associated with the structure were filled rapidly after a short period of use, suggesting that they were contemporary with the rapid rubble ditch fill, a view supported by the discovery of a sherd from the north ditch, from the same vessel as another in the hole for one of several large support posts.

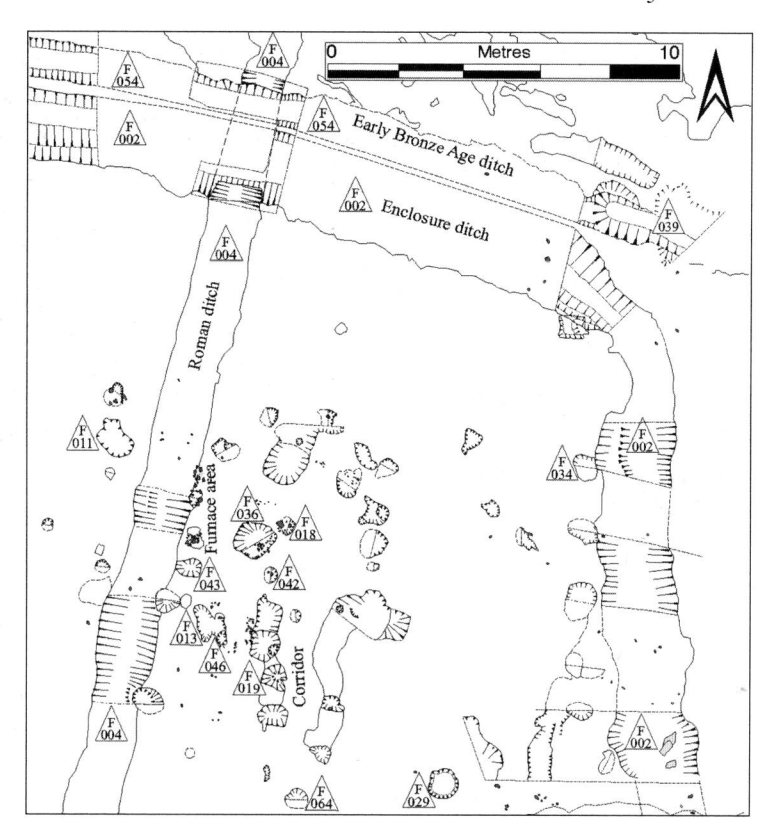

32 Sigwells: plan of features associated with the metalworking structure

The north end of the enclosure is protected by a thin prehistoric soil but the surface of the southern third has been degraded by modern ploughing, cutting off the tops of features and almost certainly removing the shallowest entirely. Two postholes (Trench 9) and slight intermittent gullies were identified (Trenches 9 and 10; *29*) but the extent of the destruction was highlighted by the damage to a cattle jaw placed in the upper fill of the ditch terminal. However, the lack of strong magnetic signatures in the south suggests that during the enclosure's life this was a fairly open area, contrasting with the unexcavated north-west interior, where there are several significant anomalies. Even without excavation, the proximity of a concentration of scrapers in Trench 8, and bone points elsewhere, suggest that skins were worked, whilst across the enclosure a minimum of five different saddle querns testify to the production of cereal-based foods. The querns offer further insight into the function of the enclosure; they were from at least three different sources. A red igneous and a greensand quern, placed side by side in the west enclosure ditch (*colour plate 7*) were from Hestercombe, approximately 40km (25 miles) west and Pen Pits, 15km (9 miles) east of Sigwells, whilst another in a posthole is of Mendip Old Red Sandstone from at least 22km (14 miles) north. If this

Cadbury Castle: The Hillfort and Landscapes

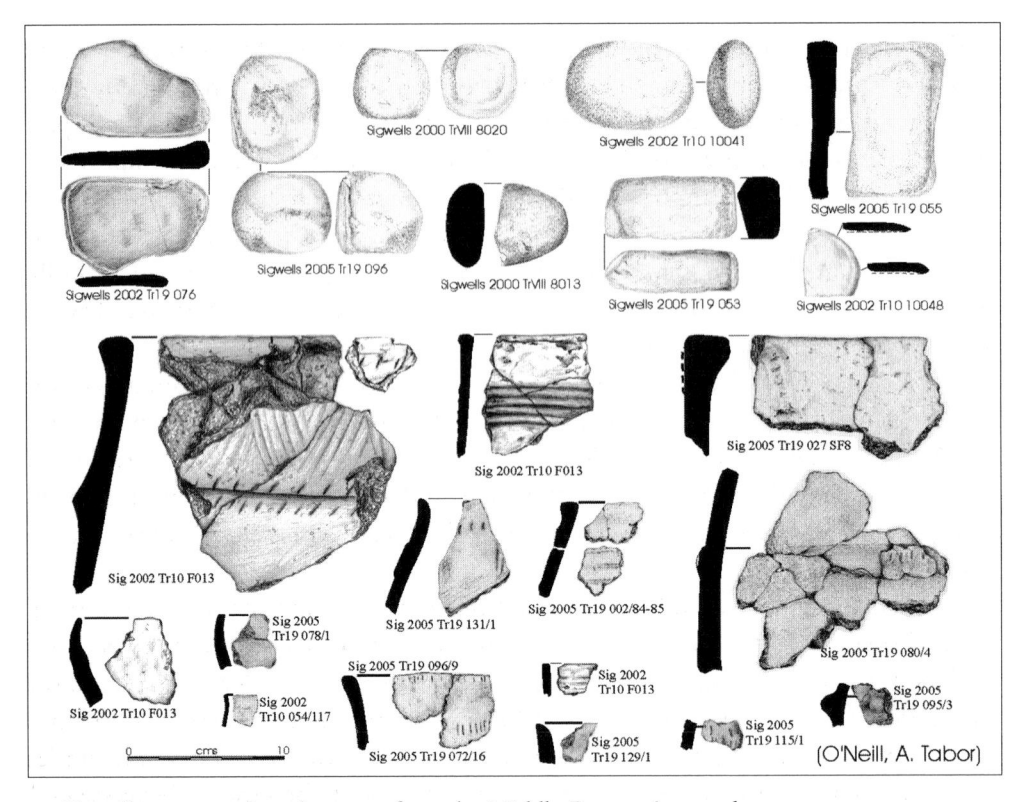

33 Sigwells: stone tools and pottery from the Middle Bronze Age enclosure

enclosure phase had been used over decades or more, it would be acceptable to argue that the querns had been imported from time to time by a local population. This is an unlikely explanation when the period in question was no longer than a few weeks.

    These more mundane crafts were sideshows to the main attraction: weaponry produced by peripatetic metalworkers, who were perhaps from Cornwall given the location of the most distant quern stone and bearing in mind attested Cornish Bronze Age tin extraction. Copper, the essential ingredient of bronze, has been mined there in modern times but there are no known prehistoric extraction sites and it is equally possible that the raw material and craftsmen had travelled from Wales, where Great Orme provided a contemporary bronze source. There have been finds associated with bronze-working along much of the Severn Valley, from the Breiddin hillfort (later than the Sigwells examples) in the north to several sites around Tewkesbury, perhaps tracing a long-lived route, although in a recent study based on the distribution of clay mould fragments and crucibles, a Bristol University postgraduate, Christoph Skowranek, found no evidence for topographical preference. It may be the territorial marginality of the land which was important.

First transformations

Skowranek noted that mould fragments in scoops adjacent to the metalworking structure were far more fragmentary than necessary to extract the finished product. He believes that the producers intended to break them beyond recognition as part of a conscious concealment of their craft. Nonetheless he has identified impressions from spear, sword, rapier, chape and socketed axe, several showing affinity with pieces from a hoard found at Wilburton, Cambridgeshire. Remarkably, he has refitted several hilt fragments from one of the scoops (*32*, F011) to a beautifully preserved sword (*colour plate 6*), found during the nineteenth-century building of the railway station at Midsomer Norton, Somerset, 37km (23 miles) north of Sigwells. Conventionally, the Wilburton style had been dated to the tenth century BC but in the 1990s radiocarbon dating of material directly associated with tools and weapons (for instance wood from a spear shaft preserved in the socket) from the hoard itself and analogous finds elsewhere, indicated that an inception as early as 1150 BC was likely. The pottery at Sigwells suggests an even earlier date is possible.

In drawing together members of several different communities from the region, the craft fairs provided not only an opportunity for the exchange of goods and animals but also a chance for feasting, reinforcement of alliances and, most importantly, intermarriage (*colour plate 8*). The construction of the enclosure would have been completed before the arrival of the metalworkers by a substantial workforce drawn from more than one community. In itself the process demonstrated planning and communication over considerable distances and it should probably be regarded as part of a long-term cycle of craft fairs. As the next chapter will show, Sigwells may have hosted more than one event. But why at Sigwells, a place without its own water supply and 3km from the nearest intensive settlement? Its very marginality offered a neutral space with the advantage of intervisibility with more distant places.

How would this temporary community have been sustained? Much of the food must have been brought on the hoof. Clare Randall's analysis of the excavated animal bone identified a conservative minimum of four cattle, four sheep or goats, two pigs and a single red deer. Some of them may have been roasted but the representation of bones from all parts of the bodies of at least three sheep in the cooking pit implies that boiled meat formed part of the diet. The pit would have been lined, either with hide or with clay (there were slight traces of yellow clay on some of its sides), then filled with water brought to the boil by adding hot stones. Carbonised residues on the outsides of pot sherds show that some vessels were used for cooking over a fire, whilst others lacking the residues would have been used for decanting food into bowls for individual servings. Water might have been brought-in daily but a trough-like pit inside the south entrance and another, 4m south-west of the cooking pit, would have made effective cisterns if lined with hides. Water consumption would have been high to meet the domestic needs of people and animals, as well as industrial processes, so similar features may remain to be found in other parts of the enclosure.

With the exception of the metalworking building there is little positive evidence for shelter. A few isolated posts, one just inside the enclosure's south entrance, and very shallow plough-damaged arcing gullies in Trenches 9 and 10, may have supported hide 'tents' but much of the south areas appear to have been open, perhaps reserved for important open-air gatherings and events.

Ritual deposits in the postholes of the circular building demonstrate that it was dismantled and the ditch and cooking pit were backfilled when the craft fair had run its course. If the process was carried out by most of the visitors it would have been a great deal quicker than its construction, quite possibly being completed in less than a day.

The perceptible residues associated with the rites of closure deserve special attention. The first in the sequence was a toothless cattle lower jaw resting on the very bottom of the north ditch. It could have been placed there at any time from the moment the ditch had been re-cut to immediately before its backfilling. In contrast, at the south end there were cattle lower jaws with teeth in the middle and uppermost fills. None were found in the west and east ditches, although an example found in the upper fill of a 6m length of segmented ditch to the north, associated with the Early Bronze Age linear (*19*), suggests that this was already an established pattern of deposition. The rubble filling the next segment may well be the upcast from the enclosure ditch, so that the quern in it may belong to the fair episode rather than the Early Bronze Age. The contrastingly coloured green and red querns from rubble in a section across the west ditch have already been mentioned (*colour plate 7*). Although both were worn, neither had been used up and they are unlikely to have been discarded casually, a view reinforced by the lack of any other whole or fragmentary querns from the ditch. Lying face down, side by side, but derived from sources at opposing points of the compass, each is likely to have been brought and used by a different group of people. These two instruments of sustenance represent a new or re-affirmed alliance, perhaps consecrating and safe-guarding a marriage agreed at the fair. In contrast, a scatter of limestones burnt to a blue hue seals the uppermost fill of the enclosure's north-west corner, symbolising its closure, its death.

It is impossible to state with certainty whether or not the pottery in the cooking pit was placed there as a matter of practical convenience or as part of the overall scheme of ritual closure. On the other hand, several objects in the metalworking building's postholes were demonstrably placed with care and in a position which indicated that the post had been removed. Of the large postholes, the richest example includes much of a quern, a bone point and a bevelled hammer or grinding

First transformations

stone, as well as decorated pottery (*32, F036*). One of the most intriguing deposit types took the form of burnt red stones placed on the bases of internal wall posts (*colour plate 9*). An elaboration of the theme included a buff red cylindrical loomweight with the stone in a very similar posthole, next to a scoop filled with burnt stone and refractory material (*colour plate 10*). We can only speculate about the circumstances in which lightly roasted fragments of human skull were placed in a post setting on the west side of the entrance corridor (*32, F019*).

THE QUIET CENTURIES?

Prior to the project's work, Cadbury Castle was presented as first the main, almost exclusive, area of activity in the study area during the Neolithic, then as a place where nothing perceptible happened. It was assumed that activity in the surrounding landscape was correspondingly sparse, a view now so obviously wrong that arguments for the abandonment of the hill are barely sustainable, despite the lack of evidence from Alcock's excavations. During a span of over 2000 years, humans transformed space and their consciousness of it. In the Mesolithic it is probable that spaces were circumscribed but not by means which created a long-term impact. Demarcation of space was part of consciousness but not yet rendered concrete by ditches and banks. The act of demarcating space by such means transformed a community's consciousness of it, indeed, made it tangibly theirs. In doing this, people altered their understanding of what they could do with the land and they became agents consciously engaged in that process.

Initial clearances and marked paths did not have a huge impact in themselves but they created the imaginative scope for more ambitious projects in the Early Bronze Age, requiring ever greater communal effort. We can measure that ambition not only in the number and length of ditches but in the depth of hillwash on the valley sides and bottoms and the corresponding depletion of soils on high ground, where intensive ploughing left its mark. Evidence from the Wessex chalk has suggested that this long linear manner of land division originated in the Late Bronze Age but at Sigwells we can demonstrate that they were created at around the same time as, and before, Early Bronze Age barrows.

At some point in the later second millennium BC people changed their means of subsistence and large-scale soil movement ceased. Either there was a reversion to greater animal husbandry or arable agriculture became more sustainable. Certainly some of the lower valley sides and bottoms had accumulated deep, light tractable soils in a more sheltered environment where erosion would have been slower.

We can say little of the character of dwelling. The Early Neolithic sunken floor at Milsoms Corner supported a lightweight structure whilst postholes on the hilltop provide tantalising possibilities of substantial timber buildings. There are no identified dwellings from the Early Bronze Age but we can identify two types of settlement in the Middle Bronze Age. The floor and enclosure at Woolston was an isolated, farmstead-like, short-lived settlement, perhaps serving one family for a single generation. The orderly plots and structures at Milsoms Corner and burnt mounds in Homeground evidence long-term settlement for a sizeable group which made prolonged use of a specialised ritual enclosure on the spur and repeatedly feasted below the north slopes of Cadbury at what were probably seasonal gatherings. Their proximity to an important settlement implies either a phase (cordoned pottery at Homeground probably pre-dates the material from the Sigwells enclosure) when diverse groups felt comfortable with meeting on another's territory or that the festivities were exclusive to the community.

The Sigwells craft fair offers important glimpses into economy and social organisation at a regional scale. We may say with confidence that certain crafts were left to designated peripatetic specialists who travelled from a considerable distance to manufacture and exchange their products, probably during the summer months. What did these craftsmen receive in exchange? It is easy to see that their immediate needs for shelter and food were provided for by the host communities, but they must also have returned with items that made it worthwhile to make a journey which lasted several weeks. Did they have a home community which tended their flocks and crops while they journeyed between craft fairs or were they able to live on the proceeds? At the very least, we may guess that they were enriched by their craft.

The implications are important, giving metalworkers attributes quite unlike those of any other people. As long distance travelling workers they had a degree of autonomy over their lives which was not afforded to members of their community of origin or to those they visited. Much of their time was spent in spaces between those determined by human settlement, rendering them less accountable than other people, including the local headmen. They had a pivotal role in exchange networks which would not have been restricted to the supply of metals. Their own products – weapons – had no direct relationship with sustenance-based needs such as food or clothing, yet they required a great deal of labour investment. Casting and distribution was at the end of a process which included extraction, smelting and transport. There were also 'administration' costs involved in organising labour and advance communication with the communities responsible for setting up fairs. Were many of these processes carried out by the smiths themselves or did they have a retinue which ran the infrastructure to free them to perform their craft? At the very least their 'payment' must have included food to cover the periods of travelling, with the implication that some of it must have been on the hoof. No members of Bronze Age society in Britain were better placed to acquire the range and amount of material goods which represented the wealth of the time. Such wealth translated into influence and power.

We should also consider why, if metalworking was the work of peripatetic craftsman, Somerset and the neighbouring areas of Devon and Dorset have produced a very distinct style of local bronzes from a century or so earlier, with a marked resemblance to material found in Germany. Did travelling craftsman create a particular style for a particular patron? Were the bronzes imported, despite the fact that far more have been found in Somerset than in Germany? Or were the producers themselves from Somerset?

Around Cadbury, the Middle Bronze Age field system was a manifestation of a new authority breaking from the past, a sign of prestige as well as a means to prosperity. In creating the system, decisions were made about the apportionment of territory, even about who could travel through which parts of the restructured landscape. How did a particular individual or group reach a position of such power in a world previously dominated by kinship and lineage? A large part of the answer lies in the means to metal technology. A lithic-based technology required great skill but it could be learnt by many members of the community. Its greatest socio-political significance was gained through its acquisition from the chalklands. Whilst controlling the sources of copper, tin and latterly lead would have been a great advantage, the knowledge of production techniques was even more potent. Furthermore, plasticity in design was achieved through casting created objects which could be varied according to demand but repeated where there was a desire for uniformity, reinforcing a communal or territorial identity.

To maximise their power, producers needed to establish links with consumers, which meant giving them something in return, necessitating the generation of agricultural surplus and intensification of land use. Those who could provide the sites and facilities for fairs, such as that at Sigwells, would have gained rapidly in status (partly through sheer display, partly through the indebtedness of those who used the facilities) through the paradoxical good fortune of their geographical location close to a marginal but visible space. This natural advantage might take the form of control over land or waterborne routes, productive soils or defensible positions. A further paradox lay in the consequence that individuals or groups striving for increased power to secure their advantage had a general destabilising effect on larger society, not because of an absolute pressure for productive land but because of a desire for particular preferred spaces. David Yates' valuable synthetic work shows that much of the ensuing drama was played out along the Thames Valley and the coast and inland watercourses of south-east and southern England but SCEP's work shows that Cadbury Castle would also have had a part.

Over nearly 3000 years, the landscape developed from woodland with clearings and paths to one which was increasingly defined by human intervention, resulting not only in the introduction of long-term boundaries but changes in the balance of flora and fauna. Excepting the apparent hiatus in the Late Neolithic, it was populated in isolated settlements which were gradually abandoned in favour of a marked focus around Cadbury by the Middle Bronze Age, a trend which was to become more pronounced during the early first millennium BC.

4

A CENTRAL PLACE

In the previous chapter we saw how land around Cadbury became the pre-eminent focus of settlement during the Middle Bronze Age. By the beginning of the first millennium BC there had been a radical shift as it became the exclusive site of settlement within its particular locale. As a consequence, previously loosely defined Early Bronze Age territories and the spaces between are more obviously discernible, the settlements within the former situated increasingly on, or very close to, enclosed hilltops spaced at least 3km (1.9 miles) apart, reflecting tensions between territorial groups. It is tempting to suggest increasing insularity, although the presence of bronze artefacts and a half gold bracelet of the tenth to ninth centuries BC on Cadbury Castle are physical proof of contact with a wider world, in particular with seaborne trade. Two roughly contemporary gold bracelets were found in a midden deposit at Brean Down, close to where the north Somerset River Axe issues into the Bristol Channel, and two others have been found in spots close to the river but much further inland.

Cadbury itself is at least 10km (6.2 miles) from any river which would have been navigable, and more than 30km (18.6 miles) from the Axe; although most gold bracelets of the period are from near the coast there are notable examples from inland. A single rare object sheds very limited light on Cadbury's wider links to the world, but the issue is an important one in current research. Barry Cunliffe has outlined a general model of maritime contact for the first millennium BC linking west Britain to the western fringes of Europe and ultimately to the Mediterranean. This Atlantic zone is distinct from Channel and North Sea zones linking central southern and south-east Britain and the east coast to their European neighbours. Cadbury's situation at the neck of the south-west peninsula is on the notional eastern boundary of the Atlantic zone, where it was well-placed to be an intermediary.

Cadbury Castle is one of the very few prehistoric sites which can demonstrate a continuous span of occupation through the first millennium BC, and before advancing further the reader needs to be aware that there remains considerable disagreement over the all important dating of the pottery. It is a crucial matter in establishing the story of Cadbury and its landscape, so a short section is devoted to presenting the case for the chronology preferred by SCEP, covering the Late Bronze Age and the whole of the Iron Age. In all the following chapters there will be extensive reference to the archaeology of Cadbury Castle itself, but the aim is to give a clear sense of the hillfort's relationship with the wider landscape through time rather than to provide a detailed account of the hillfort interior, which can be acquired from other books. There are exceptions where I have argued for interpretations at variance with those publications.

DATING IN THE FIRST MILLENNIUM BC

The significance of material residues, their dates and cultural associations, remains an issue fraught with difficulties. Writing in 1972, Alcock was reluctant to discard invasionist theories which had largely been abandoned for a decade. His perspective was informed by the belief that he could identify a distinctly varied pottery sequence extending from the Late Bronze Age and through five Iron Age phases. He considered that the decorative motifs of the Early Iron Age represented a stylistic rupture with indigenous potting traditions, whilst stressing that the Bronze Age/Iron Age transition itself was gradual. He went on to discern stylistic similarities to material from northern France, southern Germany and the Netherlands, while pointing out the similar geographical affinities for some of Cadbury's bronzes (*colour plate 15*).

In pointed contrast, the authors of the English Heritage report published in 2000 sought to 'avoid the many pitfalls of a spurious chronological accuracy'. Certainly, by the time the report was being assembled, the archive was showing its age; stratigraphical records were sometimes elusive and in any event budgetary constraints led to drastic and highly selective 'sampling' of two crucial elements: bone and pottery. The former deficit is being addressed by Clare Randall. There are no plans for the latter to be resolved.

Alcock's ceramic classifications in an important 1980 paper on the first-millennium BC pottery were broadly right except, perhaps, for the first centuries BC/AD. The problem lay in the categorisation of the many thousands of featureless sherds and, on an extremely busy settlement, the probability that many were moved one or more times after their initial deposition. The currently prevailing opinion of pottery in southern Britain is that there was no rupture in the styles requiring a special explanation and that Cadbury was no exception.

The solution offered by the later report's authors was to blur the chronology, emphasising continuity in the shape of persistent traits and activities of social reproduction. In so doing the over-determined periodisation by technology (Bronze Age, Iron Age) was largely removed from the narrative to be replaced by Early Cadbury (roughly from the foundation of the settlement to around 300 BC), Middle Cadbury (roughly 350 BC to AD 100) and Late Cadbury (AD 50 onwards). In broad terms, the middle period coincides with the building of the ramparts and occupation of the hillfort by people with a material culture which had embraced local term traditions, as well as some traits from central southern England and Europe. The scheme is subdivided where stratigraphy allows discrimination, notably on the ramparts and south-west gate, and where there were alternating bands of soil and cobbling on the east of the plateau. Without doubt full analysis of the ceramic assemblages from pits would have greatly increased their datability but the budget did not allow for this.

Whilst we have literary evidence for the division of the year by the people of north-west Europe in the Late Iron Age, we do not know how they counted the years passed. Written genealogies derived from oral traditions imply an evolving chain of events with no absolute reference point. Archaeologists frequently correlate events to such a point or, failing that, to identifiable, but undated, events. They are also faced with the issue of measurable duration, fundamentally a concept imposed after the event and hence alien to people and places who are the objects of our study. If we take Early Cadbury as an example, perhaps representing a period of seven centuries, the number of pits and possible structures becomes very important to ascertain whether or not the settlement was a place of regular seasonal occupation, or one which was used intermittently on an *ad hoc* basis. For understanding the dynamics of the community, it would be useful to have a strong idea of whether or not key industrial processes took place before or after the hill was enclosed, probably protected, by massive banks. Did the population swell before the banks were constructed or were people drawn to the hill because they existed? The combination of shortcomings in field-recording and restrictions on the amount of data analysed meant that some of the most crucial aspects of the Cadbury narrative have not been addressed by the English Heritage report.

Where in 1980 Alcock had stressed that the Cadbury pottery series ought be considered in its own terms, Ann Woodward rightly set it within a scheme developed at Hengistbury Head, Dorset, and refined at Danebury. Although the respective assemblages are distinct, they share enough traits to allow chronological alignment. Comparisons of a particular jar type found at Danebury and Houghton Down (a site targeted by the former's environs programme), JB1.3, bears a close family resemblance to similarly named vessels assigned to Alcock's Cadbury 6 and to a lesser degree Cadbury 5. It is a class which Barry Cunliffe and his colleague Cynthia Poole have given a date range of seventh to fifth centuries BC (Danebury ceramic phase or cp1-3), close to Alcock's scheme but up to two centuries earlier than that

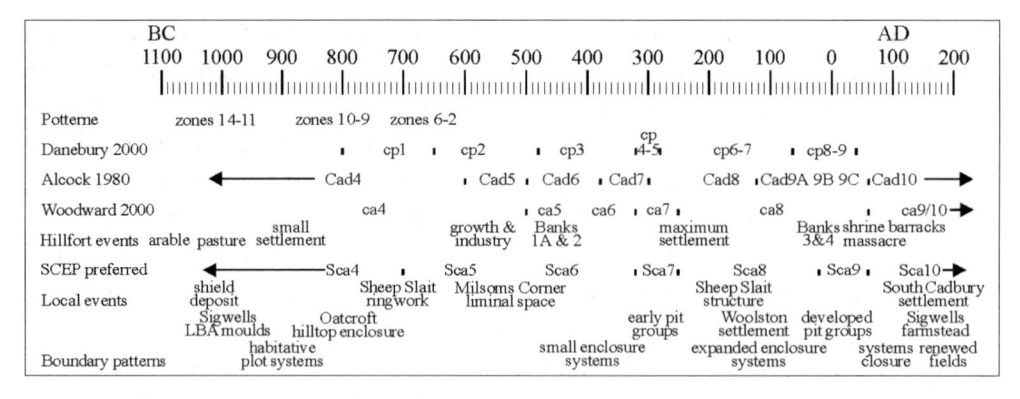

	BC											AD		
	1100	1000	900	800	700	600	500	400	300	200	100	0	100	200
Potterne		zones 14-11		zones 10-9	zones 6-2									
Danebury 2000				cp1		cp2		cp3	cp 4-5		cp6-7		cp8-9	
Alcock 1980		←		Cad4		Cad5	Cad6	Cad7		Cad8	Cad9A 9B 9C	Cad10	→	
Woodward 2000				ca4			ca5	ca6	ca7		ca8			ca9/10 →
Hillfort events			small			growth &	Banks			maximum		Banks shrine barracks		
	arable	pasture	settlement			industry	1A & 2			settlement		3 & 4 massacre		
SCEP preferred		←		Sca4		Sca5		Sca6	Sca7		Sca8	Sca9	Sca10 →	
Local events		shield deposit			Sheep Slait ringwork	Milsoms Corner liminal space					Sheep Slait structure			South Cadbury settlement
		Sigwells LBA moulds		Oatcroft hilltop enclosure						early pit groups	Woolston settlement	developed pit groups		Sigwells farmstead
				habitative					small enclosure		expanded enclosure		systems renewed	
Boundary patterns				plot systems					systems		systems		closure	fields

34 First-millennium pottery in the study area

preferred by Ann Woodward, who has moved the whole series forward in varying degrees. The Danebury Environs Programme chronology is supported by a substantial battery of carbon dates so, where correlation seems appropriate, SCEP has leaned towards it. The inevitable consequence is a reassessment of some of the structural history of the hillfort, as will emerge below, summarised in a table (*34*).

The most significant disagreement between the systems of Woodward and Alcock relates to the first centuries BC/AD. Alcock had observed a clear break between Cadbury 8, characterised by the highly decorated Glastonbury style and saucepan pots, and the Cadbury 9 Durotrigan Wares, amongst which bead rim bowls and jars predominated. In retrospect Woodward noted that in the bank and associated contexts, Cadbury 9 material always occurred with diagnostically Romano-British pottery or metalwork and, citing work in other parts of Somerset, she has asserted that Durotrigan vessels did not reach the Cadbury area until around the time of, or soon after, the Roman invasion. Drawing on the local archaeological literature, she observed that the Glastonbury style persisted until but not beyond the invasion. In contrast, Alcock envisaged the arrival of 'quite alien' Cadbury 9A Durotrigan Ware as early as the first half of the first century BC and that there were two further discernible subdivisions from a period leading up to a massacre episode in around AD 60. Both authors noted that while Cadbury 8 material dominated the pit assemblages on the plateau, it was comparatively under-represented in the banks.

Some of the areas investigated by SCEP have provided a much sharper focus on a particular time precisely because they have been used less intensively or for a shorter period than Cadbury itself. Later phases have not degraded and destroyed earlier ones and particular ceramic ranges can be defined clearly. Even here there are qualifications: some of the material from test pits has been dated mainly by fabric and finish rather than the more reliable form. The problem is more acute during periods, or at sites, where there is little decoration on the pottery as quite simply there are fewer fragments with diagnostic potential. During the first millennium there are two phases where this is true. Alcock's Cadbury 4 assemblage broadly equates with the so-called Post Deverel Rimbury or Late Bronze Age Plain Ware range. In crude terms it is the filling of a chronological sandwich between the Globular Urn style pottery from Sigwells Middle Bronze Age enclosure and the Earlier Iron Age Cadbury 5 and 6 vessels (*33*), as well as some highly decorated material from Milsoms Corner (*52*) and especially Sheep Slait (*50*), described in the sections below. The specialised character of these sites ought to sound a warning bell: to what extent is the chronology distorted by function? If we look at the material from Sigwells it is easy to see stylistic relationships with some vessel classes from Sheep Slait; the Plain Ware assemblage must overlap both.

There is also important evidence regarding the Late Iron Age pottery from an enclosure sequence and pits in the north-west of Sigwells. Here the later pits and ditches contain a great deal of Dorset-sourced Durotrigan pottery but not a single diagnostically Romano-British sherd. Immediately south of the enclosure and pits, Romano-British and Durotrigan material were found in later banks bounding a trackway. The pottery in the pits and ditches is unlikely to have accumulated over a very short span of time. After they had been filled, several pits containing Dorset material, some accompanied by shell-tempered Cadbury 8 sherds, were cut by later pits also containing it. The same was true of the two latest phases of the enclosure ditches, although a brooch from the uppermost fill of the latest ditch phase had currency in the late second to third quarters of the first century AD. It is hard to avoid the conclusion that a considerable amount of Durotrigan pottery was circulating well before the invasion of AD 43. Alcock's early first-century BC date seems unlikely but its arrival in the late part of that century is quite conceivable. This is the chronological framework adopted for this and the following chapters (*34*; the 'SCEP preferred' row).

LATE BRONZE AGE (*35*)

In the Late Bronze Age grassland easily exceeded woodland within the study area, although some of it had become scrubby and the extent of cultivation may have been less as wealth and food were largely on the hoof, rather than in the form of crops. Many pre-existing enclosure systems may have continued in use although the only field ditches proven to have been open by this time were at Milsoms Corner and Sheep Slait, Poyntington Down (*47*, below), both of which were in core areas of activity. Woolston Manor Farm is a third area from which there was slight but compelling artefact evidence for activity, most dramatically associated

Cadbury Castle: The Hillfort and Landscapes

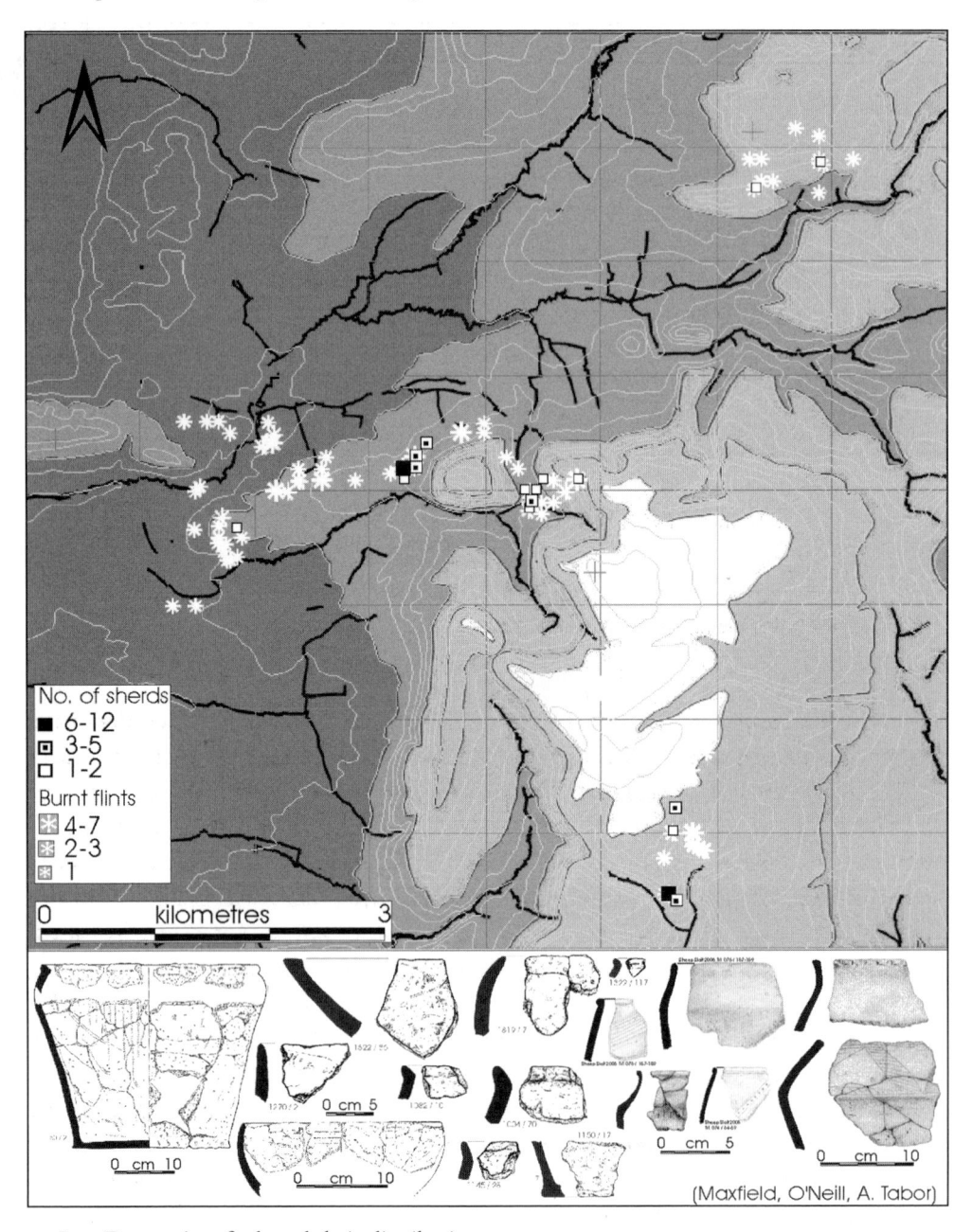

35 Late Bronze Age finds and their distribution

with ditches surrounding a narrow ridge. Only its east end has been surveyed but it seems likely to have been a defended hilltop (*36, 37*). The pottery distribution, taking Cadbury 4 Plain Ware as the marker, shows a retraction of settlement to within these three core areas.

A central place

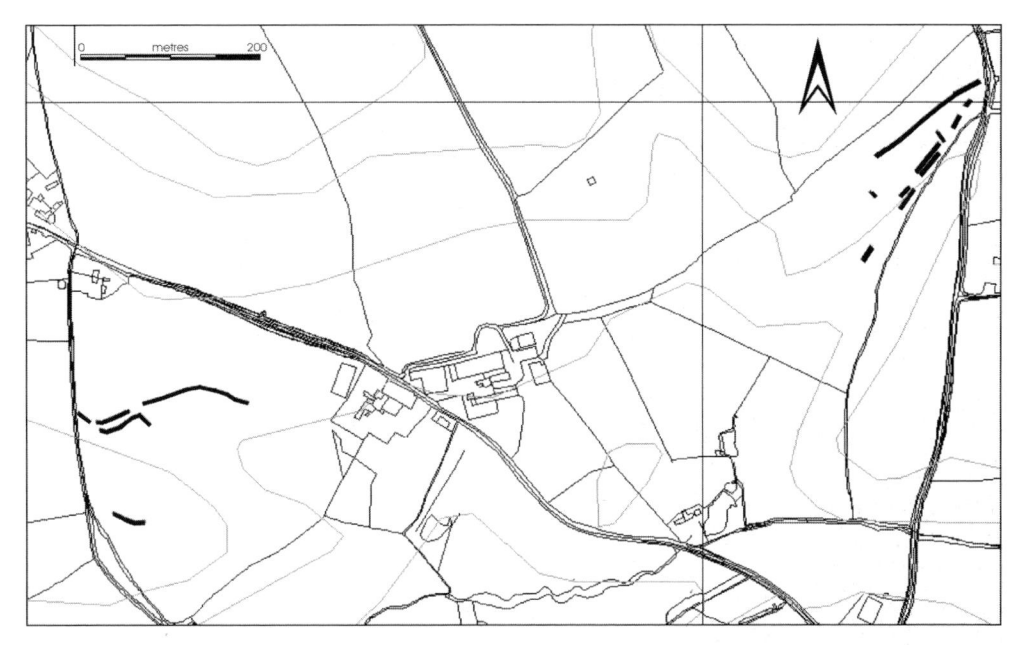

36 Woolston Manor Farm: the Late Bronze Age hilltop and linear boundaries

Mould fragments for between eight and twelve different bronzes (*38*) deposited in a pit 150m north-west of the Sigwells craft fair enclosure indicate that the plateau south-east of Cadbury continued to host craft fairs at least until the tenth century BC, although no contemporary enclosure ditch has been identified. It seems highly likely that travelling craftsmen were still plying their trades and the mixed styles of the manufactured objects imply influences from more than one tradition. During the first half of the first millennium BC there was a shift to local metalworking. Previous accounts suggest that much of the Late Bronze Age material found on Cadbury was scrap destined for reuse but there is no unambiguous evidence for metalworking on the hilltop until the Early Iron Age. An alternative view of the significance of the metalwork will be outlined below.

The explosion of developer-funded archaeology across Britain since 1990 has led to a huge growth in the discovery of Middle to Late Bronze Age long boundaries, field systems and enclosures south of the Humber. They tended to be close to the coast or along major watercourses, most notably in the middle and lower Thames Valley. In general the best soils were favoured but in some areas of south-east England the pressure for land was so great that even heavy clays were being used by the Late Bronze Age. During this period a new form of circular enclosure or ringwork emerged, typically associated with the intensification of land use manifested in field systems and often in key locations through which high status could be acquired by control over traffic. Until 2005 such ringworks were

Cadbury Castle: The Hillfort and Landscapes

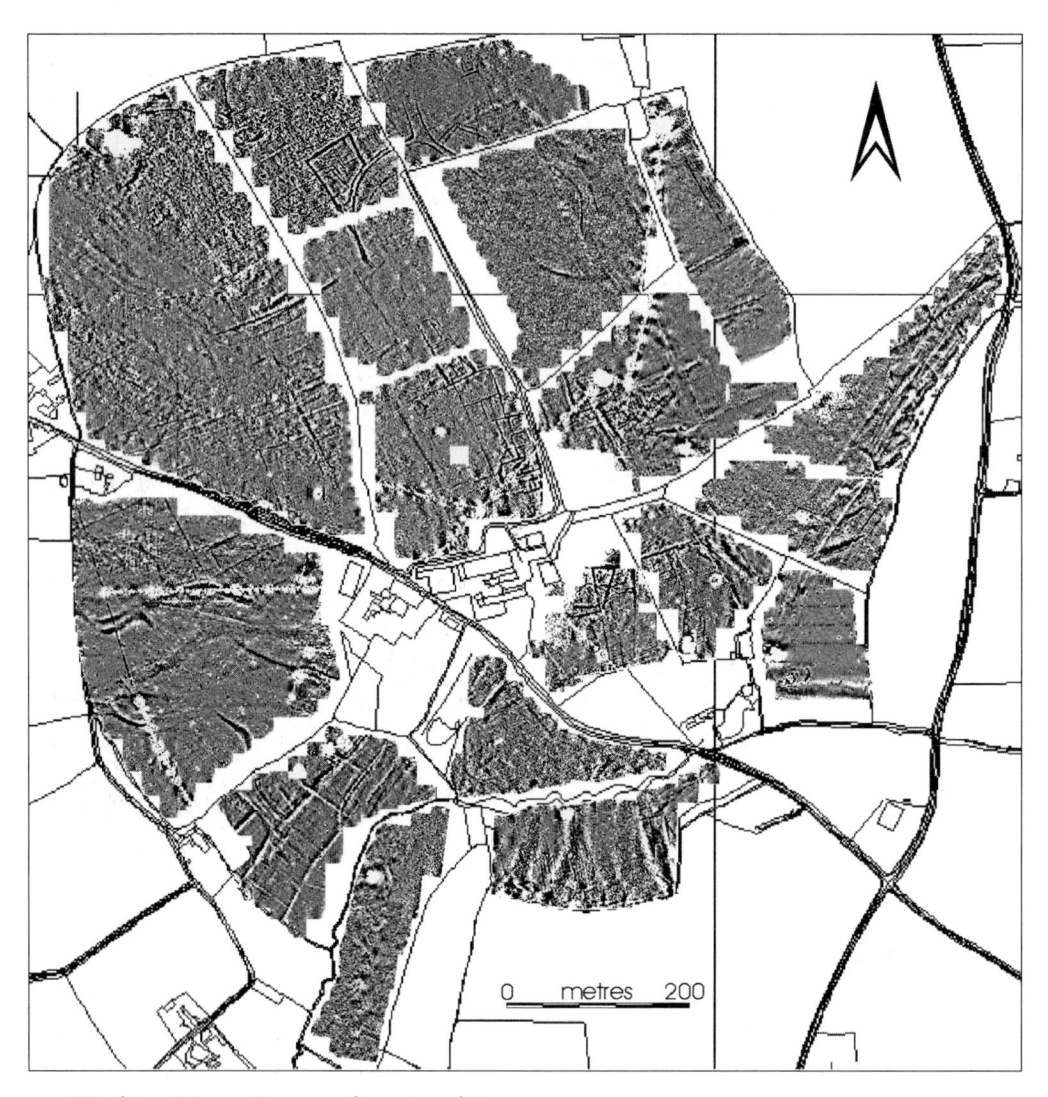

37 Woolston Manor Farm: gradiometer plot

considered exclusive to the east of England. David Yates has argued that these examples of 'aggrandising' architecture are a clear sign of far greater economic growth there. It is an assertion which ought to be qualified. The remarkable multi-hectare Wiltshire hilltop middens at Potterne, East Chisenbury and Whitesheet Hill, with others emerging through ongoing research, are each testaments to hugely agriculturally productive communities with extensive wider connections exemplified in the ranges of objects sealed in their rich soils, and only 4km (2.5 miles) south-south-east of Cadbury is a ringwork, 160km (100 miles) south-west of its nearest neighbour.

A central place

38 Sigwells Trench 4: Late Bronze Age weapon moulds. *Graham Norrie*

Cadbury in the making

The resumption of activity on the hill was marked below the south-west gate's Iron Age defences by a gully and a line of 50cm (20in) deep postholes, several packed with stones and interpreted by Ann Woodward as a field fence sealed by a near sterile red soil bank including an antler which yielded a radiocarbon date in the later second millennium BC. A soil sealing it was brown and charcoal-flecked, indicative of more intensive human activity and the return of settlement to the hilltop. A gravelly red soil, sealed beneath an Early Iron Age turf under the southern Iron Age defences in Site D, suggested that the plateau was ploughed after the settlement was established and probably before as well. The best dating for the cultivation came from the cutting through the north bank, Trench A. Charcoal-flecking in a plough horizon, sealing a sterile hillwash, may have derived from burning-off scrub or regenerating woodland.

No absolute dating exists for any interior features, but on the east end of the plateau there are at least two post-built rectangular structures and arcs of a gully and stakeholes, which would have formed respectively 14m (N042) and 10m

Cadbury Castle: The Hillfort and Landscapes

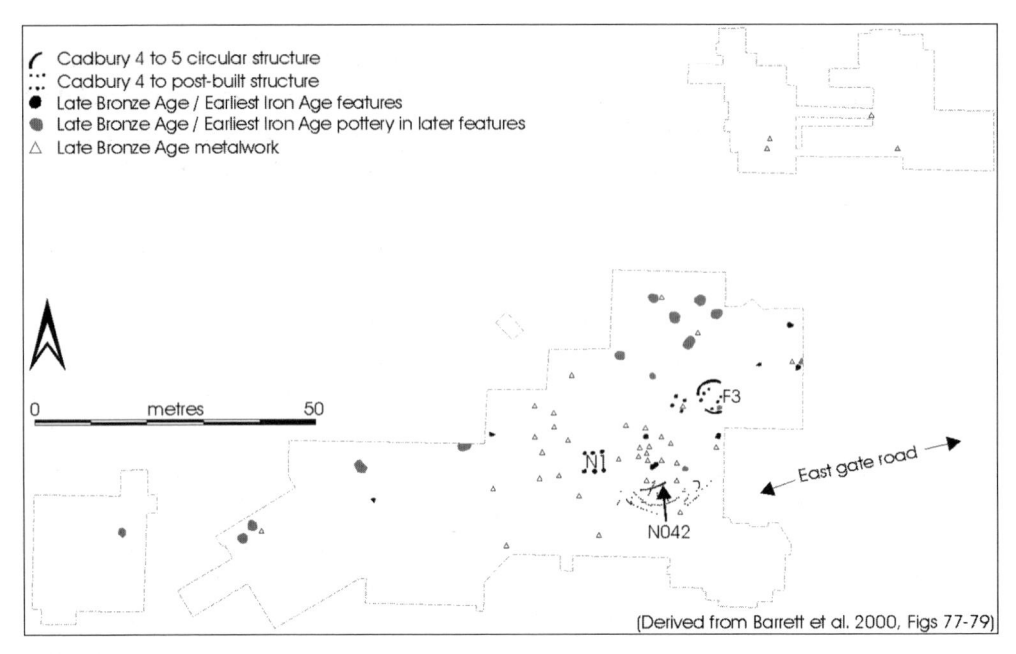

39 Cadbury Castle: Late Bronze Age features on the plateau

diameter circles, broadly contemporary (*39*) and sealed by later cobbles. These and other stakeholes may have been for buildings or for lightweight fences. The latter option was preferred in the English Heritage report where, as incarnated in the Late Iron Age, they are seen to define the limit of a rubbish layer. The north of the area, taken in by a putative circular fence, would have enclosed the space in which a considerable number of bronze objects was to accumulate, a process which might have started by this time. The ground to the north was very disturbed by later hearths and furnaces, so ephemeral traces of shallow bedding gullies or stakeholes were unlikely to have survived.

The most substantial feature was a pit filled with ashy soil and a collapsed large jar, graphically portrayed by Alcock as breaking while a 'Bronze Age housewife' prepared a meal. No doubt the accident happened as she plucked her eyebrows with tweezers, found in a nearby posthole (*colour plate 15*). Alloy analysis of bronze pins dated to the Early Iron Age but Alcock shows that several are significantly earlier, with a chronological span stretching from around 1100 BC (roughly contemporary with the later Sigwells metalworking) to 800 BC. More Late Bronze Age pottery was found in Iron Age pits on the north-west side of these structures over an area of roughly 40 x 20m along with apparently stray metal objects, including an Early Bronze Age axe. They may be explained best as ritual inclusions in a longstanding midden, part dispersed and part sealed by subsequent activity. It was not on a scale to rival the Wiltshire middens but it does have similarities with Brean Down; not only were both associated with contemporary settlement but they incorporated high-status objects in the shape of their respective gold bracelets. The Brean examples were similar in style to one from the Potterne midden and may be slightly earlier than that from Cadbury.

The metalwork lay on either side of a rectangular building, N1, the greatest density to its east. The building was the first in a succession which extended into the mid first century AD, all with a similar orientation, reflecting a particular relationship with firstly the metalwork and the rubbish layers, and subsequently cobbled surfaces and animal burials. They seem to have opened towards the east gate and appear to have been shrines marking the spiritual heart of the settlement. Roughly 8m south of N1 was a similarly sized rectangular building, N5 (*91*, see below), with a foundation trench showing that it undoubtedly faced east. Built in the first century AD, it is widely accepted as a shrine. N1 is one building in this area which has not been described by the term, yet the artefacts around it and the organisation of space surely make it a very good contender. The shrine interpretation has spawned several lookalikes, not least in a wholly comparable central location on Danebury, where Cunliffe has suggested it marked a place of special religious significance throughout the Iron Age (for further discussion see *The hilltop ascendant*, p. 103).

The best-preserved structural traces on the plateau lay east of N1, in a slight hollow, and were protected by a layer of cobbles. Late Bronze Age pottery in Iron Age pits at the west end suggest that there would have been buildings there, too, but that their traces have been entirely removed by ploughing. Similar pottery sealed by the later ramparts (and it is important to remember that the rampart sections represent only a very small sample from the entire length of the inner bank; (*3*)) show that activity was widespread and no doubt there was a considerable number of other buildings. Paul Johnson's geophysical survey revealed possible circular structures within the ramparts on all sides, but very few coherent anomalies on the west of the plateau. By analogy with the excavated areas the majority of the structures are likely to date to the Iron Age but some were probably Bronze Age or on the site of Bronze Age structures. The survey would not have identified lightweight stake or post-built structures.

The geophysics also showed holloways routed towards the north-west, south-west and west emerging from the east gate, probably the most ancient surviving opening onto the hilltop. Two of these routes skirt around the steep dished face which obscures the plateau, but the westward route leads directly to the east of the plateau after a slight kink over the dish. All three tracks may well have served the Late Bronze Age settlement, the south-west route probably linking up to a holloway revealed by Johnson, emerging from under what later became the west inner bank.

The latter track appears to have been well established before the building of the ramparts put it out of commission, indicating a considerable volume of traffic in the form of herds, beasts of burden and people. The steep ascents to both the east gate and the now invisible west gate would have deterred most wheeled vehicles. At the base of the hill the traffic from the west would have passed north of the Milsoms Corner spur, an area of special importance to the early settlers.

Milsoms Corner shield

The south and east ditches of the Middle Bronze Age enclosure on the spur at Milsoms Corner had silted up gradually to about a third of their depths when the sides stabilised. Research on experimental earthworks at Overton Down and elsewhere suggests that once this stage has been reached there is no reason for a ditch profile to change without significant external intervention. During the period of silting, or more probably after it, a circular structure stood on the east side of the enclosure, revealed in excavation only as a sunken floor sealed by an abandonment level much disturbed by subsequent Iron Age activity. During or after the life of the structure there were several discrete episodes of deliberate filling of the ditches. Clearly internal banks had survived in a very degraded state as the material thrown in was a mixture of natural silty sand and soil. A localised deposit of gritty burnt stone, sealed by one of the first of these episodes, was probably derived from the hearth of the circular building. It began a sequence of singular bone deposits, some shoulder blades but typically lower cattle jaws, laid and covered in the ditches at irregular intervals (*28*).

As originally dug, the ditches were level-bottomed and the distribution of silt was even when it first reached equilibrium, excepting an area of collapse from the inside of the enclosure on the south side. The deliberate deposits of soil and upcast occupying approximately the middle third of the fills were much less even, at their highest in the narrow junction of the ditches, and had remained so as silt accumulated slowly over the top of them. Clearly the process of deposition was important rather than the mere filling of ditches. A second phase of slow silting to a point where the depth of the ditch was no greater than 30cm (1ft) implies considerable soil movement but with little sign of habitative settlement near or in the enclosure.

There followed a brief episode of intense activity in and around the enclosure which pottery places in the earlier first millennium BC. The size of the trench (*40*), and the areas within it destroyed by later Iron Age occupation and modern ploughing, prevented the exposure of the event's full extent but enough remained to gauge its general character. A roughly 2 by 1m spread of burnt stone (F051), rounded on the upper surface, was found next to a substantial posthole (F150) in the south-east of the enclosure's interior. A shallow scoop (F165) immediately south of the enclosure contained a single layer of burnt red stones (*colour plate 9*) under

A central place

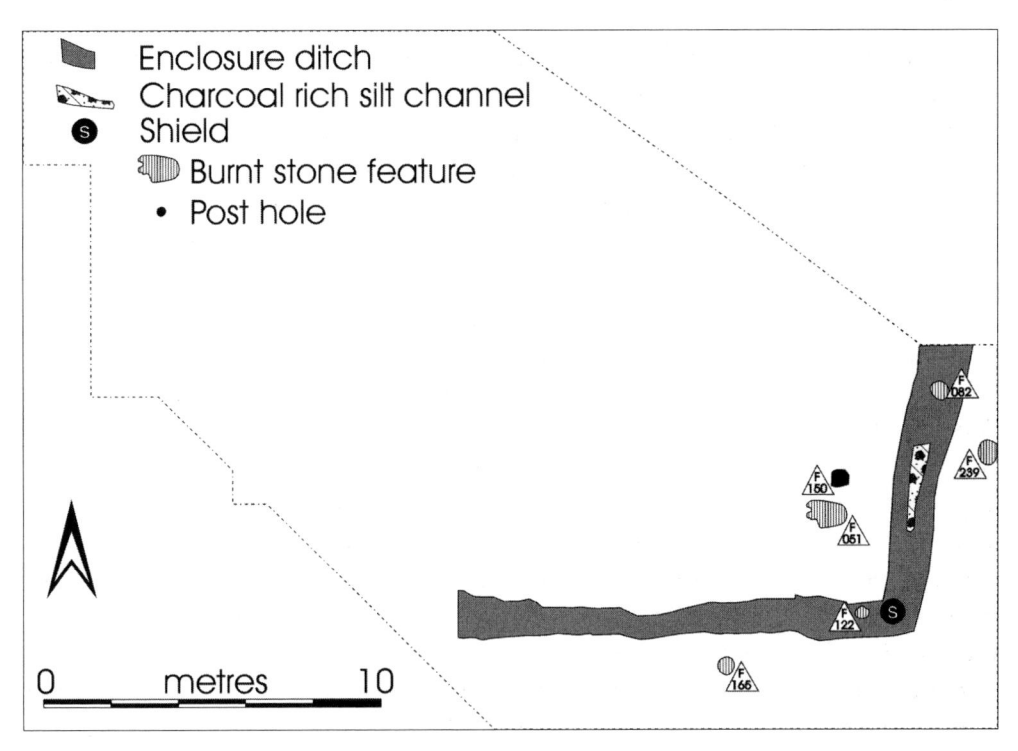

40 Milsoms Corner: shield and contemporary features

a small, charcoal-rich deposit in the middle, a single burnt flint and a rim sherd from a bowl to the south. A single cattle rib was placed immediately south of the feature, snapped into two roughly equal halves. Immediately east of the enclosure several shallow scoops (F239) contained charcoal-rich soils sealed by a 1m long, 50cm (19in) wide pile of burnt blue stones.

The most complex remains were reserved for the enclosure ditch itself. A large jar, filled with burnt stones and the remains of a bowl (similar to the one lying on the red stones), had been placed in a purpose-dug pit (F082) into the upper ditch silts. A metre to the south, a soil rich in charcoal, including some large lumps, filled a channel from the approximate level of the surviving height of the jar on a slight decline towards the junction of the ditches. One metre west of the junction, a small pit had been filled with layers of stone (F122) on one side, with an area of soil bounded by a large pitched stone on the other. This was the only posthole constructed with such care and complexity amongst several hundred from the many phases identified in the trench. What made it more exceptional was the discovery of a human lower leg bone in a state of arrested decay identical to that of the surviving knee joints where the Early Bronze Age burial had been cut by the Middle Bronze Age ditch. There is no reason to doubt that they belonged to the same person.

85

41 Milsoms Corner: discovery of shield

The most spectacular find was a complete bronze shield, lying flat on its face, at the junction of the ditches, the first example from the Bronze Age to have been found during an excavation in north-west Europe. A Birmingham University postgraduate student, Josh Williams, spotted a green arc emerging from a section (*41*) he was cutting back by a few extra centimetres late in the afternoon. He called for help and within minutes we realised that it was probably a shield. By this time rain was falling but most of the students remained until we were digging under car headlights in an effort to lower the level of the soil around it to avoid water damage. Crucially, a red deer or cattle hip bone was in the silt immediately below the shield and touching its rim. The bone later produced a radiocarbon date of 1050-830 BC. By 10pm the shield was covered and secured for the night. Somerset County Museum had been informed and called in specialists from the Wiltshire Conservation Centre. They arrived in the middle of the following morning to

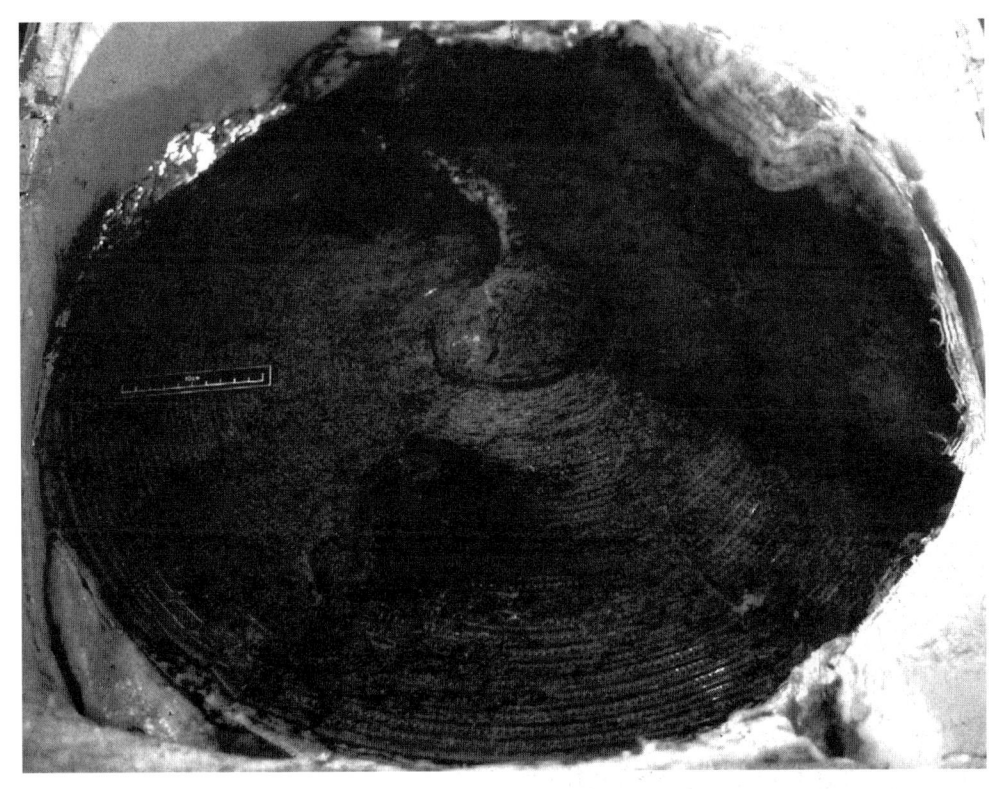

42 Milsoms Corner: front of shield

remove a thick soil sandwich, wrapped in clingfilm and on a metal plate. Several weeks elapsed before X-rays revealed a complete shield.

Inevitably the manner of the shield's removal caused some damage to the contexts immediately underneath. Nonetheless, the socket of a substantial stake survived to a depth of 30cm. Seven months after the discovery, once funding had been found (and it is surely a powerful indictment of current law regarding portable antiquities that such an important artefact, from which no one stood to make a personal profit, had to compete for funding through the same channels as those used to acquire material from treasurer-hunting metal detectorists) microexcavation of the shield was able to start in the Wiltshire Conservation Centre. The work lasted nearly a year and earned Andrew Wilson and the laboratory the 1999 Museums and Galleries Commission Award for Conservation.

Wilson's work revealed impact damage on one area of the rim, probably pre-depositional, and that after it had been placed face down in the ditch it was penetrated three time by a fairly crude instrument (probably a stake) which had driven flakes of bronze several centimetres into the soil below (*colour plate 12*). Its large dome-shaped central boss (*42*), only 0.4mm thick, would have been very

43 Milsoms Corner: handle of shield

susceptible to crumpling but had survived intact because it was lying in the stake socket. Otherwise, despite almost total corrosion, it was possible to show very little sign of wear on the external surfaces.

Before discussing the events associated with the deposition of the shield we need to understand the significance of the object in its own right. The project was extremely fortunate in having the foremost expert on Bronze Age shields, Professor John Coles, examine it and set it in context with other examples from Britain and Europe. He established that it was fashioned from a single sheet of bronze reduced to 0.6mm thickness and a diameter of 66cm (26in) after hammering on a yielding surface or former of over 6000 small bosses around the central boss in 25 concentric rings, each divided by a strengthening circular rib. A thicker bronze sheet was wrapped around a tin core and rivetted in harmony with the innermost ring of bosses to form a handle (*43*) behind the large boss. Two rivetted bronze tabs provided anchors for a leather shoulder strap. The technical prowess and investment in time is daunting even to contemplate but reconstructions have demonstrated that the resulting object was not strong enough to resist a single blow from a contemporary spear or sword. Its value was exclusively symbolic rather than practical.

Between 40 and 50 later Bronze Age metal shields have been found in Ireland and mainland Britain and a comparable number of regionally varied types extend in an arc from Spain to Sweden. All were found accidentally, typically during peat digging, river dredging or ploughing of former wetlands. The Cadbury example is of the type most commonly found in the British Isles, named after Yetholm in Roxburghshire, Scotland, where three were found in a peat bog. Most have been found on the east side of Britain, either close to the coast or to major water courses, including the River Thames, although this may have more to do with the distribution and intensity of modern activity than with the original pattern of deposition. The Cadbury shield is the only one of all those from the British Isles not to have been found in a wetland context. It is also the most southerly in Britain, nearly 120km (74 miles) south-west of its nearest neighbour in Oxfordshire.

Yetholm shields had been assigned a manufacture date between 1000 and 800 BC but analysis of the alloys by Peter Northover shows that along with six others sampled, the Milsoms Corner shield has a very strong correspondence with later Middle Bronze Age metalwork. It is likely to have been made before the end of the twelfth century BC.

In summary, the shield appears to have been well over a century old but in nearly new condition when it was placed in the ditch. It conforms to a widespread pattern of deliberate damage and deposition of weapons in the Late Bronze Age, particularly frequent in the Fens and Thames Valley, though much less so in the case of the hoards and individual deposits around the Somerset Levels. Arguably the shield was divorced from the particular symbolic associations which required its production and acquisition, yet its careful preservation indicates a potency enhanced over time, elaborated in the complex events which culminated in its deposition.

I have listed several areas with remains which appear to register the effects of particular events that the site stratigraphy showed to be broadly contemporary. But the question is how contemporary? Are they close enough in time, perhaps a few days, even hours, to be treated as parts of a single event? My view is that they are but with some important caveats. As already noted, the pelvis from immediately below the shield produced a radiocarbon date centering on the mid tenth century BC, but the snapped rib associated with F165 gave an unhelpful bimodal result of 900 to 750 BC or 720 to 520 BC (all at 68 per cent confidence). The most economical explanation would be that the pelvis belonged to the earlier, if very long-lived (bear in mind the date of the Middle Bronze Age mandible from the upper middle ditch fills) sequence of singular bone deposition and that the earlier of the two date ranges from the rib apply both to the scoop and to the deposition of the shield.

Corroboration for this chronology is offered by a roundhouse, dated by pottery to the Late Bronze Age (*44*), built on the fully backfilled enclosure ditch and later in the site sequence than all the features putatively linked to the shield. Although

Cadbury Castle: The Hillfort and Landscapes

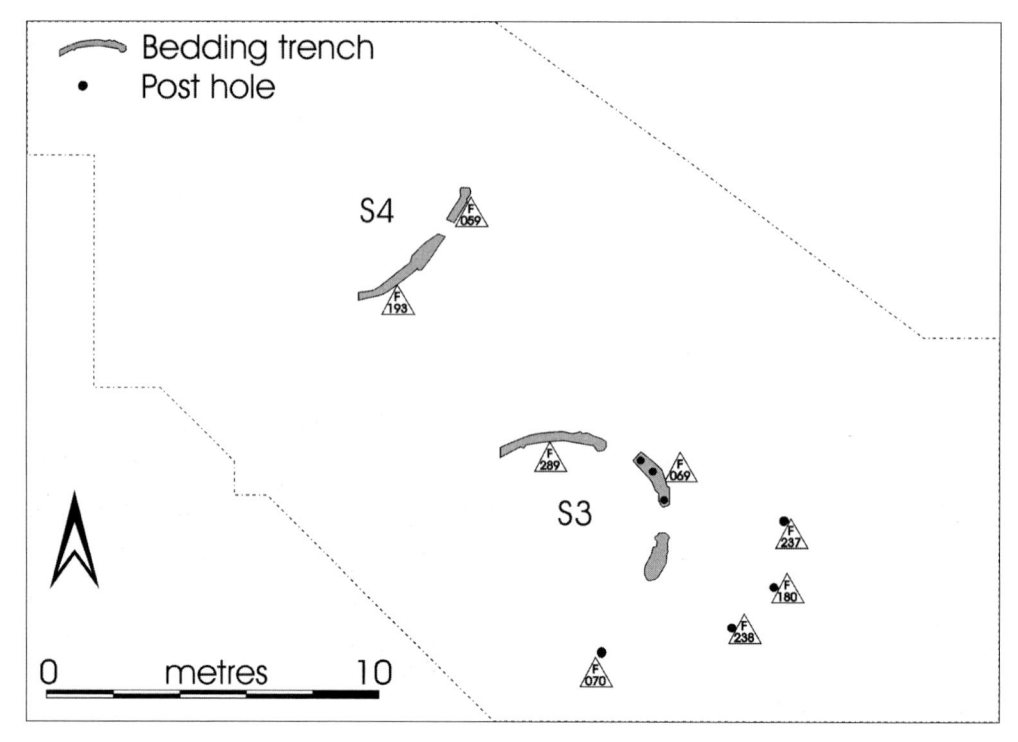

44 Milsoms Corner: selected Late Bronze Age features

the general space around the junction of the ditches remained a continuing focus for ritual observance, it seems more probable on balance that the group of features were residues of a single event.

Feasting played a part in the event. The bowls associated with both the large jar and the burnt red stones would have been used in the consumption of food, and the small mound of burnt blue stones was a residue of food preparation outside the enclosure. The cobble-like spread of burnt blue stone formed a hard standing as well as a base for a fire and was either where people gathered for warmth or where more food was prepared, perhaps using a spit. In an interesting parallel with the Sigwells cooking pit, sheep was the dominant species represented in association with the jar and with the cobbles. At both sites this represents an interesting contrast with the cow jaw deposits in the enclosure ditches, although these clearly pre-date the festivities associated with the shield.

In the previous chapter there is a brief reference to burnt red stones at the bottom of postholes and burnt blues stones marking the closure of the metalworking enclosure's north-west corner. The pattern is repeated here. Red stones line the bottom of the scoop whilst a pile of blue stones seals the fills of several small scoops. The latter pattern persists into the Late Bronze Age (see the following section).

A central place

45 Milsoms Corner: Closure. Amanda Tabor

The nearest neighbour to the stakehole below the shield was the posthole, F122 (*40*), packed with several layers of predominantly blue burnt stones in which the lower leg bone from the Early Bronze Age burial was placed, probably after the withdrawal of the post. It seems likely that the stake from the hole covered by the shield had been used to display it. If the standing stake was paired with the packed post, the shield would have faced either north or south if suspended between the two. During a solstice it would have provided a startling reflection of the sun's passage through a day (*colour plate 13*). When the shield had completed this last function it was dispatched with utter finality, first by a blow to its rim and then by three piercings as it lay across the empty trace of its support. Of course, there was another ending: the long-curated lower leg bone was placed in the other empty socket after being preserved for several centuries (*45*).

We can say with confidence that the event included feasting and that the status of the shield and the human leg, and the care with which the red stone feature was created, indicate an occasion of great moment. Given the early first millennium BC date, it seems highly likely that the events marked something of special significance on the hilltop. The festivities were surely too late to mark the foundation of the renewed settlement, or even the death of its first chief, but they may mark its ascendancy over rival hilltop settlements in the area. The re-interment of the ancestral relic and depositing of a shield, which was of an age to have been handed down since around the settlement's foundation, imply the legitimation through kinship (though possibly illusory) of authority over the territory.

Within a few decades the enclosure ditch ceased to have any active function. A made-up earthen floor was laid over its south ditch surrounded by a post trench which cut the upper fills in providing the foundations for a substantial circular building (44, S3). The complete outline of a pot base (the base itself had been taken out) had been placed at its centre before being sealed by a new layer of flooring. The pot was made of clay tempered with calcite, typical of the Late Bronze Age over an area extending from the Somerset coast to north Dorset. The building appears to have been kept fairly clean and little of the detritus of daily living survived for the archaeologist, providing a marked contrast with the messy east end of Cadbury's plateau. The building may have had a specialist use which was neither domestic nor industrial, but successive floors of an Iron Age building have obscured or, more probably, destroyed all evidence for a hearth or entrance.

Well-made postholes supported a fence which followed a widening arc from the building's south-east side, separating it from the area of special deposits around the shield. Their area of deposition seems to have remained special in the long term, as the density of later cut features was a great deal lower in this part of the trench (44, 55). A second stake and post-built circular building (S4) 8m north-west was roughly contemporary and may have co-existed with these features. A calcite-tempered jar base was found in its post trench, a fabric comparable with the base circuit from the floor of the other building. Over half of the building outline has been destroyed by ploughing on the west side.

It may be tempting to interpret the structures as dwellings on the periphery of a small settlement taking shelter through its situation low on the west-facing slopes of the hill. However, the relative scarcity of domestic waste seems to point to a specialised use and postholes on the inside of the backfilled enclosure ditch seem to cut off the spur from the main body of the hill at what was its narrowest point before Iron Age remodelling. The protection of the area around the shield, including the ancient burial and its re-buried lower leg bone, suggest in was regarded with awe. Perhaps it was taboo to approach it, although given the proximity of the roundhouses it might have served as a shrine.

'Aggrandisement' at Poyntington Down?

Sheep Slait, a long, narrow, banana-shaped hill at Poyntington Down, steeply cut by valleys on three sides and at an unknown time separated by a massive ditch from the greater plateau in the north of Locality 4, is an area which the project had contemplated with relish. In the event, much of its west end had been thoroughly degraded by Mediaeval ridge and furrow which in turn had been utterly

A central place

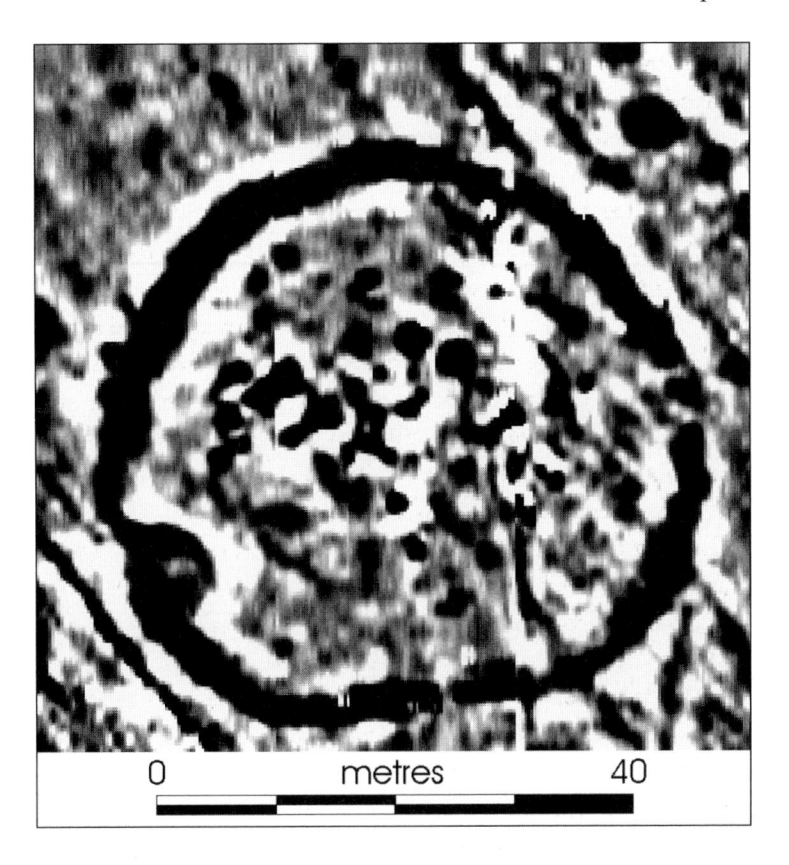

46 Sheep Slait ringwork: gradiometery

erased as earthworks by ploughing in the twentieth century. Linear anomalies presented tantalising magnetic signatures but little in the way of surviving cut features. However, on a slight shelf protected by trapped soils, gradiometry revealed a very substantial circular ditch with an outer diameter of 50m (*46*). The location, slightly below the highest ground and on a tongue of land above the source of the largest local water course, the River Yeo, has a commanding view of the valleys and as a ring ditch and bank it would have been an impressive feature visible from the ridges to the east and south, and in glimpses along small valleys to its north and west. A test pit 60m south-east of the circle targeted a ditch, producing pottery closely akin to the material from the Sigwells metal working enclosure. By extrapolation, the field system laid out over Poyntington and Seven Wells Downs (*47*) was certainly extant by the Late Bronze Age and its form and orientation would be consistent with an origin several centuries earlier.

The results of survey within the circle, supplemented by ground-penetrating radar, suggested that there were pits (see Ditches in transition, p. 142), particularly in an arc on the west side and towards the middle, a much smaller discontinuous gully or ditch concentric with the ringwork and a large area of heat-related activity

47 Sheep Slait: ringwork and contemporary linear features

in the middle. The magnetic survey revealed possible openings on the west, south and east sides of the ring, and in 2006 a trench was excavated extending from the latter to just inside the west side of the ring. The sheer number of features evident after initial trowelling prohibited the full investigation of the area, resources being biased towards the centre where highly complex deposits, contributing richly to the Middle Iron Age narrative, obscured the heart of the initial concept.

Excavation of the ringwork's north terminal revealed three phases of cutting. In the first, the north and south terminals of a shallow, flat-bottomed, ring's east-facing main entrance were divided by a line of posts (F051, F003, F027 and F028) which probably supported a fence sharing its orientation with the field system (*47, 48*). An arcing funnel projecting from the inside of the ring's south-west arc provided a rear access and a narrow breach to the south may have been a third (*46*). In the second phase it was massively re-cut (F025) to a depth of nearly 2m and a width of 5m. A concentric, arcing, substantial palisade or screen (F001 and F015) was raised, concealing the centre of the enclosure from the entrance and interrupting the line of posts, which was probably dismantled. Fills on both sides of the north terminal ditch show that it silted fairly slowly but was then re-cut to its base in a

A central place

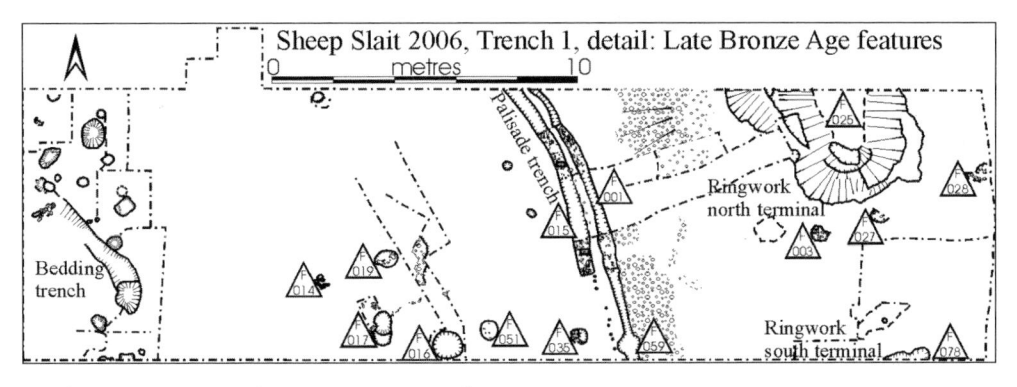

48 Sheep Slait ringwork: Late Bronze Age features

49 Sheep Slait ringwork: north terminal section

third phase, before being rapidly refilled with rubble (*49*), presumably from the upcast internal bank, traces of which survived despite cutting and dispersal by Mediaeval and modern ploughing. Two shallow postholes cutting into the fills of the first ringwork re-cut may have provided revetting for the bank, in which case the berm between ditch and bank was very narrow.

The magnetic survey suggested that the inner ring continued in an interrupted arc on the south-west side of the enclosure, but no trace of it was found within the west end of the trench. An irregular cluster of postholes north of the ring's centre indicate that a rectilinear building, probably first constructed with the earliest ringwork, was refurbished over several generations, possibly succeeded by, or overlapping with, a circular structure supported by massive posts cutting through the base of a shallow circular gully. The circular building would have dominated the whole of the screened area from its central position, but details of its interior have been entirely erased by the subsequent Iron Age activity.

At least eleven of the posts and the palisade were deliberately dismantled and closed with deposits of burnt stone, typically of an oxygen-reduced bluish colour, a mode adopted previously in the north-west corner of the Sigwells metalworking enclosure. Of the eleven, at least nine belong to the general period but only a few can be regarded as closely contemporary with any confidence, notably four forming a line from the entrance towards the palisade, the last to the west of it. Five of the closed postholes were packed, predominantly with burnt stones which can reasonably be taken to imply that they post-date the first phase. The burnt stones in the palisade trench were sharply subangular but those filling the top of the feature were rounded by weathering, a clear sign that they remained exposed for a considerable time after closure.

Contemporary finds of all kinds were comparatively sparse from surface deposits and cut features within the enclosure, contrasting strongly with the volume and quality of material from the rubble fill of the final ring cut. The lower rubble contained a small plain bowl at a slightly lower level than an antler, close to a stone almost certainly selected because of its similarity to the appearance of the latter. The rubble was sealed by a thick layer of a very humic charcoal-rich soil, in turn capped by several thin alternating lenses of rubble and similar soil (*49*). The regularity of gently concave boundaries between each lens indicates that there was a significant settling time before the introduction of the next deposit. In effect, the first deep rubble fill was sealed by a midden layer which was then capped and the depositing and capping of midden material was then repeated several times in discrete episodes. Finds from all the lenses were in fairly fresh condition, excepting the uppermost in which the material was severely weathered as it was sealed by a slow-forming stony silt. The thick soil and lenses all included an abundance of bone (a typically Late Bronze Age range of cattle, sheep and pig, although more of the latter than is usual) and pottery (*50*), much of it decorated in a style with a strong resemblance to that dated between 800 and 600 BC from the midden at Potterne, Wiltshire.

The lower Thames Valley is at the core of the distribution of this class of Late Bronze Age landscape feature, the ringwork. Others occur on the east side of England from Kent to Yorkshire but none were known west of Oxfordshire before the discovery at Poyntington Down. They vary greatly in size, with rare large diameters reaching 230m compared to small examples of around 35m. The scale

1 Looking north-west from the Sigwells twin barrow: Brent Knoll is the hill on the left, Brean Down is a hazy outline to its right and far right is Glastonbury Tor, the Mendip Hills forming a backdrop

2 Cadbury Castle from Hicknoll Slait

3 Milsoms Corner: pottery, burnt flint, baked clay and charred hazel shells in an Early Neolithic pit. The detail shows a Cornish stone axe and pottery found lower in the pit

4 Sigwells metalworking enclosure: cooking pit with pottery exposed

5 Sigwells metalworking enclosure: cooking pit after excavation

6 Sigwells metalworking enclosure: mould fragments from excavation (F011) to refitting on the Midsomer Norton sword

7 Sigwells metalworking enclosure: red and green querns in west ditch

8 Sigwells Middle Bronze Age craft fair. *Amanda Tabor*

9 Sigwells metalworking enclosure: burnt red stone deposited in a posthole

10 Sigwells metalworking enclosure: loomweight and burnt red stone in posthole

11 Milsoms Corner: Late Bronze Age ritual feature

12 Milsoms Corner: the reverse of the shield

13 Milsoms Corner: feasting and displaying the shield. *Amanda Tabor*

14 Sheep Slait: rhyolite quern, quartz crystal and some of other finds from the ringwork terminal

15 Cadbury Castle: Late Bronze Age and Early Iron Age jewellery

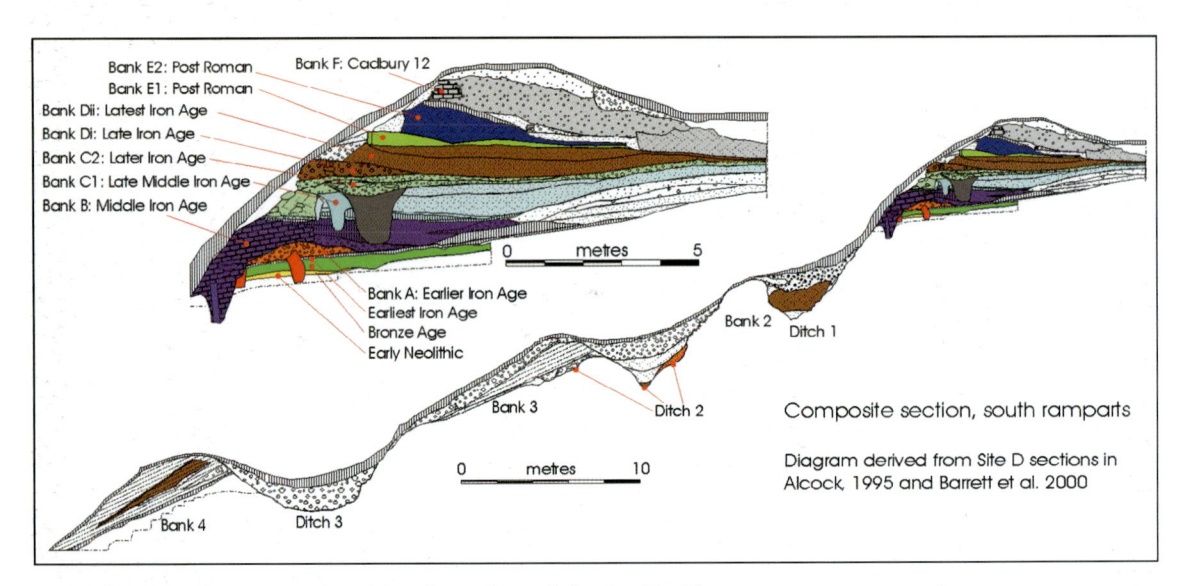

16 Cadbury Castle: composite section through south banks, Site D

17 Cadbury Castle: view from Sigwells at around the beginning of the first century AD. Amanda Tabor

18 Cadbury Castle: antler and bone weaving combs

19 Sheep Slait Trench 1: Late Iron Age hearth and and fire-reddened floor slabs

20 Sigwells Trench 12: yellow-eyed cattle skull with slag in a Late Iron Age pit (F004)

21 Sigwells Trench 12: pair of fused horse mandibles overlying rocks sealing its skull in a re-cut Late Iron Age pit (F025)

22 Sigwells Trench 12: excavation of the horse skull revealing a daub 'tongue' under the front teeth (F025)

23 The Moor Trench 3: Middle Iron Age upturned cattle skull and quern in ditch (F008)

24 The Moor Trench 2: remarkable later Iron Age ditch closure deposit including a Durotrigan jar (left), structural material, a collapsed jar with lower cow jaw and a small local jar (right)

25 Cadbury Castle: burnt deposits in the south-west gate. Note the firing of the natural rock. Cadbury Castle archive

26 Cadbury Castle: human remains sealing the burnt deposits (25, above). Cadbury Castle archive

27 Devastation in South Cadbury valley: local people fill in their ditches under Roman supervision. *Amanda Tabor*

28 Sigwells Trench 12: zoomorphic design on a Late Iron Age bowl. Note the fine lines for hair

29 Cadbury Castle: bronze plaque found amongst the massacre deposits in the guard chamber. It has both Celtic and Roman features

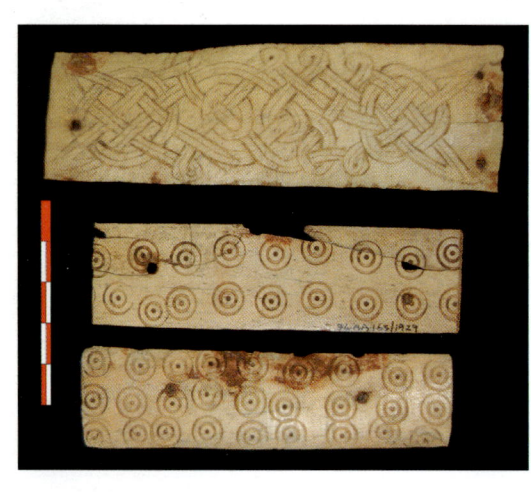

Top: 30 Cadbury Castle: late fifth- and sixth-century Mediterranean amphorae and tableware sherds, and a Saxon pendant/buckle and gilt brooch

Above: 31 Cadbury Castle: view from the plateau towards the south-west gate of a military muster. *Amanda Tabor*

Left: 32 Cadbury Castle: Late Saxon bone plaques, probably from a casket

A central place

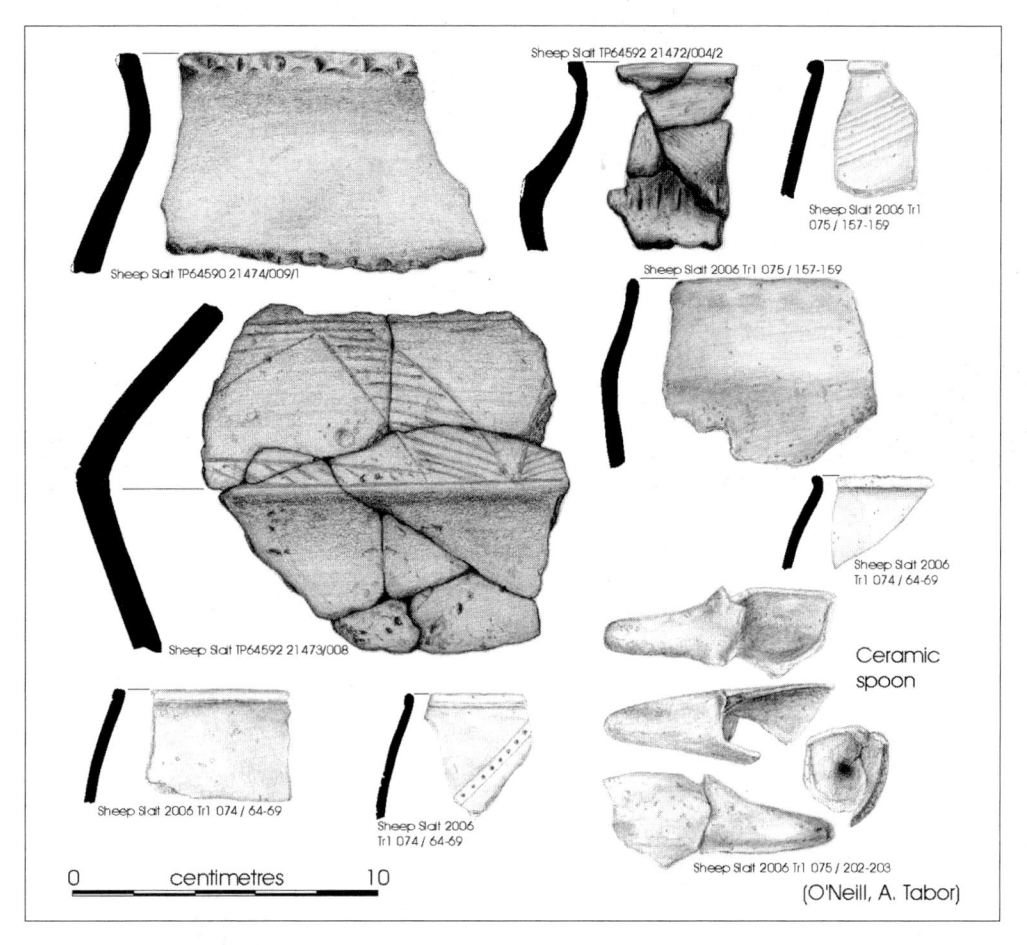

50 Sheep Slait ringwork: pottery from the terminal

and layout at Sheep Slait have striking similarities to the north ring at Mucking, Essex, but with the sequence reversed. During the latter's first phase, a slightly concave fence obstructed access from the east to two circular buildings and the centre of the ring, although a smaller breach in the south-west of the circuit provided a 'back door'. In the second phase, a gully cut through the fence line and separated the north-east and south-east quadrants of the enclosed space. Five further posts extended the line of the gully, leading the visitor to the entrance of a single circular building.

This apparent theme of a compelling welcome to the central space is enhanced elsewhere. The line from a four post structure immediately inside the first phase ringwork entrance ushered the visitor to the elaborate porch of a single central circular building at South Hornchurch, another Essex lower Thames Valley site. The internal route was parallel to a droveway which structured the wider field system, an echo of the organisation of the Sheep Slait ring's first phase. The Hornchurch ringwork appears to have been built before the droveway impinges on it, constricting it to around half its full width. It is precisely this sort of manifest imposition on passage through the landscape that has led Yates to assert that ringworks were an architecture specific to an emerging and highly competitive elite class of individuals or chiefs.

Other authors have been more circumspect, noting their lack of consistent association with high status goods and highlighting the dangers of assuming that a common architecture signifies a similar function or status. It is just as feasible that the Hornchurch layout was a matter of local agricultural convenience, not for controlling a major route. Most ringworks were linked to field systems and most had associated industries, including salt extraction, metal and textile working. Unfortunately many rings investigated in the Thames Valley are on acid soils and little bone survives, depriving the archaeologist of a major resource for understanding their economy. However, the terminals of the inner circuit of the double ring at Thwing, Yorkshire, produced large amounts of animal bone, paralleling the third-phase terminal fills at Poyntington.

Although we have no direct evidence for the character of Late Bronze Age activity in the centre of the ringwork, the volume of burnt stone used in the packing and closure of the postholes and palisade trench is strong evidence that pyrotechnical industry was of continuing importance. Thick ashy deposits, sealed by a stone Iron Age floor and a large hearth or furnace associated with slag-like material, evoke a tradition of metalworking extending into the second century BC. We have already seen that many centuries earlier participants at the Sigwells craft fair consumed a considerable amount of meat prepared or presented in decorated vessels over a short period. It may well be that something very similar took place at Sheep Slait but with significant differences: at least some of the structures were used and refurbished over a considerable time and the ringwork is intimately integrated into a field system rather than being appended to a linear boundary. A rhyolite quern and quartz crystal (*colour plate 14*) found in the terminal's lower rubble fills, both of the south-west peninsula from either north Dartmoor or north Cornwall (180km, 110 miles), again testify to long distance contacts, albeit from a different point on the compass.

Wood-based structures when left empty do not last well. Without the heat of a fire and regular maintenance, a roof and wall would soon collapse. This circumstantial evidence is enough show that the buildings inside the enclosure at least were visited by a caretaker on most days or that they were permanent shelters. The comparative lack of casual refuse is an argument against the latter but the negative data is weak as only a comparatively small area of the enclosure and its immediate exterior have been explored. The deposits in the terminal strongly suggest episodes of conspicuous

51 Sheep Slait: Owning the land. Amanda Tabor

consumption attended by people from well outside the immediate community, but they were either hosted by that community or by a high-status individual or subgroup within it. Whether or not some of the craftsmen who worked there were local or still peripatetic, the ringwork was situated at the heart of a particular thriving agricultural community (*51*) rather than on the periphery.

The evidence from around Cadbury, Poyntington and probably Woolston (see above) shows that communities living in the area during the early centuries of the first millennium BC had more in common with the purportedly prosperous areas of the south-east than previously thought. For some people there were great opportunities in a period of flux, but for others anxiety was probably an ever-present emotion as reliably repetitive modes of production were threatened by those wanting to maximise their own positions. A period of ostentatious affluence is sustainable for as long as the crops are plentiful, the lines of communication allow access to raw materials, craft skills and exchange remain open and labour remains willing or at least compliant. It is equally true that prestige can only be enhanced by providing others with what they have difficulty obtaining; if there is a surfeit there may be a need to restrict supply before the bottom drops out of the market. Ambitious individuals or groups gain by taking risks in unstable situations: foolhardy promises as a basis for alliances, dubious claims to key tracts of land, even robbery with violence. Perhaps those who thrived in these circumstances did so because they had the good fortune to inherit the most naturally defensible local hill, Cadbury. However, as we shall see below, although Cadbury's potential competitors did not rival it in status, there are signs enough that they survived.

EARLY IRON AGE (52)

Although southern Britain is far from lacking Early Iron Age settlements, they are rare when compared with occupation areas of the Late Bronze Age or Late Iron Age. In particular, whilst there has been an explosion in the discovery of Middle and Late Bronze Age field systems through development-led archaeology, there have been very few identified as Early Iron Age. It is hard to accept that this negative evidence reflects an actual radical change in either the agriculture or population density of the time. It should be noted that the Danebury Environs Project successfully identified settlement after constructing the best regional ceramic series for the first millennium in Britain. Mitigating factors might include a narrow time frame, thorough de-silting or re-cutting of ditches continuing into the Late Iron Age, a failure to recognise characteristic pottery or even a period during which pottery was restricted in the main to high-status sites. Even allowing for all these factors, there seems to have been a marked diminution in wider activity which, although apparent in the South Cadbury study area, should not be overstated.

The firing quality and components of pottery visible under a hand lens ('inclusions') can provide a rough guide to the period of manufacture, but characteristic forms and decorative motifs are far more reliable. It is fortunate that during the Late Bronze Age the dominant, calcite-based, fabrics were very distinctive to the point where sherds composed of it are classified as diagnostic. The reverse is true for the Early Iron Age, during which fossil shell was the dominant inclusion, a characteristic shared with some local pottery of the Neolithic, Middle Bronze Age and Middle Iron Age periods. The only ray of light is that the shell fragments are often larger plates rather than the more consistently crushed varieties of later fabrics. One of the great advantages of using test pits instead fieldwalking or shovel pitting is the increase in the number of sherds recovered with diagnostic traits. Although the prehistoric assemblages include more formless pottery than rims, bases or shoulders, there are enough feature sherds to narrow the date range.

Analysis shows that while we have distinctive forms from most prehistoric periods, the survey work has generated very few belonging to the Early Iron Age. Excepting a few sherds in the South Cadbury valley and around Sparkford and Weston

A central place

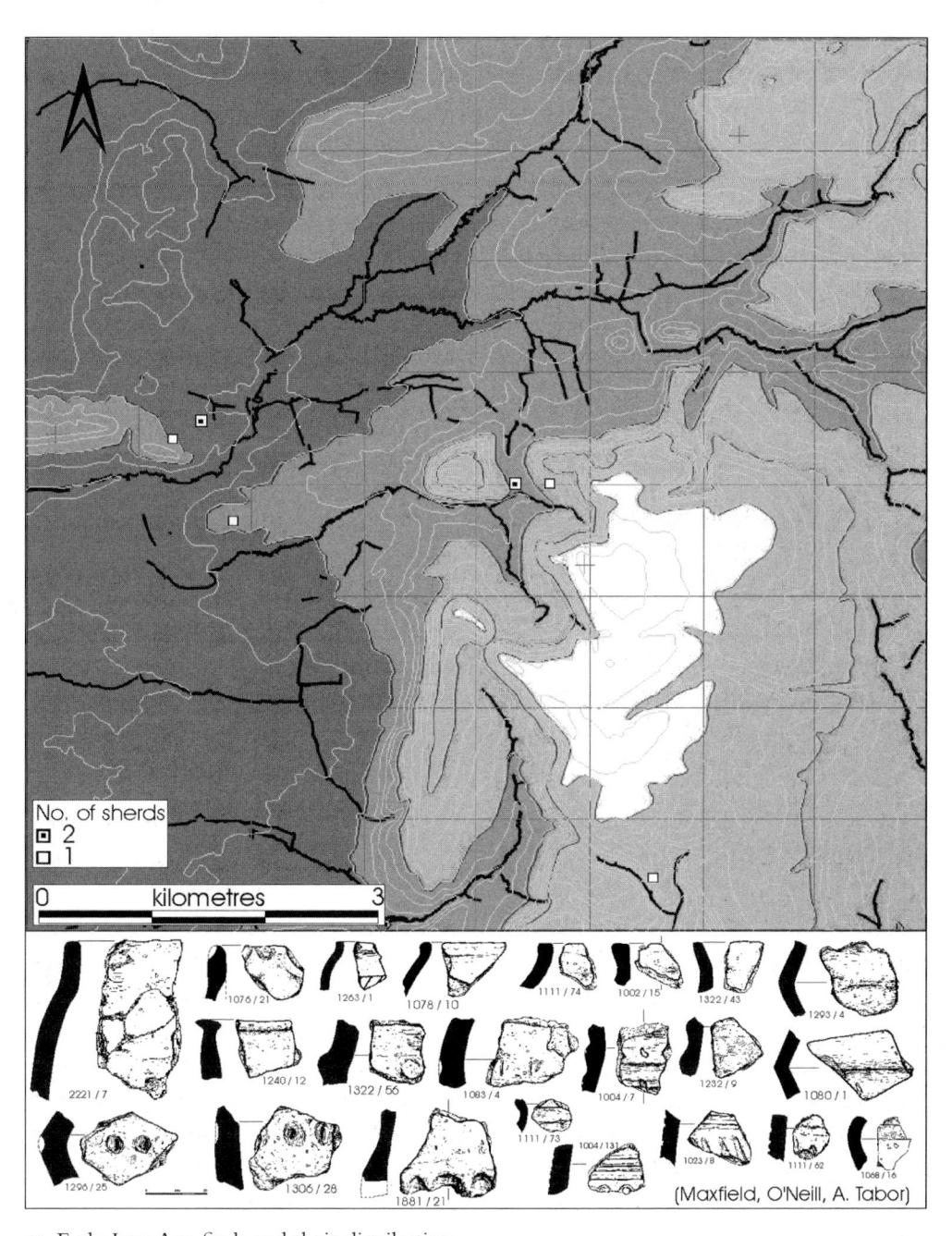

52 Early Iron Age finds and their distribution

Cadbury Castle: The Hillfort and Landscapes

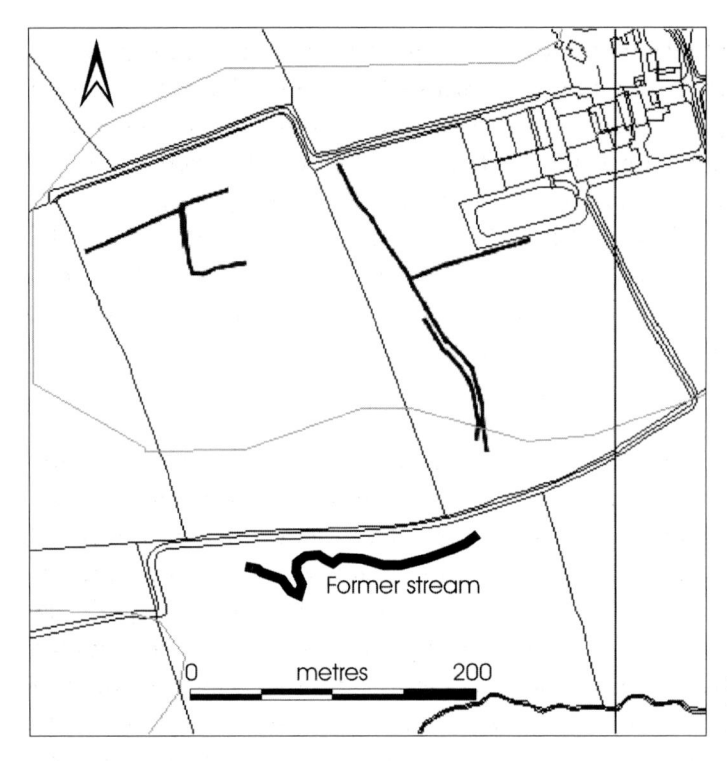

53 Weston Bampfylde: Early Iron Age long linear and enclosure

Bampfylde, the only finds definitely belonging to the period are from the interior of Cadbury Castle and from Milsoms Corner. The Weston Bampfylde sherds are from a long linear ditch (*53*) which may originate from the Bronze Age, allowing the possibility that a Middle Iron Age farmstead alongside it originated at this time. Some of the pottery from Sheep Slait dates from the Bronze Age to Iron Age transition and may reasonably imply a continuing low level of activity there, perhaps seasonal, perhaps in the form of specialist industry, but there is no sign of the previous flamboyance. Rare diagnostically Early Iron Age sherds at Woolston may understate the persistence of settlement there. The Late Bronze Age hilltop enclosure bank and ditch at Woolston was still a sufficiently impressive earthwork in the Middle or Late Iron Age to cause the modification of an otherwise strictly oriented system of rectilinear enclosures (*36*, *82*). Although little can be made of two find-spots in Sparkford, at Great Woolfester the location of a single sherd in slumping upcast from an upslope quarry allows the possibility that a natural river cliff overlooking the River Cam had been settled.

The project's methodology is neither fine enough nor sufficiently extensive to assert that it has identified the full extent of Early Iron Age activity, but it is probably fair to say that it has characterised the general pattern. At least some of the ancient Bronze Age field ditches had been backfilled and the natural traps formed by their subsided fills only started to accumulate material again when the very distinctive Late Iron Age to Romano-British Black Burnished Ware entered circulation. The former, or potential, competitors were eventually subsumed into one larger territory centred on Cadbury Hill, which not only offered the best natural defensive situation but had the great advantage of springs on its slopes. It also overlooked what already would have been an ancient route to and from the south-west peninsula and its important minerals. Overall, the extent of habitative settlement appears to have decreased, but there was a marked increase of intensity on the pre-hillfort and the Milsoms Corner spur.

The hilltop ascendant?

We know something about the outcome of this stage of Cadbury's life: it became a hillfort. Equally we can see that geological processes had made it the local hill best suited to being transformed in this way. Why did it undergo this transformation? This particular investment in the reorganisation of space was not inevitable, it was a choice, perhaps intended as a long term solution to a particular set of problems or aspirations. In the Middle Bronze Age there appears to have been a very limited range of habitative settlement forms: a small number of houses, usually round, often enclosed, probably intended to keep stock in rather than keep people out, and gradually moving around the favoured tract of land as one generation of housing was replaced by the next. Yet the seeds of change had already been sown by the inscribing of large-scale boundaries across the land. Boundaries conceived as long-term, even permanent markers conceal an inherent contradiction which is expressed when others are inspired by the example to draw their own lines. The very act of asserting possession defines a desired space for one and may highlight its desirability to another. If the new system is productive it will be taken up by others and the population will grow.

By 800 BC there was a burgeoning range of landscape boundary and settlement models to choose from. The desire for stability led to increasing experimentation in the search for solutions. Different groups had to decide whether to compete for land or to follow what might be termed the village model, in which a number of families living as a community have affiliation to a particular tract. Such a model has a number of characteristics, one of which is the division and specialisation of labour and the potential for surplus production to support it. Ultimately the village would no longer depend on outside or peripatetic manufacture, even though it would still need to engage in exchange to acquire raw materials. The village model would have changed the pattern of biological as well as social reproduction, although once again there was a range of options. Within cultural systems which have survived over a very long period of time, elaborate kinship taboos evolved, no doubt through learned experience, and consequently a healthy gene pool was

Cadbury Castle: The Hillfort and Landscapes

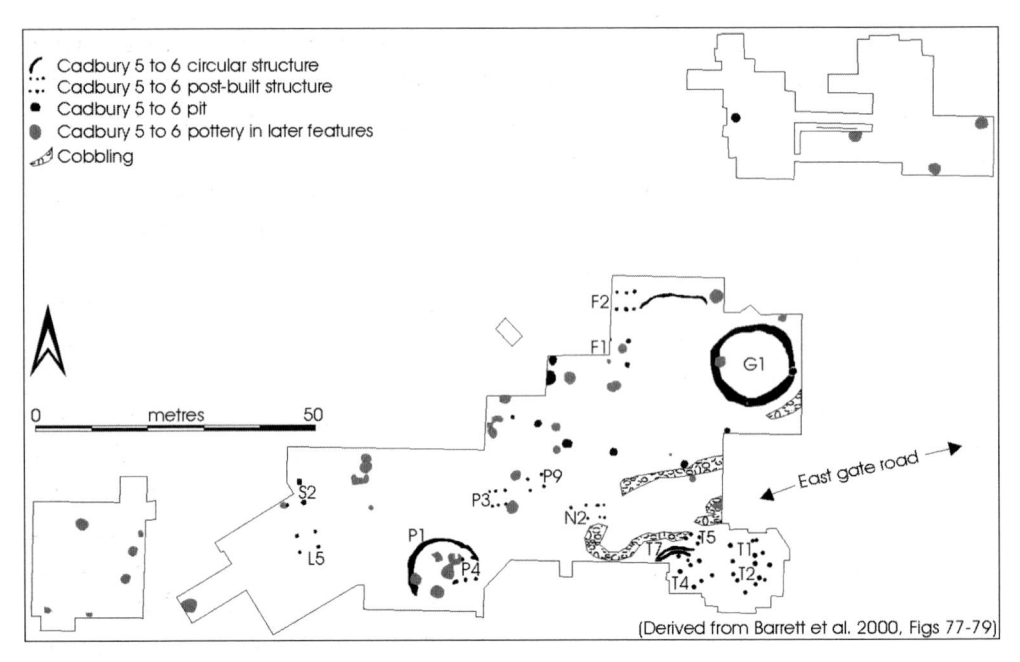

54 Cadbury Castle: Early Iron Age features on the plateau

maintained. When a village system first developed, new ways of viewing the world would have been introduced and some of the old knowledge would have been lost. At the outset it would have been perfectly viable for marriage to be an intracommunity affair but over a longer period such self-sufficiency may have engendered problems.

There was a marked growth in the extent and sophistication of the settlement on the east side of Cadbury's plateau towards the middle of the first millennium BC, fitting the village model. The shrine, N1 (*39*), associated with Cadbury 4 and 5 pottery (*35*), may have survived from the previous phase but was eventually replaced by N2 (*54*). If it opened to the east it would have faced directly towards the track from the east gate, before it veered southwards to avoid the steepest descents from the plateau, and would have overlooked the area in between, where by far the greatest density of Bronze Age metalwork from the hill was found. If the detailed plan included in the English Heritage report's inventory of structures is accepted, the central posts on its west and east sides were aligned on the find-spot of the oldest piece of metal from the hill, an Early Bronze Age flanged axe lying 13m to the east. The bronze artefacts in between included a spearhead, a razor, a knife, two gouges, an awl, pins and a gold-plated ring, all dating to the last three centuries of the Bronze Age or the earliest Iron Age. This is the area which appears to have been enclosed in the Late Bronze Age and which may have remained fenced. A significant but much thinner spread of similarly dated material lies within a 10m arc to the west side of N1 and includes the half-gold bracelet. More generally across the east of the plateau there are two Middle Bronze Age spearheads, more awls, tweezers and pins.

Two bronze razors of a distinctly continental style can be placed with some confidence in the eighth or seventh century BC and at least three of four pairs of tweezers (*colour plate 15*) were roughly contemporary, but some of the pins attributed to this phase were probably manufactured earlier, as noted above. Whilst they had been for personal adornment, it is possible that they were small parts of scrap intended for recasting, a view first favoured by Alcock and the currently favoured explanation for such assortments. The same explanation has been offered for a strikingly similar group of bronzes, on this occasion a hoard in a small pit at Danebury. If the razors, pins and tweezers are placed alongside the earlier flanged axe and the Middle Bronze Age spearheads mentioned above, they make an apparently incongruous group. In both cases the latest objects dated to the seventh century BC but both groups included objects cast up to 1000 years earlier. It surely stretches credulity that objects could have been cared for over so long a period only to be melted down. Barry Cunliffe's alternative suggestion is that the Danebury material constituted a ritual deposit possibly shortly before the construction of the first defences there.

The dispersed character of the Cadbury objects makes the latter explanation harder to sustain but the general lack of other material and features from the Early and Middle Bronze Age give the objects a special status. We should note that there was an established tradition of curating ancient objects most potently exemplified by the shield and the human lower leg bone at Milsoms Corner. Most archaeologists at some time experience a sense of almost tangible contact with a notional ancestor when they find a particularly striking object. Such feelings are even more acute when an heirloom has passed through a family for generations. In an age before writing, the potency of the tool which formed part of an ancestor's world would have given substance to stories about him or her which informed later generations' senses of themselves. The discarding of a 200-year-old shield or a 1000-year-old axe with or without other objects either severed a direct link to the past or preserved it in a safe place. It must have been a moment of great significance. It is tempting to see it as physical testimony to the end of a family line but the examples from Cadbury and Danebury may both mark transitions to new beginnings.

N1 (*39*) may have been abandoned by the time substantial ditches encircled G1 and P1; roundhouses of diameters exceeding 10m gave an air of permanence to the settlement. They are dated by Cadbury 6 pottery, as are four and six post rectilinear structures, T1-5, south of track junction and probably indicative of increased above-ground storage (*54*), although their overlapping outlines show that they cannot all be exactly contemporary. Several were standing on the plateau when the first ditch and bank system encircled the hilltop. A few more pits were dug into the natural rock, some cylindrical but often subrectangular or irregular in plan. The pits of this phase were generally smaller than those of the Middle Iron Age and they often appeared to have been backfilled in a single episode.

Later a cobbled surface was laid over the filled features and a significantly brown soil. The natural soil on Cadbury is red. It only became brown with the addition of humic material, whether through the addition of manure to a plough soil, the accumulation of a midden, or the abandonment of structures, tools or other waste high in organic content. The soil's proximity to areas of industry and habitation indicates that it formed from one of the latter processes and it is a clear sign of intense use over a substantial period. During phases of refurbishment and expansion the cobbles served both as a road surface and as a working platform, notably providing a base for large hearths or furnaces which, on occasions, may have been used in metalworking. Crucible fragments were found in a shallow hollow, lined with stone slabs, some of which were stained by copper, and a similar feature revealed evidence for iron working. Although a neighbouring group of features failed to produce in situ metalworking debris, a significant amount of bronze casting waste and iron slag was found amongst the cobbles. Alcock recorded the presence of loomweights but their proximity to several structured areas of burning lends circumstantial support to the interpretation that they were oven bricks, implying that there had been high-temperature industrial work.

Textile production is to be expected on most Iron Age settlement sites of significant size, but the evidence for it on Cadbury is extremely thin for this phase. Neither spindlewhorls nor weaving combs were found in demonstrably Early Iron Age contexts. Forty-two are recorded as stylistically of that phase in the English Heritage report, nearly 80 per cent of which were made from red deer antler, but subsequent passages suggest that the attribution may be a slip of the pen. Unfortunately none of the bone of this period was analysed in the report so it is not possible to make inferences about the likely use of wool on the basis of the age of slaughter of sheep, or indeed any other aspects of animal husbandry.

In the centuries leading up to the construction of the hillfort there was a marked trend towards nucleation of settlement and there may have been a retreat from the agricultural use, particularly arable, of some of the land surrounding former settlements. This may have reflected a decline in the population but equally might be a sign of the increased effectiveness of crop production on the plateau and low lying areas close to Cadbury. A single small enclosure linked to the linear system at Weston Bampfylde may have been for stock rather than cultivation, a sign that beyond the core settlement animal husbandry was more important.

The hilltop enclosed

The digging of massive earthworks was established as a practice in the Neolithic. Some causewayed enclosures survive as earthworks and the largest of all that period's ditch and bank enclosures, Avebury, Wiltshire, remains a daunting presence. Engineering on this scale had long been in decline and it has been suggested that it only resumed during the British Iron Age under the influence of mainland Europe. Better understanding of European chronologies has undermined this view so hillfort evolution is better understood within an indigenous framework. There were enclosures on hilltops, and even some enclosed hilltops, during the Bronze Age but their banks and ditches were not of a depth or height comparable to later Iron Age examples. They served to contain stock, to mark boundaries and to structure special events such as the Sigwells craft fair. This changed with the advent of ringworks. Deeper and wider ditches provided the material for substantial banks which had the potential to play a defensive role.

Chris Musson, Alcock's assistant director at Cadbury, went on to plan and implement a major programme of excavations from 1969-76 on the Breiddin in the Welsh Marches. He chose not to excavate during the summer, as at Cadbury he had observed that many features simply lost their distinctive soil colours at that time of the year, effectively rendering them invisible to the digger. He believed that the problem had been particularly acute in the lee of the ramparts on Cadbury where deep stratigraphy was often reduced to a homogenous baked dark soil, eliminating possible structural evidence. Musson duly found roundhouses sheltered by the ramparts at much the time that Cunliffe made similar discoveries at Danebury. The close relationship of the buildings to the ramparts provided important evidence about the range of activities contemporary with different phases of the defences. The combination of the ground conditions and the comparatively small area explored behind the inner bank on Cadbury leaves the character and date of settlement activity there unknown. Without a stratigraphic link between the inner bank and the plateau it is impossible to say with confidence which phase of interior activity coincided with the massive hillfort construction project.

Alcock's decision to cut trenches through the inner rampart in four places proved wise, although in retrospect the use of a machine was sometimes excessive and led to confusion. The best continuous sequence was revealed in Trench D, on the south side. On the west and north sides (Trenches J and A) much of the Iron Age bank could not be reliably identified. The remains of the bank explored in the two Trenches J were mainly post Iron Age and appeared to show that the later remodelling of the defences was set well back from the original structure, which had been cut away or tumbled into the ditch below. Problems in the excavation methodology in Trench I, on the east side, obscured important aspects of the structural sequence, but distribution of finds suggests that preservation of the Iron Age banks was better there.

At Cadbury the dating is entirely dependent on the pottery and as we have already seen that is no longer the reliable indicator it once seemed. Pottery from a former turf which formed over the Bronze Age lynchet and was sealed by the first bank, was of Alcock's Cadbury 5 type, the most distinctive vessels being fairly sharply shouldered bowls. The pottery from the bank itself, designated Cadbury 6, included jars with fingertip decoration and haematite-coated bowls comparable with those from Milsoms Corner. This suggests that the first defensive bank originated in the sixth or fifth century BC (*32*). Interpretation of this and subsequent deposits has been complicated by the collapse and deliberate cutting away of earlier structures to provide a good foundation and not least by the burrowing of rabbits. Despite these difficulties, the analysis published in the English Heritage report has generated a coherent earthwork sequence which I have adopted here (*colour plate 16*) but with some qualification of the dating.

The initial conception may have comprised two concentric banks and ditches. The most detailed plan of the first phase was obtained from Site D on the south side of the hillfort, the only trench to cut through all the defensive banks. The surviving structural evidence for the first phase of the inner bank suggested that two or, more probably, three concentric rings of posts at intervals of 1.5-2m supported a framework for containing a dump of reddish brown soil and gravelly limestone rubble which included a few sherds of Cadbury 6 pottery. A ledge inside the outer posts provided a slot for the lowest part of a wall made up of horizontal planks up to 20cm (8in) thick which shored up the dumped material. The posts may have been given added stability with horizontal tie-beams linking the rows.

Authors of the English Heritage report asserted that by the end of the Early Iron Age the holloway, which by the first century AD was an established approach to the plateau from the north-east gate, was already in existence. The evidence that it was a major route, if a route at all, before Cadbury 8 is thin indeed. The published section drawings are inconclusive, although it has been noted that the same silts which filled the platform left by roundhouse BW6 (*60, 62, 63*) filled the holloway. By definition the silts over the platform which had been cut into natural before the house was built could only have formed after the building had collapsed or been demolished. The arcs of two further roundhouses (BW1 and BW5) which have been loosely assigned to the Middle Iron Age, but without any firm evidence, would both have overlapped the track. As there was no evidence that either cut it, the conclusion must surely be that the track post dates them. This would place the holloway's inception as a major route well into Cadbury 8.

An earthworks survey has confirmed that the east gate is integral to the rampart system and I have argued above that it was one of two early established approaches

A central place

to the hilltop. It would be unusual to have had three approaches, but there are plenty of early hilltop enclosures with a west and east approach. It is likely that when the first banks were built both the steep traditional routes were retained but without a north-east gate. This would imply that most transport was on foot or hoof, but not on wheels. When draught became more important, these long venerated tracks became obstacles to access, necessitating adaptation in later phases.

The heavy degradation of the first bank by the one which succeeded it has removed all evidence for possible tie-beams in Trench D. The material for the bank was upcast from an outer ditch dug where the hillslope began to fall away steeply. This ditch was subsequently re-dug to a greater depth and would have required regular clearance due to erosion from the bank above it in later phases. The original outline of the ditch may have been entirely erased.

There is some evidence from the long section (*colour plate 16*) that Ditch 2, the outer of the two, was relocated, possibly because the local geology rendered the ditch and bank unstable. Alternatively the subsequent relocation 5m northwards and upslope presented a much steeper approach. Like the inner, the second ditch was subject to clearance but a trace of the second phase outline and early silts survived in places on the north side. The latest diagnostic pot sherd from the silts was a Cadbury 6 type rim, with the implication that Ditch 2 was in use at the same time as Bank A.

Although we cannot be certain that the first bank was built around the entire perimeter, it almost certainly was, giving a length of just under 1100m. Two rings of uprights would have required around 1800 posts and Alcock estimated that around 21,000m (70,000ft) of timber would have been required for the breastwork. Allowing that each timber would have had a diameter of between 30 and 40cm (11.8 to 15.7ins) the number of suitable trees is high. He postulated that this first enclosure was a communal work by peasant farmers. If Bank 2 was contemporary with it, even allowing that both were of a relatively small scale, a considerable amount of labour would have been required, as well as readily accessible wood. It may be rash to assume that the bank builders were descendants of those who had deposited the shield and that items such as the gold bracelet may still have been in circulation, but at the very least they were well-connected peasants with a proud history.

Bank A survived long enough for turf to form over a tail extending from its rear. We do not know how much effort went into maintaining it but while Cadbury 6 pottery was still current, the outer face was dug away to create a ledge into which postholes were cut to provide a firm base for a wooden framework which supported a stone breast work. Partly built from blue lias, the nearest source for which would have been a river cliff by the Cam 2km (1.2 miles) to the west at

Sparkford, the extraction and transportation of the stone would have been as challenging an undertaking as the actual building work. The laminated stone would have produced an impressive vertical façade, flattered by its appearance, as it was structurally weak. At only 25cm (10in) deep it was structurally weak and even the surviving lower courses (as many as ten in places) tilted outwards under pressure from the over 3m-wide rubble bank retained by it. Timber posts along its interior show that it had a vertical rear revetment, while laid slabs on top of the bank provided a walkway. The few sherds from within the bank were of Cadbury 6 type and if we are to assume that occupation of the enclosed area had been continuous, they surely date to the late fifth or very early fourth century BC.

The rear of the bank was prone to collapse and in places additional irregularly spaced postholes were a symptom of ongoing repairs. The pottery in the material which built up behind it, belonging to the Middle Iron Age Cadbury 7 assemblage, was another sign of the bank's longevity.

EXCLUSIVE SPACE

The most coherent evidence for Early Iron Age activity is from the Milsoms Corner spur (55). The Bronze Age roundhouse cutting the backfilled enclosure ditch (44) was replaced by a building with a hearth slightly north-west of its centre. The main door, marked by two deeply set posts, opened to the south-west but a break in the circular gully defining it may be a narrow access on its east side. Deposits of sandy clay made up a level platform. The surrounding gully was filled with large stones which at the time of excavation was interpreted as a means of drainage rather than packing in a bedding trench.

When the building was constructed the door posts had been packed with material from a hearth. Eventually the building was demolished, the posts withdrawn from their sockets and the north door posthole sealed with large wall slabs from a plain storage jar. A posthole on the east side produced a penannular bronze finger ring and included large quern fragments lying across it, suggesting that these were also closure deposits rather than packing, the latter provided by slabs of lias. This may have arrived in the area at the time of Bank B's construction but it seems more likely to have been re-used after some of the breastwork collapsed.

The other Late Bronze Age roundhouse was replaced by industrial activity. Shallow, dish-shaped, scoops reminiscent of those on the edge of the Sigwells metalworking structure were closed with gravelly burnt stone, one with a complete cuboid perforated oven brick set into it. The underlying fill included greeny-yellow material, probably derived from cess. Postholes were associated with three of the scoops. It is possible that urine was being collected for the dyeing of textiles which

A central place

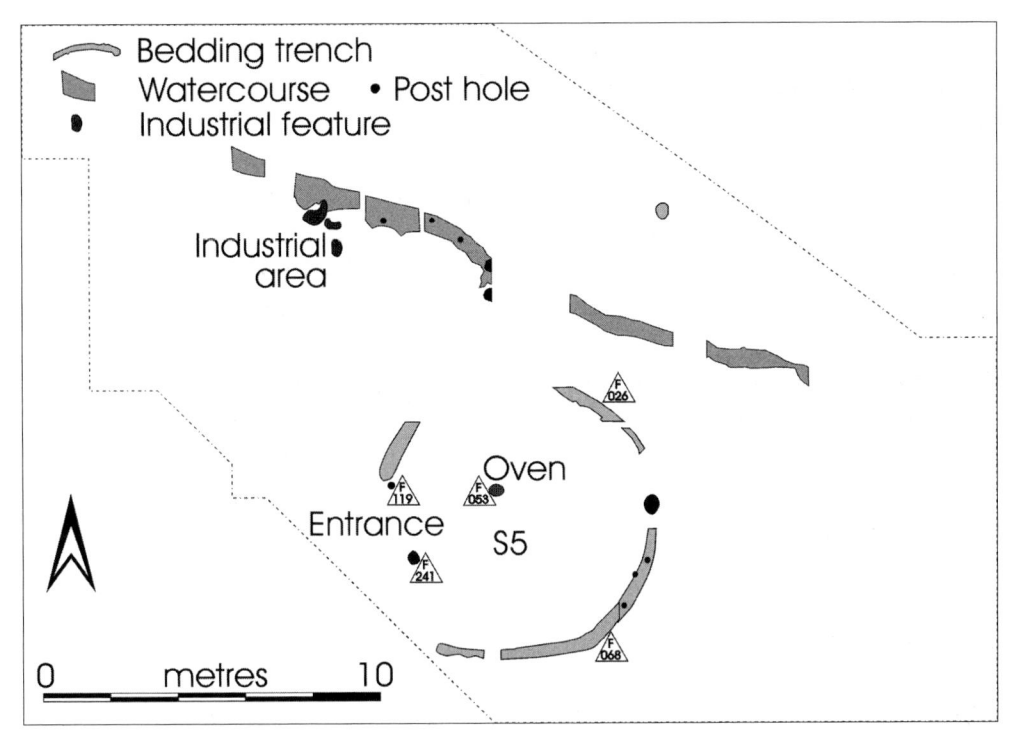

55 Milsoms Corner: selected Early Iron Age features

were suspended from the posts but the evidence is extremely tenuous, amounting to the presence of sheep bone. A drainage gully appeared contemporary with the scoops as the burnt gravelly closure deposit from one had slumped across the lower fills of the gully. Unfortunately this was an area of the trench badly damaged by modern ploughing so that a full plan of any associated structure was beyond recovery.

Up to 150 postholes within a trench with maximum dimensions of 30 x 21m belong to this period. There appears to have been frenetic restructuring within a small area, which surely gained its significance as the threshold to the hill looming behind it. Two pairs of substantial posts seem likely to have supported a gate through a fence, in part following the line of the east enclosure ditch, showing that the division of the spur from the hill persisted. The pottery characterising this phase was often decorated with fingertip impressions on the outer rim and on cordons applied to the shoulder or lower neck. There were also rare examples of sherds decorated with sharply defined stabbed or impressed circles and horizontal lines (only one sherd of the type was recorded from Alcock's excavations), furrows with bird bone impressions, and a few with haematite coating. The latter correspond well with Early Iron Age material from Wiltshire and, judged against an admittedly incomplete record, it represents a higher percentage of finewares than occurred on the hilltop.

When the finds assemblage is measured against the number of potential structures, it offers meagre resources for a dwelling area. A hearth in a roundhouse need only have provided heat and a modicum of light, rather than a regular supply of cooked food, yet the substantial fence on the east side is a clear sign that in some respects the activities here were outside the scope of the everyday life of the community of which it must have been part. It is tempting to suggest it was the gatehouse to the hilltop community but, while that arrangement might make some sense, once the massive defences had been constructed it would seem grandiose to 'protect' a beaten track to the earlier small, unenclosed, settlement. If we take into account the already long tradition of funerary rites, of which the shield's deposition may be part, and the opening of the roundhouse door onto the winter setting sun, a role in the disposal of the dead seems very possible.

Firm evidence for the disposal of the dead throughout the Iron Age in southern Britain is rare. In the later Bronze Age, cremation was widespread and from the Late Iron Age there have been some instances of seemingly opportunistic burials in pits (notably at Danebury and Suddern Farm, Hampshire) and crouched burials in Dorset and parts of Somerset. Otherwise the dead are present as odd fragments of skull or limb and little else. There is increasing evidence that much of this scattered human material occurs in carefully structured deposits, sometimes associated with particular bones from a limited range of other species or with certain artefacts. Butchery marks are rare on the human bones, but their fragmentary nature shows that some control has been exercised over their remains for a long time after death. It is widely accepted that excarnation (leaving the dead body exposed to be consumed by birds or other animals) is the practice which would best fit the evidence. There are no storage pits at Milsoms Corner and a feasible interpretation of the wealth of post settings is that some provided the supports for excarnation platforms. Against this interpretation is the lack of fragmentary human remains from the spur, although we should bear in mind that mortal remains from the Late Iron Age are usually found in close proximity to the living, often in midden-like deposits in pits and ditches. They may have been cleared up.

MIDDLE IRON AGE (56)

The earliest specified political divisions in Britain are from classical sources. There should be caution in their application as they may be no more significant than the designated states created in the Arab peninsula and Africa for the purposes of administration by European imperialists. The first geographical account after the

A central place

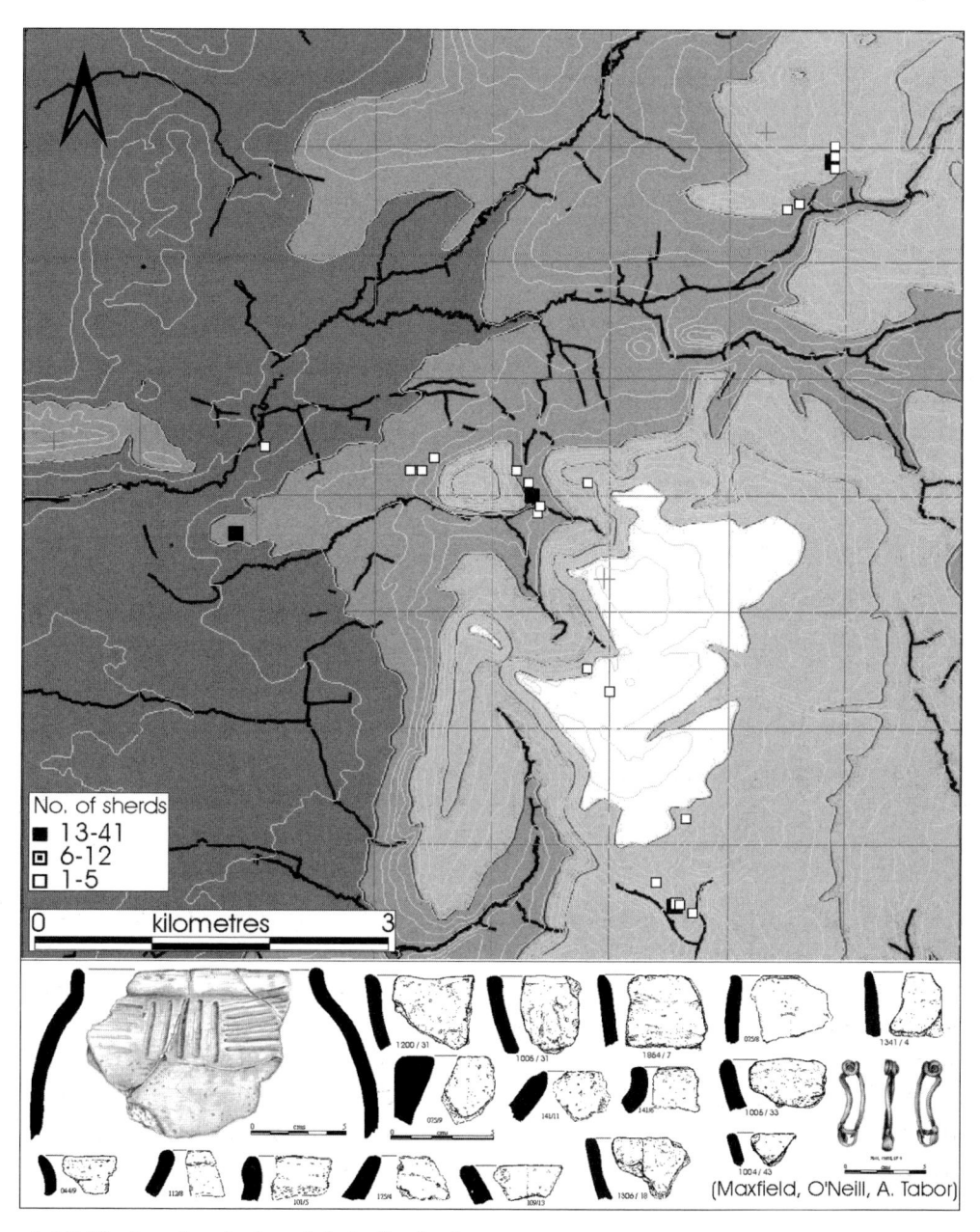

56 Middle Iron Age finds and their distribution

Julian invasions of 55 and 54 BC was Strabo's from the first quarter of the following century. Tacitus gave much fuller descriptions at the end of that century and in the second quarter of the second century AD, Ptolemy provided much more specific information about tribal locations in Britain. Archaeological evidence based on the distribution of pottery styles and, in particular, Late Iron Age coinage suggests that Cadbury's community was affiliated to the Durotriges, a tribe centred on Maiden Castle. The Dobunni were to their north and the Dumnonii to the west and south-west. In the first century BC there may have been a political shift due to the arrival and ascendancy of the Belgae in Hampshire to the east. The greatly increased structuring of the landscape by hillforts and field systems suggests that the three western tribes may have at least Middle Iron Age origins.

A key objective of SCEP was to test claims that there was little if any extramural habitative settlement close to developed hillforts. This lack was first noted in the report of survey work around Maiden Castle in 1991, the year before SCEP was founded. The issue was raised again with the publication of the Danebury Environs Project in 2000, coincidentally the year before this project received funding from the Leverhulme Trust to go full time. The restatement of the claim at the end of such an outstanding programme provided added impetus as the author recruited and galvanised a team of willing, and increasingly skilled, regular volunteers, who sieved ever more soil and dug foxholes regardless of the ground conditions! The crucial datable finds were crushed shell-tempered sherds from generally undecorated straight-sided and gently curved saucepan pots and jars. The effort paid off as the concentrations of such pottery show (56).

By the third quarter of the first millennium BC, enclosure systems in the focal areas were growing and spreading, except in the vicinity of Sheep Slait. In peripheral areas such as Weston Bampfylde, land divisions which had originated in the Early or Middle Bronze Age persisted and so probably did the associated animal husbandry. In Worthy, a double-ditched track led from the settlement to a former stream detected by gradiometry. A double-ditched droveway on the north-facing side of the Weston Bampfylde ridge may have existed already to funnel traffic and herds from Cadbury towards the crossing of the River Cam at Sparkford (57). Certainly it became an important feature as the hilltop community exercised increasing influence over the landscape. There are traces of ditches south of the droveway but most of the heavy soils on the ridge remained outside the systems of arable and stock farming, providing pannage for pigs and wood for fuel and building.

One important change was the development of trackways and an elaborated field system at Sigwells. Its orientation in the east half of the field (57) may have been influenced by the later phases of the Middle Bronze Age enclosure and its pronounced north to south orientation suggests an inception roughly contemporary with the prominent Middle to Late Bronze Age system west of Cadbury. Its great expansion during the Middle Iron Age has been demonstrated in trenches but barely registered in the regular test pits. The intensive agricultural production here may have replaced the more extensive system 1km south at Poyntington and Seven

A central place

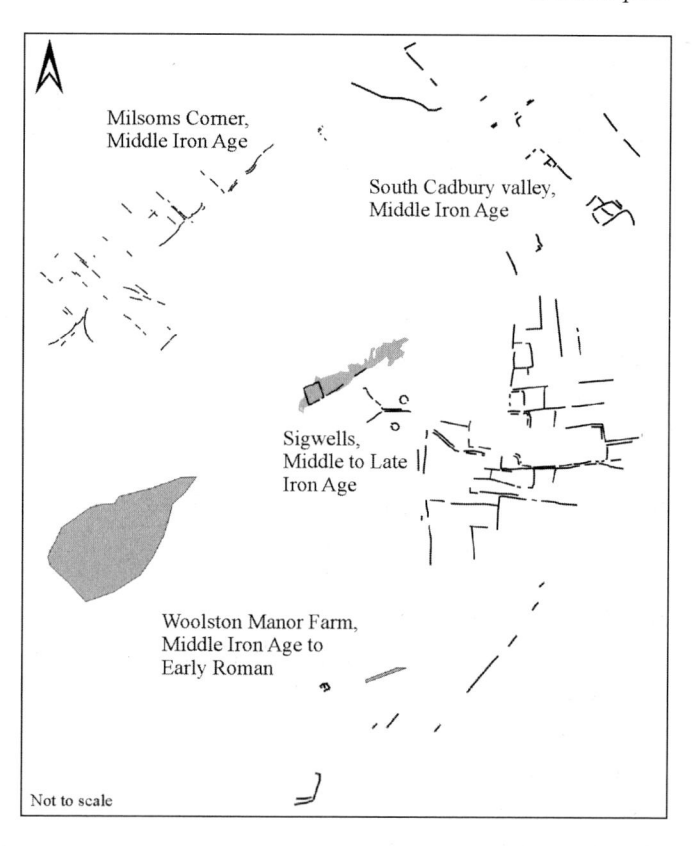

57 Middle Iron Age fields and tracks

Wells Downs. The marked concentration of Iron Age pottery within Sheep Slait ringwork, and the slight scatter spreading from it, may not be linked to permanent or habitative settlement.

Intensification below Cadbury Castle itself was marked by expansion of the field system in the valleys to its south-east and east, and an entirely new scheme developed along a south-west to north-east axis, broadly following the outline of the north-west side of the hill and entirely replacing the later Bronze Age system (*57*). An ancient trackway leading south from Cadbury, to cross what is now a partly underground watercourse below Sigwells at Whitcombe, would also have passed by field systems on gentle west-facing lower slopes (*colour plate 17*). On this side of the hillfort, the pattern is one of adaptation and expansion rather than wholesale replacement. The number of small pot sherds in the enclosure ditches in the east valley provides sure signs of associated settlement.

An expansive field system developed at Woolston, oriented with a west-south-west to east-north-east valley, extending from a dry plateau down a steep south-south-east facing scarp and onto the level ground below it. A concentration of pottery from targeted test pits, some in cut features, showed surprisingly that at

Cadbury Castle: The Hillfort and Landscapes

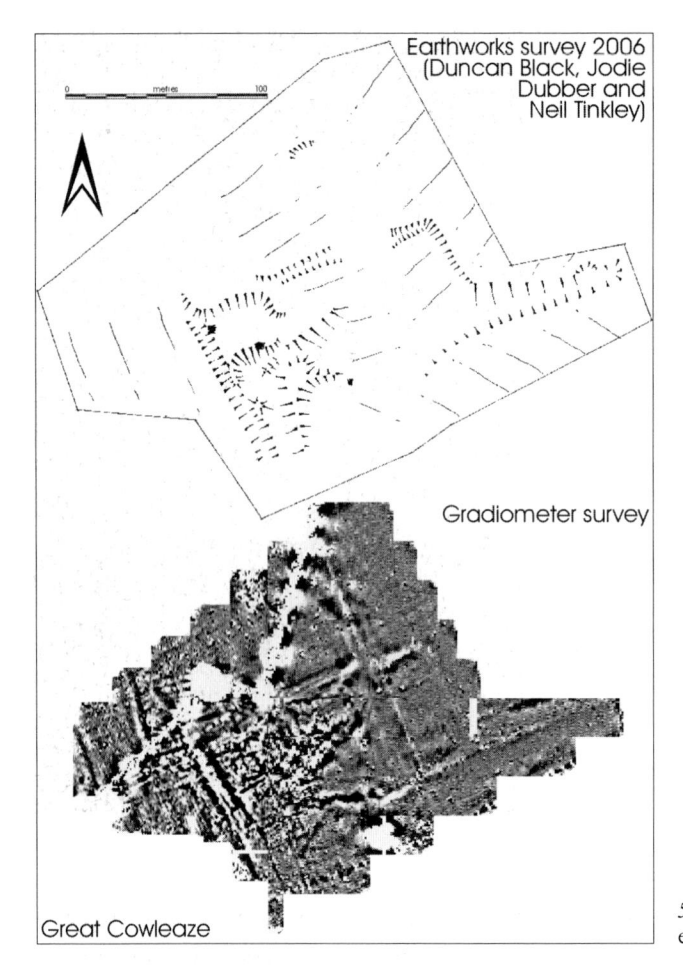

58 Woolston Manor Farm: earthworks in Great Cowleaze

least some of the surviving terracing and platforms (*58*) on the lowest slopes of the east side of the scarp were Middle Iron Age.

Safe and Plentiful

Cadbury Castle's Middle Iron Age defences can be bracketed crudely by the use of Bank B and the construction and use of soil Bank C1 which was a glacis (i.e. with a sloping rather than vertical outer face) (*colour plate 16*). The phase was dated by its association with Middle Iron Age Cadbury 8 pottery, representing a total span of between 250 and 400 years (*34*). As noted above, Bank B appears to have been constructed during the currency of Cadbury 6 pottery, but the material in soils which built up behind it were Cadbury 7. The distribution of this assemblage is weighted towards the lee of the ramparts on the south side of the hill and, by analogy with other hillforts, it is likely that domestic activity was focused in this sheltered zone.

A central place

59 Cadbury Castle: slingstones and infant deposit. Cadbury Castle archive

The picture from the excavations of the south-west gate is also muddy. Everywhere the banks required periodic refurbishment or rebuilding but in the area around the gates there was a permanent structural crisis where traffic caused rapid erosion of the trackway, which deepened leaving the banks on either side in danger of collapse. As a consequence, episodes of refurbishment and structural adjustment were even more frequent at the gate. Although banks from earlier phases survive, traces of the entrances do not. During Cadbury 7, a fire destroyed a 6m-diameter post-built circular building, which may have been a guard house or lodge on the north side of the entrance. As it had at least two structural phases it probably stood for a long period, a view supported by Early Iron Age pottery recovered from the postholes. This would suggest that the first south-west gate, as opposed to west, was either a feature of Bank B's construction or an adaptation during its currency. In either case we may surmise that for the first time wheeled vehicles became an important feature for transport. The same transport needs would have precipitated the construction of the north-east gate, where the natural gradient was much gentler than that below the east gate.

Following the lodge's destruction, a midden-like layer formed which was sealed by layers considered to be possible floor levels of a rebuild culminating in a well-defined new circular structure. Pebbles in a scoop beneath the floor were described as slingstones, effectively an ammunition store, although some of the pebbles were far from aerodynamic. A dish-shaped scoop in the top of the pebbles nested a neonatal infant (*59*). The association of the two has been described as a boundary-defining deposit, as have later deposits in the south and east banks. Alternatively it may be an example of the most typical identifiable Iron Age burial practice: the interment of a child under the floor of the house. The lodge floor was dated by early Cadbury 8 pottery, making it roughly, or even exactly, contemporary with the first surviving guard chamber, hewn out of the rubble bank and underlying natural rock on the east side of the passage. Within a few decades a guard chamber had been added to the other side of the passage and through constant refurbishment survived into the mid first century AD when it accumulated testimony to the massacre. By then, the floor of the chamber had been lowered by the height of a sentry below the floor of the original due to the rampant erosion in the busy gate passage.

There is a comparative lack of narrowly dated cut features of this phase on the plateau, in particular pits; there were more dated to the earlier phases and a far greater number belonging to Cadbury 8. This can in part be explained by the relative brevity of Cadbury 7, which occupies no more than a few decades either side of 300 BC when reinterpreted as Woodward's ca7 and linked directly to Danebury's cp4-5 (*34*). An additional reason may have been that in the main, storage of harvested crops was above ground during the earlier part of the Middle Iron Age and certainly there were comparatively few pits on the plateau during the long Late Bronze Age and Early Iron Age occupation.

Continuity from earlier times was illustrated by repairs to the cobbles and by the similar siting of buildings and industry on the plateau (*60*). The survival buildings with some refurbishment or slight relocation leave little room for periods of abandonment, and the construction of a new roundhouse, T6 (*61*), associated with Cadbury 7 pottery over the area to the south of the track junction, indicates an expansion of dwelling space (*60*) at the expense of the former above-ground storage buildings.

Even in the earlier phases, when the hilltop was comparatively open, there was a preference for rebuilding either on, largely overlapping with, or next to, an earlier building. It is hardly surprising that this trend remained very pronounced in the Middle Iron Age as the population grew rapidly. The even distribution of the roundhouses on the hilltop may well reflect family plots, in effect surrounding a core communal open area given over to religion and industry. We may wonder why some people dwelt on the most exposed part of the hill whilst others sheltered

A central place

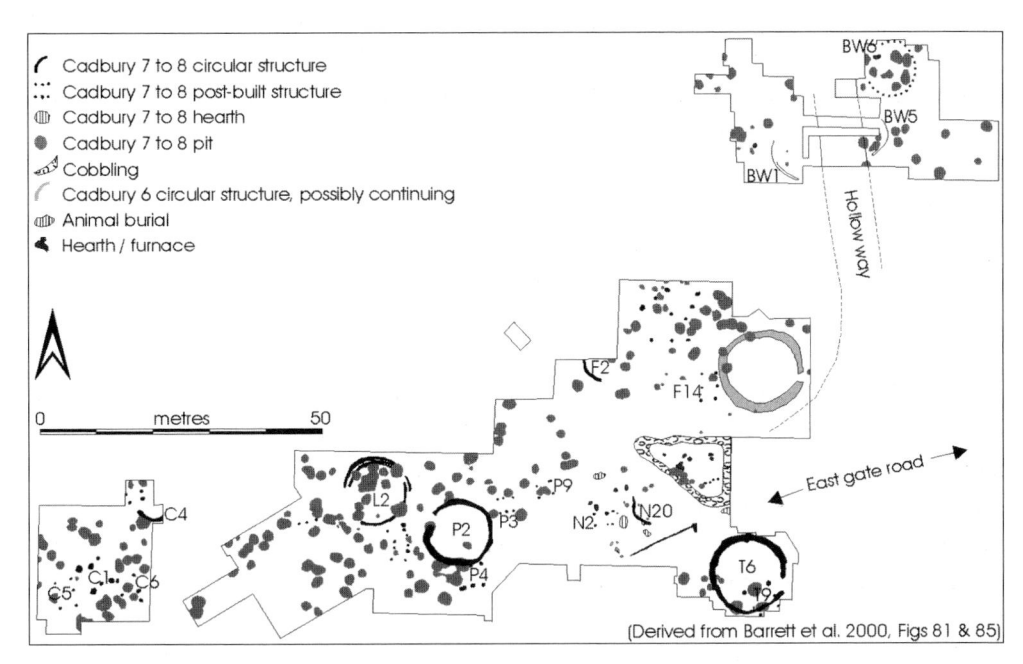

60 Cadbury Castle: Middle Iron Age features on the plateau

61 Cadbury Castle: Middle Iron Age roundhouse T6 ditch. Cadbury Castle archive

Cadbury Castle: The Hillfort and Landscapes

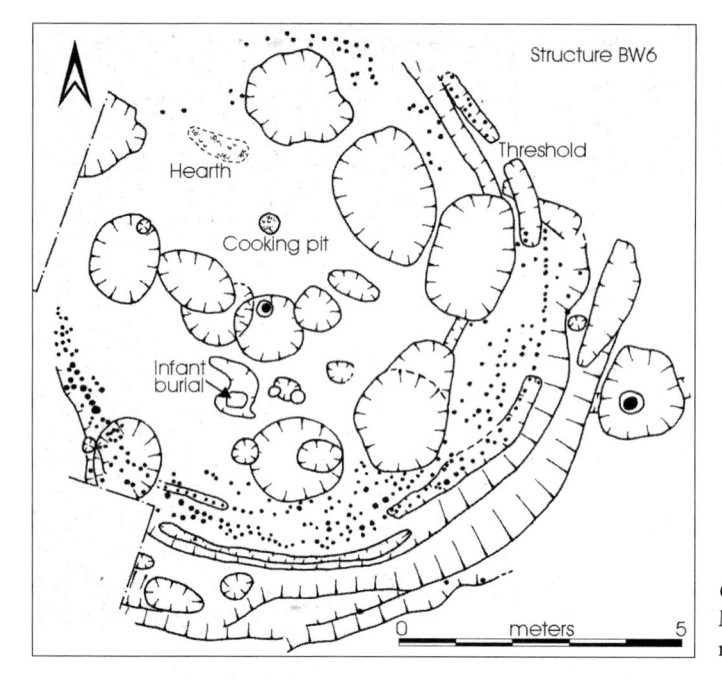

62 Cadbury Castle: plan of Middle Iron Age roundhouse BW6

behind the ramparts, but wattle and daub provided excellent insulation and leading figures in the village surely felt that geographical pre-eminence symbolised and reinforced their status. The area of evenly distributed habitation continued to expand westwards well into the later stages of the Middle Iron Age. A short length of ring ditch, C4 (*60*), cut filled pits which contained Cadbury 8 pottery.

Growth also occurred along either side of the north trackway and it was here that deep stratified deposits, filling a terrace cut into the hillside, provided the clearest insight into roundhouse construction. Even without ploughing, a fractured natural rock makes the identification of postholes difficult because the small stake cuts tend to be irregular and indistinct as the downward movement of the stake levers stones from the side. In Trench B/W, on the slope between the plateau and the north-east gate, the natural was sand so that the cut line of a stake left a clear impression which showed well when filled with a brown sandy silt where the stake had rotted or been removed. The initial construction appears to have been very similar to a Late Bronze Age structure at Milsoms Corner. Slightly offset pairs of stakes and, in places, a single row were set into or around the edges of a circular bedding gully. This pattern can be seen most clearly on the north side of building BW6 (*62*). On the south side the picture is confused by an abundance of pinpricks with only the most general curving pattern. A photograph of the trench side (*63*) shows that the ground on the south side is considerably higher than that on the north. The gap between the outer circuit of stakes and the natural sand into which

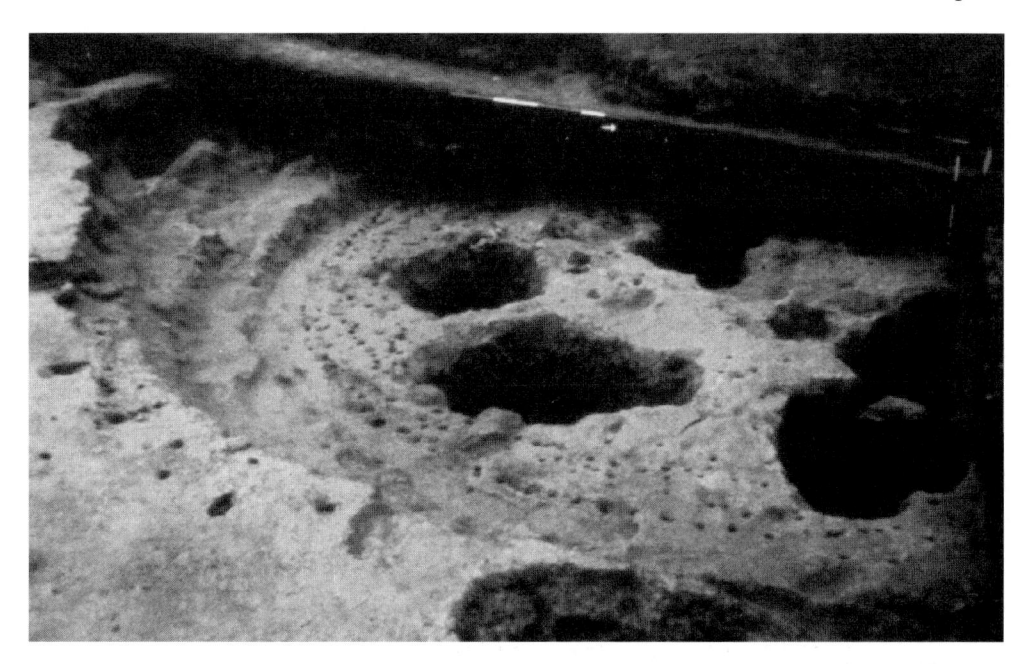

63 Cadbury Castle: fills over Middle Iron Age roundhouse BW6. Cadbury Castle archive

the terrace had been cut formed a trap for hillwashes moving downslope. This prompted the strengthening of the building from the inside, incurring the loss of a significant amount of living space. Later pits have cut away evidence for internal division but interestingly there appears to have been a cooking pit as well as a hearth, the latter disconcertingly close to the north wall.

There was a huge growth in the number of pits during Cadbury 8. Alcock dug a total of 375, of which 362 were fully excavated and had not been subject to substantial disturbance by later features. Analysis of pottery from 272 of them suggested that 23 pits were earlier than the Middle Iron Age and 41 had included Late Iron Age Cadbury 9 material. Of the remaining 208 assigned to the Middle Iron Age, 189 were dated by Cadbury 8 pottery. If we try to conceptualise that in terms of the number of pits being dug per year and over the whole of the interior, compared with other phases, by multiplying up, we gain some idea of the increase in storage represented. During the Late Bronze Age and Early Iron Age an average of one pit was dug every three years; an average of three were dug each year during Cadbury 7, rising dramatically to eight pits per year in Cadbury 8 and falling back to four pits per year in Cadbury 9. The early and late figures may be inflated, bearing in mind that, at least on the plateau, occupancy was restricted during the early phase. However, the figure for Cadbury 8 is probably understated, as borne out by the welter of pits at Danebury. The digging of in excess of 10 new pits each year would not be untoward and Paul Johnson's geophysical survey has revealed probable pits covering most of the interior. There are further caveats: most obvious is the balance between over- and underground storage but we should also note that the pits appeared to get larger over time, a trend confirmed at Sigwells, and many would have remained in use over several years. We can be confident that well over 2000 pits were dug during Cadbury 8.

Despite the growth in the number of pits there are discernible clusters, typically linked to roundhouses. In some cases, when a building moved or replaced an earlier building, pits were dug into the old floor surface. Some pits may have been dug inside existing houses although this is difficult to demonstrate. Analysis of the fills suggested that around 65 per cent were backfilled with a single deposit and that the majority of the others had contained three to five layers. It was noted that the earlier pits tended to have the least layers. In some pits, particularly the later ones on the west end of the plateau, there were probably ritual deposits with various mixtures of animal skulls, odd pieces of human bone, reconstructible pots and, rarely, metalwork, worked bone and querns. The percentage of single deposit pits is extremely high when compared with the data from Sigwells which is presented in a separate section below and forms the backbone of a discussion of Iron Age pits.

The area where N1 had stood in the Late Bronze Age (*39*) was increasingly cramped by an expanding area of successive hearths, marking a strong link to the traditions and spatial organisation of the past. During the Cadbury 7 phase, a greenish rubbish layer had built up over the early cobbles and the industrial features overlying them and was itself sealed by metalling associated with Cadbury 8 pottery, into which the bases of more stone and clay furnaces, or hearths, were cut.

There is no reason to think that many of the furnaces were in use at exactly the same time. There may have been the occasional episode where particular need warranted the use of more than one, but otherwise the sequence of one hearth cutting another, or the building of a new hearth a few metres away suggests that this was a general work area where this sort of activity took place when it was needed. Once a furnace had been used it was abandoned and collapsed to be gradually incorporated into and under an ever-growing expanse of detritus resulting from generations of similar activity. Although this midden spread was damaged by Mediaeval and modern ploughing, the average size of pottery sherds within it was larger than other surface deposits. There had been a minimum of contemporary trampling and other disturbance, suggesting a reduction in the intensity of activity on the plateau towards the later stages of Cadbury 8.

An assemblage of 10 La Tène I iron and one bronze chape fragments (apparently from as many different objects) is exceptional in Britain. Sword blade fragments are harder to typify but may well share a third-century BC date. The extremely rare swords and accessories of the period have come usually from riverine contexts in the east of England, typically in isolation and probably continuing the Bronze Age tradition of the deliberate discarding of weaponry in wet environments. Their discovery in surface deposits requires explanation. Pits were the most common places of deliberate deposition of iron tools generally, and Cadbury has its own hoard from behind the south rampart. It is hard to imagine that undoubtedly highly valued objects were left carelessly on a surface. Plough disturbance is equally unlikely to offer a satisfactory explanation, although it might be considered elsewhere on the plateau where surfaces were exposed to cultivation. A violent episode leading to a disorderly loss of weapons, such as might be represented by the destruction of the bank and early lodge in the south-west gate, fails on two counts: there is no evidence that the fire resulted from an assault and, with the apparently uninterrupted occupation of the hilltop, it seems improbable that weapons were simply left around. There is nothing to suggest that Cadbury was a centre of sword and scabbard making in the Middle Iron Age, although the discoveries were almost exclusively on Site N, the centre of the furnaces. An alternative explanation is that broken weaponry may have been buried in a midden, given the disproportionate lack of it in pits when compared with the range of more mundane objects. This would imply in turn that the particular space had been reserved for this purpose since at least the Late Bronze Age.

The production of textiles may have been far more frequent than metalworking but at Cadbury the surviving traces were tools rather than structural features such as the twinned postholes sometimes found just inside south-east facing entrances to roundhouses and thought to be fixed looms. The tools include needles, spindlewhorls, possible loomweights as well as decorated bone and red deer antler weaving combs typical of the period (*colour plate 18*); they appear to be fairly evenly, if thinly, distributed across the putative family plots. The same is true of tools associated with food production – querns, rubber stones and oven plates – although there is a marked concentration on the west of the plateau. More surprising is the apparent trend towards the ubiquity of metalworking. The long-standing industrial area to the east of the plateau appears to have remained a centre for casting but over time there appears to have been a marked growth in smelting in or around the buildings to the west.

This area probably came to be regarded as the traditional core of the settlement. It has already been suggested (above) that it was overlooked by a sequence of shrines which extended into the second half of the first century AD. Well before the end of this sequence, the south part of the space became a burial ground for mainly young cattle. Two carbon dates from separate whole animal burials centre on the mid to late second century BC (*91*). Although absolute dating for this period is unreliable (and leeway of 150 years either side should be allowed) the sheer number of burials and the newly emerging evidence that later graves were being dug through earlier ones, makes such a date acceptable. Its counterpart on Site D, in the lee of the south inner rampart, was a cluster of lamb burials (consistently around three months old) filling a single pit dug into the silts which had formed behind the Middle Iron Age bank.

Leslie Alcock's innovative wholesale application of geophysical survey was not always advantageous. The poor performance of the various techniques off the plateau encouraged him to investigate areas where he knew there were things to find: the plateau itself and the defences. Paul Johnson's surveys, with far superior equipment, in 1992 and 1993 showed no let up in activity on the lower enclosed areas of the hilltop. By then, thanks to the Danebury campaigns, this was no more than was to be expected. His interpretations strongly suggested that not only was there a far greater number of roundhouses off the plateau, but that there were traces of rectangular enclosures set back from the inner bank along the north to north-west side which are similar in scale and orientation to those outside the north-west side of the hillfort belonging to the Middle and Late Iron Age (*57, 82*). In both cases this organisation of the fields was influenced by topographical factors but it may also suggest that tenurial strips established within the hillfort followed a notional line across the ramparts and into the wider landscape. This might in turn have implications for which family, or other group, was responsible for the upkeep of the ramparts. It was not merely a matter of repairing the wall and de-silting the ditches; the lack of an ancient turf line on Bank 2 suggests that natural and stone-built surfaces remained exposed.

Pits in transition

The most clear-cut indicator of change in the structure of prehistoric human relationships with the wider landscape is the re-orientation, expansion and contraction of ditch systems; these will be dealt with in the next section. Apart from the practical purposes of agriculture, they offer crude indicators of population groups' attitudes: acquisitive, assertive, defensive. To gauge changes in their perception of themselves in the world we look at the organisation of personal space and, where that is elusive, at what they chose to discard or conceal and how. In the past, Iron Age pits acquired a notoriety as either for 'storage' or for 'rubbish', depending on the author, and they tended to be treated as a homogenous group. Over the last 30 years there has been a struggle to categorise them not just by their shape but in the manner and content of their filling. SCEP is making a very particular contribution to this debate, most notably through the work of my colleague, Clare Randall, although her detailed research may lead her to challenge the interpretations I present here.

We have seen that around Cadbury Castle there was a huge growth in the number of pits in the Middle Iron Age and that they may have grown in size. It

A central place

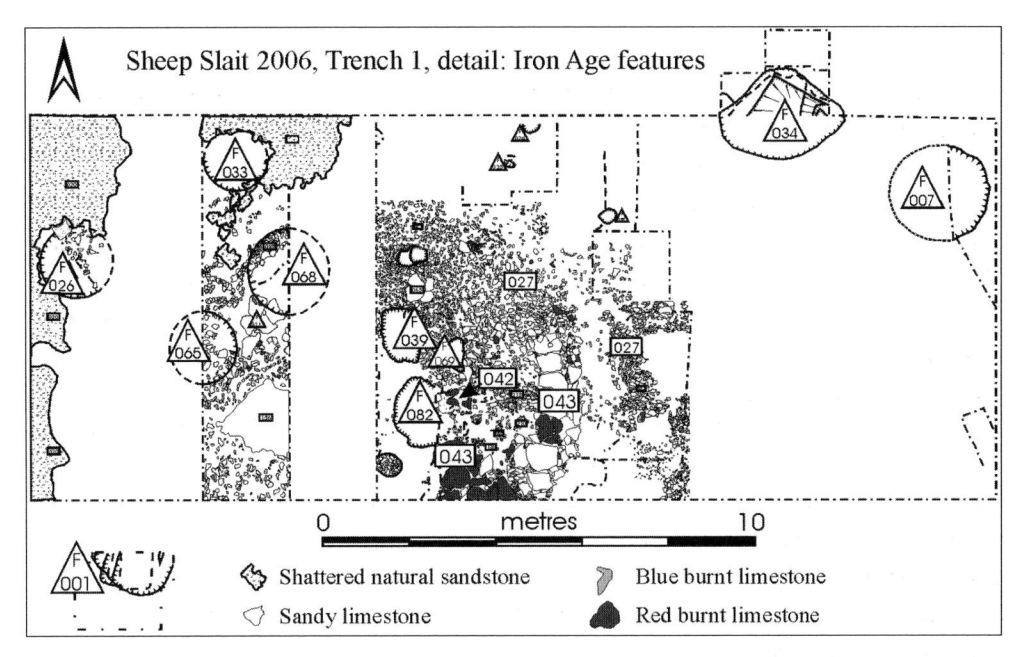

64 Sheep Slait: plan of the Iron Age features

has also been argued that the character of filling alters over time with evolution from rapid single episodes to highly complex combinations of rapid fills and deposits separated by slow silts over a long period. Pits from Sheep Slait provide examples of the range (*64*). The lower half of Pit F001 was filled with large, very fresh rubble with no soil in between, hence many voids. Clearly the rubble had been sealed with something which survived long enough for a soil to build over it without filling the large gaps. On the other hand, Pit F065 had at least partially silted up with erosion deposits before being re-cut and filled to the top of the pit with rubble, mixed with a little soil (*65*). Pit F034 started similarly. The picture was complicated by natural fissuring on the east side (*66*) but there remained a clear sequence of erosion deposit followed by re-cut, followed by rubble fill. It differed from F065 in being cut again and having a series of tips comprising charcoal and humus-enriched dark soils. Pit F007 contrasted strikingly with all the other pits in its depth (1.9m; the others were all between 0.8 and 1.20) and in its filling with lenses and deeper deposits of humic, charcoal-enriched soils. Whilst the other pits produced few, generally very fragmentary, finds, those from the upper fills of F007 included lumps of slag-like vitrified material, a bronze ring and a near complete pot from the middle fills. In this it has aspects in common with the later Sigwells pits (below).

The geophysical survey suggested that the pits were exclusive to the area enclosed by the Late Bronze Age ringwork, which by this time was reduced to a shallow

Cadbury Castle: The Hillfort and Landscapes

65 Sheep Slait: rubble Iron Age pit fill (F065)

66 Sheep Slait: mixed Iron Age pit fill (F034)

channel and a low internal bank. The earliest pits were probably those sealed by a cobbled floor which became the foundation for a floor of large slabs of sandy lime stone (context 043 in *64*), reinforced by several courses where it overlay a gully on

A central place

67 Sheep Slait: slab footings of the Iron Age structure

the east side (*69*). It is unclear which floor a central hearth cutting into the upper fill of F082 belongs to. It was made up of a bed of thin flat stones underlying 15 x 20cm of baked clay, shuttered by upright flat stones (*colour plate 19*). Several large lumps of vitrified material were found on a rubbly arc (027) around the floor, the degraded remains of the wall and an external bank. The intensity of burning on the floor slabs in the south-east of the structure might imply that there had been an internal fire fanned by the air at the entrance. There was no unambiguous evidence for a superstructure but one seems highly likely. The floors were later than all the pits which overlapped them. Only two pits, F007 and the final cut and fill of F034, were likely to be contemporary with their use.

The pits probably all fall within the currency of Cadbury 7 and 8 and possibly early 9. Those with sterile fills were probably from the early part of the sequence simply on the grounds that their soils were paler and that activity had been at a low enough level for few finds to be trapped in them. It is also worth noting that there was little residual material from the Late Bronze Age in their fills. Either the central area had been kept very clean during the ringwork's life or, more probably, it had been sealed by a turf, indicating a clean break between two phases of intensive use.

There was little sign of domesticity. Bone was very sparse from all Iron Age contexts and there were none of the tools for household industry such as weaving; a few quern fragments were present but these stones may have functioned as anvils. The test pits show it as a hot spot of Middle Iron Age activity (*56*) but it is extremely

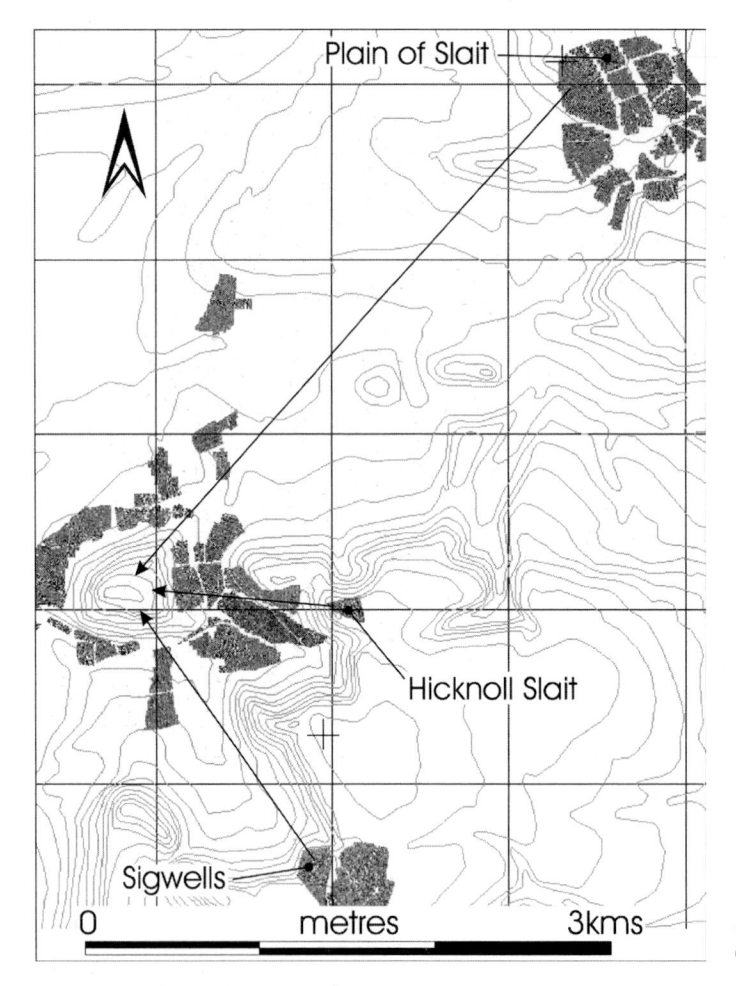

68 Pit groups overlooking Cadbury Castle

localised and there are no signs of associated field systems. The re-use of a ringwork, long divorced by time from a Late Bronze Age system of which it was the hub, surely indicates that folk memory determined the location of what appears to have been industrial activity. In this respect it has a superficial resemblance to the Sigwells metalworking enclosure; indeed, a similar interpretation might be offered for the original ringwork. However, a metallurgical researcher has observed that although the vitreous material derived from extreme heat, there is no evidence that it is metal slag.

The pits at Sheep Slait surely existed specifically in support of a relatively narrow range of activities there. They may have provided a short-term storage facility and some may have functioned as quarries for the floors. With the possible exception of F007, probably the latest of the excavated pits, there is little sign of ritual filling. Like the pits at Danebury and Cadbury, they were situated as a matter of

A central place

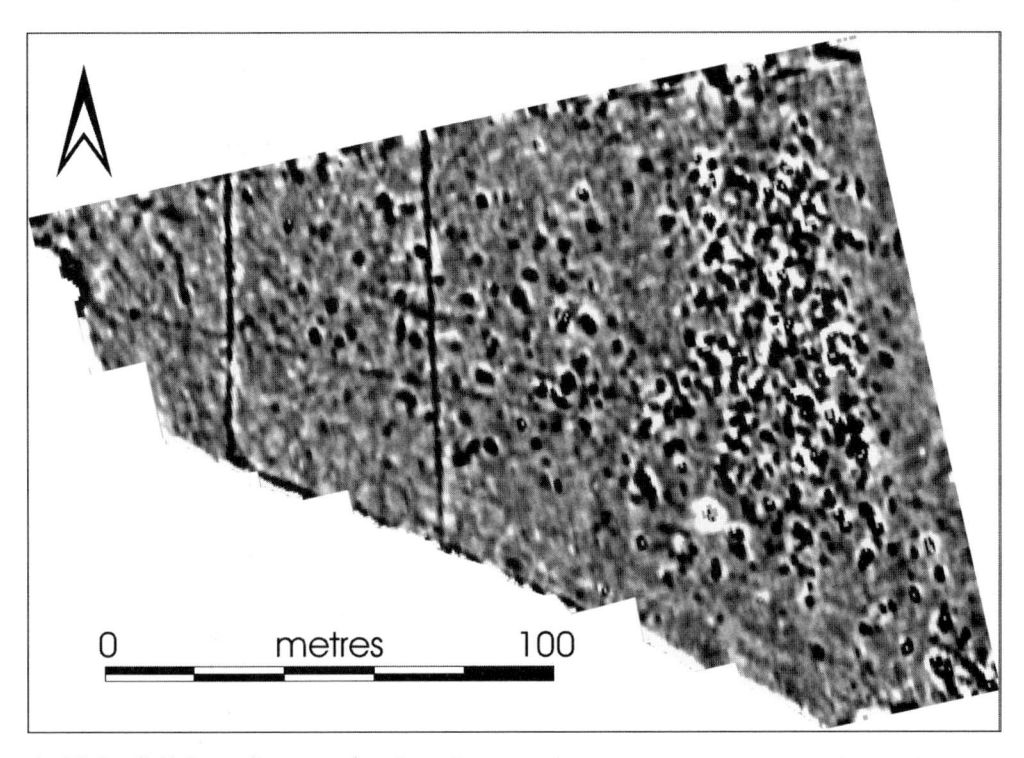

69 Hicknoll Slait: gradiometry showing pit group

convenience and most do not exist as an end in themselves. This is important when we consider other pit groups in Cadbury's hinterland.

After completing his excavations at Maiden Castle in the mid 1980s, Niall Sharples speculated about the implications for storage capacity represented by the abundance of pits, many of them very large. He believed that their overall capacity during the Middle Iron Age represented a surplus to the requirements of the hill dwellers. He postulated that it was storage for a wider community beyond the ramparts and as such gave the hierarchy leverage over the productive members of a tribal group, despite the lack of evidence for contemporary extra-mural settlement. The evidence from around Cadbury is at odds with this picture, where a massive pit group has been confirmed at Sigwells (the number may exceed that on Cadbury) and two further highly probable pit groups have been identified by geophysical survey at Hicknoll Slait, Compton Pauncefoot, and Plain of Slait, Woolston (*68*).

The grouping of pits at Hicknoll Slait (*69*) and Sigwells is very dense but less so at Plain of Slait (*70*). All three have similar topography. They were set back from a ridge or spur, effectively cutting it off from a larger plateau. The Sigwells group (*71*) was strung out over 200m along the north side of an old track or boundary, varying in width from 8 to 22m, while the other two were set on saddles. The

Cadbury Castle: The Hillfort and Landscapes

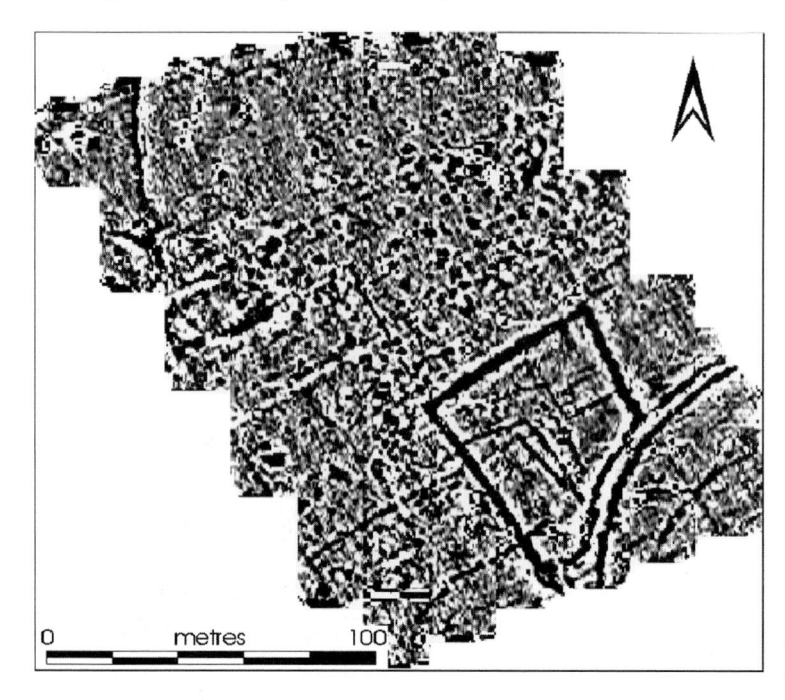

70 Plain of Slait: gradiometry showing pit group

spurs of all three offer clear views of the hillfort, seemingly a determining factor in their locations. There were traces of linear features parallel with the group on Hicknoll Slait, as well as circular structures at the head of the steep scarp which limits its northern distribution. The pits extended for approximately 104m from north to south with a maximum east to west breadth of 50m, but typically 30m. There is a significant thin scatter of pits to the west. At Plain of Slait the pits were to the north and west of a substantial multiphase rectangular enclosure, the fourth and final re-cut of which was filled during the early Roman occupation. Their maximum extent from north to south was 180m and from east to west 140m. The pits spread into the adjoining Card's Piece in an area scored by Bronze Age linear boundaries.

Pits at Sigwells were excavated from 2003 to 2005 in Trenches 12 to 14 (*71* & *72*), originally targeting an enclosure which appeared to butt onto a linear track or boundary extending south-west from the field's north barrow. The enclosure lay in a particularly exposed position, tilting towards the north-west and at the head of a steep scarp. It was no place to pass a winter. On the east side of the enclosure surviving stratigraphy included an abandonment horizon sealing all features, but to the west the ploughsoil lay directly on the natural rock. Enough remained to ascertain a robust sequence. The lower third of the ditches of the first square enclosure filled fairly slowly with silts which contained Cadbury 7 and 8 pottery, probably in the late third century BC. Its south ditch followed the line of a shallow

A central place

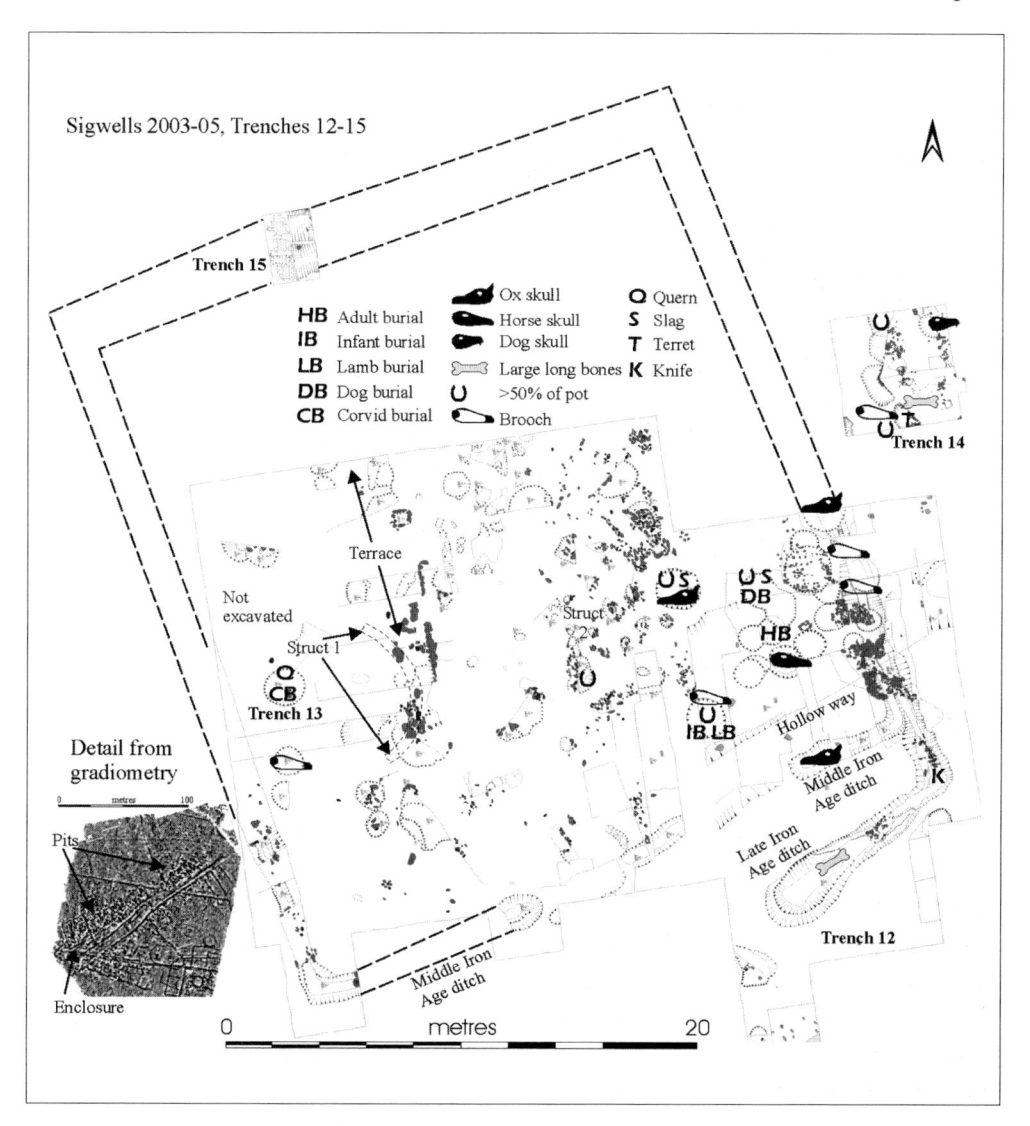

71 Sigwells Trenches 12-15: Iron Age enclosure and pits

gully which may have been the last vestige of a much earlier ditch extending from the north barrow, but was more probably a marker for laying out the enclosure. The enclosure ditch was parallel to a 3m-wide shallow holloway which had been filled entirely with fine sandy silt by the time the enclosure's east ditch cut through it. There was a single south-south-east facing entrance with a surprising width of 12m from the west to east terminal.

A 3.5-4m wide terrace or flat-bottomed ditch cut 0.6m into natural, towards the west side, may be contemporary with or slightly later than the first enclosure

Cadbury Castle: The Hillfort and Landscapes

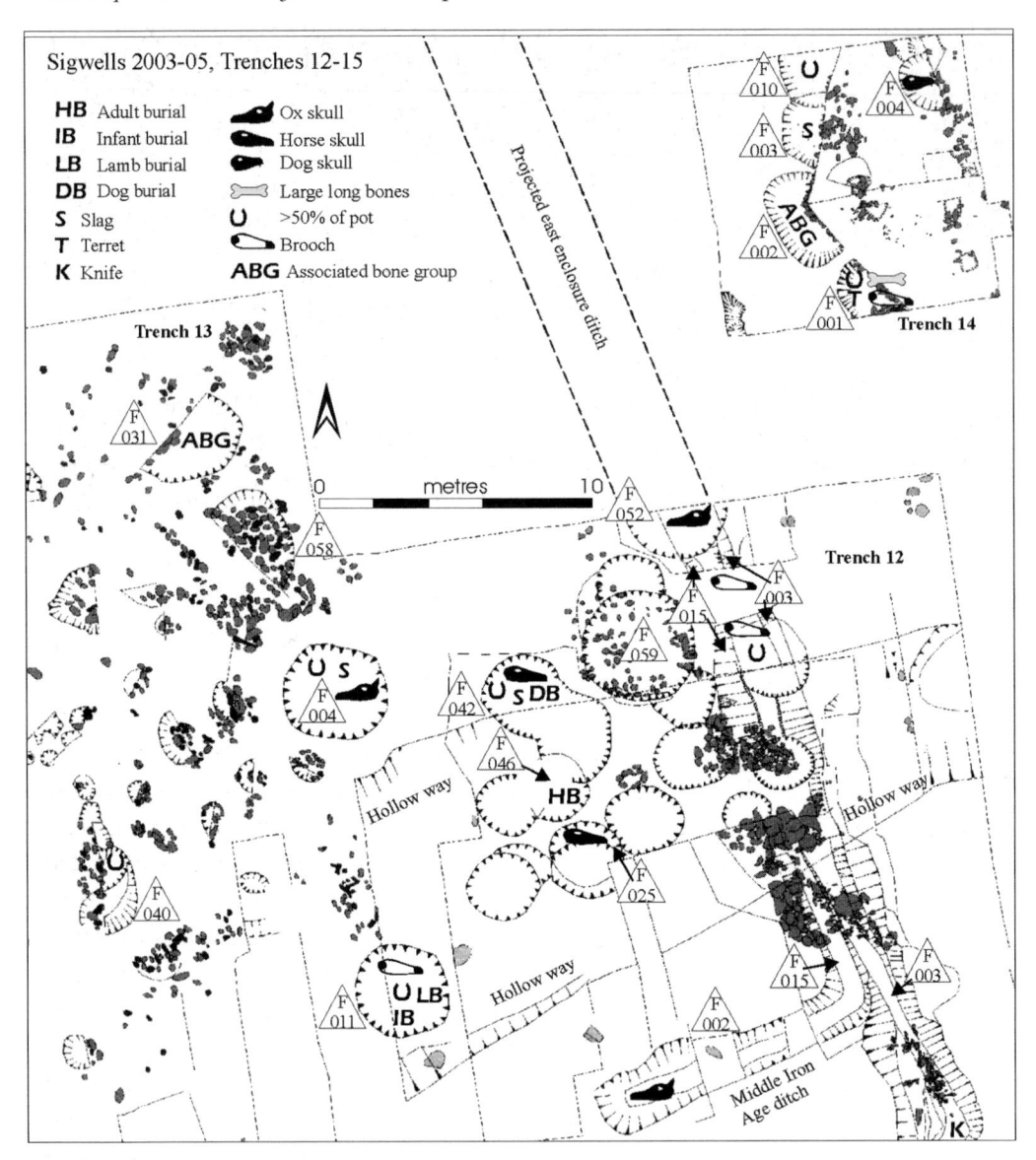

72 Sigwells Trenches 12-14: features in the enclosure's south-west corner

judging by the deposits sealing the humic soils filling it (73). The first soils may have accumulated fairly rapidly until, at a depth of around 0.5m, a straight wall was laid along the ragged line of the original cut. Up to three courses survived, matching the level of the natural where it had been ploughed. It was little more than a facade and could not have stood much higher, although it revetted an infill behind it. Slanting gravelly fills towards the west of the terrace offered a modicum of stability to a stone-footed building (Structure 1 in 71), only a quarter of which

A central place

73 Sigwells Trench 13: terrace section

has survived the plough. A single rapidly rubble-filled pit in the north of the trench cut through the terrace deposits and its natural floor.

The densest grouping of pits within the enclosed area was in the south-east, although Trench 14 demonstrated that comparable density existed outside the enclosure (*72*). A small pit, F040, was dug at approximately the same time as the first enclosure ditches, probably for the specific purpose of depositing the greater part of a large storage jar, a large piece of burnt ammonite and a bag of cremated sheep bone and charcoal (in figure *74* the very well formed mass of charred material behind the small scale indicates that it must have been contained in something organic, probably a leather bag, which subsequently decomposed; the ammonite fragment is on end, between the jar and the section). There may well have been other organic objects deposited but no visible trace remained. The pit sides were of a soft sand very distinct from the fill. As the sand erodes rapidly and no basal silt formed, the pit seems to have been filled fairly quickly with a reddish but organically enriched soil. There must have been nearby occupation or at least a midden.

The pit was stratigraphically lower than, and west of, the nearest of two parallel 4m-long trails of gravelly stones, many burnt red or blue, set 3m apart. Denser groups of slightly larger stones marked post settings for a rectangular structure which was refurbished and rebuilt (*72*). All the posts had been removed and their sockets capped with mainly burnt stone in a roughly 5m^2 area between pits F040 and the later F004. The fragile trails of stone were probably from the latter stages of the sequence and some of the postholes, particular the smaller ones, may be closer in time to the pit. The trails were oriented from north-north-west to south-

74 Sigwells Trench 13: Pot, charred material and amonite in pit (F040)

south-east and post settings at the south end were perpendicular to them and parallel to the backfilled holloway.

None of the other pits investigated were demonstrably contemporary with the ditch, although some of those with few finds and cut by later pits may have been. All of the pits on the route of the holloway cut through its silts and there was nothing to indicate that their positions were determined by it. Three pits were found to cut the earliest enclosure ditch, F015, but all of them and a fourth were cut by its two later phases, F003. Of these pits F052 included a cattle skull; no structured deposits survived in the others although substantial portions of all their fills had been removed by the re-cutting of the ditch, F003. Another five pits were butted by silts under a rough dry stone wall, built along the inside edge of the enclosure after the ditch had filled but was still settling. Only F059 contained finds of note in the shape of three small pieces of iron sealed below a rubble tip and an articulated neonatal dog. Below the iron were natural sand-derived erosion deposits whilst above the covering stones some humic soils showed tip lines. These were sealed first by slow-forming silts and then by a layer of very rounded stones which had the appearance of a well-used cobbled surface (75). Unprepossessing as this sounds, we should bear in mind that iron was rare in any form in the excavated areas. Figure 75 shows the pit on the left, with the lower rubble fill separated by soils from the upper cobbles. One of two pits cut by F059 is in the middle foreground and to the right are ditches F015 and F003, and Pit F055 respectively.

A central place

75 Sigwells Trench 12: Middle rubble and upper cobble layers (F059)

The loose use of terms such as 'deliberate', 'special' or 'ritual' to describe pit deposits tends to raise hackles. All imply forethought, although 'deliberate' need mean no more than that an agent made a decision whilst aware of what he or she was doing. 'Special' implies that care was taken and that the action was meaningful to the agent at least. 'Ritual' signifies the re-enactment of a particular pattern of behaviour which may vary from one occasion to the next, but which has enough common elements to be meaningful to the wider community, as well as to the agent. Still loaded, but a useful compromise, is the 'structured' deposit, where researchers can quantify the frequency of the association of objects and fill types. The group of pits excavated thus far at Sigwells is too small to provide a statistically viable sample, but there are nascent patterns suggesting structured deposition. If we take as an example the two pits which include bronze brooches (Trench 14, F001, Trench 12, F011) both are associated with near complete pots as well as significant bone deposits (infant and lamb burials in F011; a decorated bone in F001). Note also that only around 30 per cent of F001 has been excavated. In both cases the brooches came from the upper fills.

Where complete or near-complete vessels were associated with the burial of a complete human or animal body, or skull, they occur over it. F011 was filled to around a third of its depth with a variety soils and natural local sand before a lamb was laid above stones on the west side and a neonatal infant was placed south of the centre set in a gravelly humic soil. Large angular stones were set over the body and two vessels were placed over or broken over them (*76*). The pit continued to fill gradually before a very old brooch was placed in what would have been no more than a residual depression. Some of the same 'rules' are obeyed for Trench 12, F004. A large lump of slag was placed in the middle of the base of the 1.8m-deep pit and then covered with slanting slabs of angular stone. A weathering phase was followed by more deliberate filling until only a shallow depression remained. A re-cut was made into the depression and slag was again placed at the centre of the base. This

Cadbury Castle: The Hillfort and Landscapes

76 Sigwells Trench 12: stones and vessels concealing an infant (F011)

was covered with a gravelly humic soil which was the bed for a cow skull, made startlingly distinctive by the insertion of yellow sandstones into the eye sockets (*colour plate 20*). The skull was then covered with large stones and gravel. Immediately afterwards at least two whole vessels were smashed over the stones and lumps of slag were spread over the pieces. Although some of the stones were rounded, they must have been exposed elsewhere as the pots showed no signs of weathering.

Dogs appear to have been accorded a rite peculiar to themselves. Only one complete burial of an adult male (Trench 12, F042) was excavated (*77*) but a complete skull occurring at the cut line in a half-sectioned pit (Trench 14, F004) may have been a second. The attribute they have in common, and which occurred in none of the other pits, was a large central posthole dug through the base of the pit. In both cases the dog remains were east of the post. F042 cut away the whole of an earlier pit and cut the edge of another. The posthole was dug first (leaving a void when the post eventually rotted) and the post was inserted and stabilised while a shallow soil was spread over the pit base. The soil included a group of cattle bones which were covered with large stones (visible in the upper centre of figure *77*), some burnt. Built like an Irish Wolfhound, the dog was placed with its head under the body, turned sharply back towards the tail, fully articulated. The character of the moderately humic gravelly soil placed over the dog is not distinctive enough in itself to say whether it was a slow or rapid fill, but it must have been thrown in rapidly to support the post. There was then a hiatus during which the fill subsided and after which large stones, a horse skull, lumps of slag and a complete pot were placed in the depression (*78*). Unfortunately, recent ploughing had disturbed this final deposit.

A central place

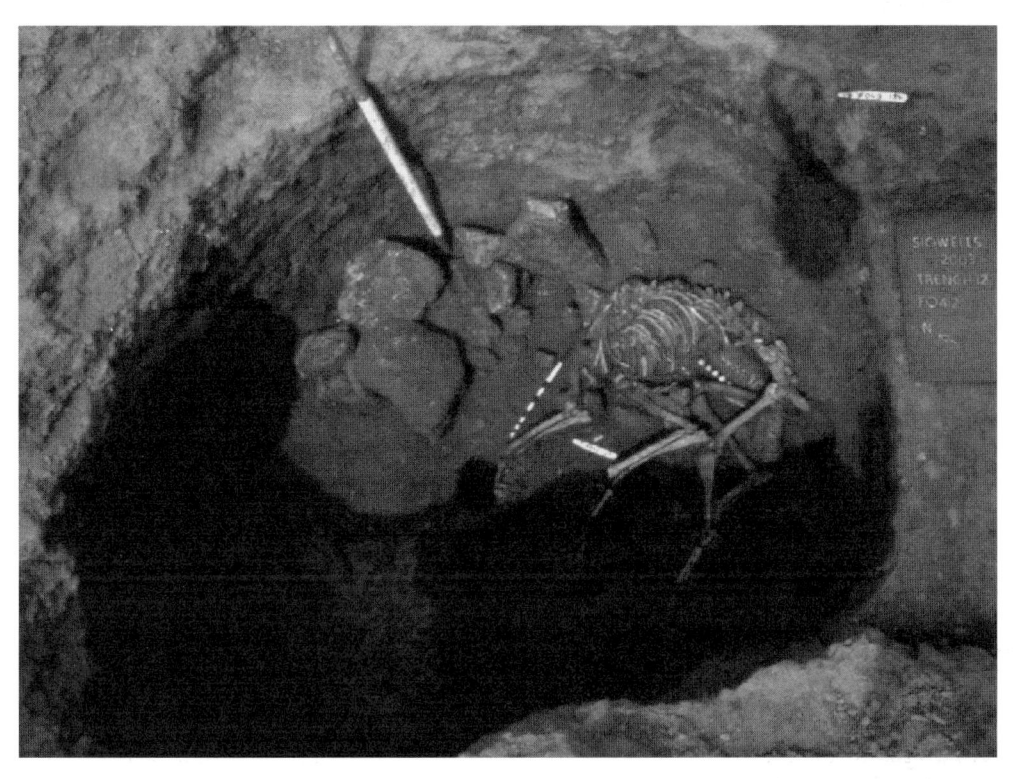

77 Sigwells Trench 12: dog burial (F042)

78 Sigwells Trench 12: upper fill of dog burial (F042)

Sigwells is not alone in having dogs buried with marking posts. Two were found in one pit at Danebury, sealed below a massive timber which may have stood more than 3m above the ground, tempting Barry Cunliffe to suggest it played the part of a totem pole. They were broadly contemporary with the first enclosure phase so were no later than Early Iron Age, centuries earlier than the Sigwells examples. After partially excavating four other similar pits, and suggesting that others were likely to be concealed beneath the Iron Age outer bank, he noted that they would have presented a henge-like spatial boundary. It is interesting to note that both dogs and large posts have in common a tendency to mark territory, as millions of telegraph poles can testify. Would such an association be the reason for linking dogs to posts in death?

A horse skull buried in Pit F025 was laid directly on natural rock and the fill of an earlier pit, the fills of which had not fully settled as they subsided further after deposition. The skull was fairly battered by a pile of large stones placed on top of it. Two opposing mandibles were placed, one on top of the other, on the stones, presumably the lower jaw detached from the skull (*colour plate 21*). A piece of red baked clay had been pushed into the cranial cavity but most remarkable was another lump protruding from below the front teeth (*colour plate 22*), appearing tongue-like. In this case, and in that of the F004 cattle skull, foreign materials were used as surrogates for parts of the body which been removed or had decayed.

The least complex, visibly structured, deposit was the tightly flexed burial of a man (F046) in his mid forties (*79*). A few small pot sherds were plainly residual and the only notable find was a small piece of non-diagnostic iron. The pit appears to have been backfilled immediately. Randall has noted a widespread tradition of sporadic articulated individual burials in pits across southern Britain, starting in the Early Iron Age, and existing in parallel with excarnation. The nearest known examples are from Dibble's Farm, Christon, Somerset and Gussage All Saints, Dorset. One other class of skeletal material deserving mention is the associated bone group, referring to an articulated or otherwise linked group. Pit F031 in Trench 13 included two groups of three sheep ribs, which, although separated from the spinal column, had been held together by flesh on deposition, and an articulated sheep skull and vertebrae. They were in a very charcoal-rich humic soil which had plainly included a great deal of organic material at the time of deposition. A similar soil in the neighbouring Pit F058 produced articulated pig vertebrae. In contrast, an articulated cow hind leg and pelvis were set in a rapid rubble fill, much of it burnt, with charcoal-rich humic soil between the stones. A period of exposure had allowed a dog to chew off its foot and it is possible that after being left open deliberately the deposit was covered by the rubble to protect it from further damage. This group of pits with structured deposits to the east of Structure 2 was quite distinct from those to its west. The only comparable

A central place

79 Sigwells Trench 12: Late Iron Age flexed burial (F046)

deposit is in Trench 13, F014, where a complete raven was buried on the pit base beneath a pile of large stones, accompanied by a large quern fragment. The central position of the bird and the very focused manner in which the stones pin it, is very striking (*80*). At Danebury, Cynthia Poole considered groups of stones on pit bases to be structured deposits in their own right. A fibula found in the upper fills of a pit 2m south of F014 undermines the brooch distribution pattern but it was the only specimen made of iron and so may have had special significance.

It is interesting to note similarities between the relative position of Structure 2 and the Cadbury shrines with respect to the burials of complete skeletons and, in the case of Sigwells, skulls. The same case might be made for the distribution of metalwork and metalworking debris (slag), although the limited number of artefacts render the association less reliable. Cunliffe noted the disproportionate number of ravens recovered at Danebury and their special place in Celtic mythology. Their carrion diet links them to the dead, rendering them disturbing figures to be treated at some remove from productive animals such as cows and sheep and those which had special roles, such as horses and dogs. The cosmological significance of the east with respect to the rising sun, birth and life, and the west to sunset and death should not be forgotten.

80 Sigwells Trench 13: corvid burial (F014)

These descriptions of structured deposits apply to pits dug and filled in the first centuries BC and AD, with the important exception of F040, which probably belongs to the late third or mid second century BC. F040 was not fully excavated but was a deep dish-shaped scoop, whereas all those between it and the line of the enclosure ditch were broadly cylindrical, some distorted by re-cutting, others precisely enough to have been marked out in advance. None of the pits in Trench 14 were fully excavated but F002 appears to have been more lozenge-shaped in plan. There would have been no technical difficulty in marking out a regular circle. A stick would be driven into the ground and a rope looped loosely around it. A pointed stick would be tied tightly to the other end and a person would then scratch an outline while maintaining tension on the rope. This method also offered a means for establishing a uniform scale of pit dimensions. Some of the earlier pits show such regularity of scale but this was much less evident in the later, generally larger pits.

The conventional view remains that the primary use for most Iron Age pits, particularly those with regular forms, was storage of grain and that once they soured they were backfilled, often with rubbish. There is no reason to disagree with the first part of this idea, although the volume of material being stored by the later Middle

A central place

Iron Age would have been very considerable. Analysis of charred remains from the Sigwells pits by Kate Blenman identified barley, oats, emmer wheat and, perhaps most surprisingly, bread wheat, as well as chaff indicating the likelihood of nearby processing. The samples also included weeds associated with arable agriculture. There is little doubt that all of these materials were introduced to the pits after their first phase of use, so they cannot be taken as confirmation of their primary function. In a few cases, notably Trench 12 F004, it is clear that the upper fills of a pit were specially re-cut to incorporate a structured deposit. In that particular case it is interesting to note the choice of slag as a foundation deposit for the original rubble fill and for the re-cut. Further examples of such repetition would imply remembrance.

Although all the pits were eventually fully backfilled, in most cases the bulk of the infill was not what had come out; that was moved, possibly used, elsewhere. The geology on this part of the plateau comprised interfacing strata of sand under sandstone beneath fissured bedded limestone which was laminate and sharply angular when first cut. Some of the latter may have contributed to the revetting on the terrace, although that too would have generated sandstone and rock. The generally more rounded rocks forming the late enclosure wall may originally have derived from the pits but must have been used or stored elsewhere first. In a few cases unweathered angular rocks have gone back into a pit (the lower fill of Trench 12 F004; the entire fill of the pit cutting the terrace fills) but usually the stone showed moderate weathering. The stones were usually weathered all around; it is doubtful that this occurred only when they were an exposed surface in the pit. They were more likely to have been piled close to the open pit.

81 Sigwells Trench 12: Burying an infant. Amanda Tabor

A few pits at Danebury were used for homogenising daub but neither Cadbury nor Sigwells have produced such evidence, probably for the simple reason that the sample of pits is much smaller. One pit at Sigwells (Trench 14 F003), with an ash then a daub layer covering the base, was penetrated by an arc of stakeholes and there was some reddening of the pit sides by fire. As there were no other pits with a similar basal deposit, it may have had an industrial use, a view supported by the recovery of a substantial amount of fine iron slag during the flotation of soil samples. Large amounts of daub in a pit 25m south of the enclosure might also have an industrial origin but could equally be the remains of a wattle and daub pit lid. The varied yet patterned treatment of pits seems to embody and integrate the mundane needs of the community with the profoundest beliefs of its members. They concealed and reveal hope, anxiety and moments of great pathos (*81*).

Ditches in transition

The humble ditch has been at the core of SCEP since its inception because it is the target feature best explored by extensive geophysical survey. The original rationale was that discrete phaseable systems would emerge which would also provide insight into land use. Test pitting and excavation have shown that, on the whole, recognition of discrete systems has been successful, allowing for modification, contraction and expansion, but sequencing, and particularly dating, have sometimes been wayward! There have also been unexpected gains in evidence for structured deposits, linked not only to individual enclosures but to extensive field systems.

By the earlier Middle Iron Age (Cadbury 7) small, paddock-like, enclosures marked the lower valley sides and bottom between Cadbury Castle and the ridge to its east (*82*). Over the following centuries infilling with small enclosures and expansion across the stream at its south end brought about a ten degree shift in the general orientation of the scheme. Parts of the Bronze Age system west of the hillfort (*26, 27*) may have remained in use at first, but during the Middle Iron Age it was replaced in its entirety by fields branching at 90 degrees from a track extending from west to north of the hill. By the first century BC/AD there had been a similar shift of orientation in this system, possibly provoked by the hillfort's expansion to include the spur and knoll at Milsoms Corner. Two circular features were probably roundhouses which, along with another partially excavated in Homeground, are a sign of movement into the productive landscape as local control over production became a priority over the security or status associated with a house on the hill. It is tempting to suggest that the same groups or families who may have controlled strip plots which extended from within the hillfort (see above) were those who moved to dwellings in the corresponding plots below.

A central place

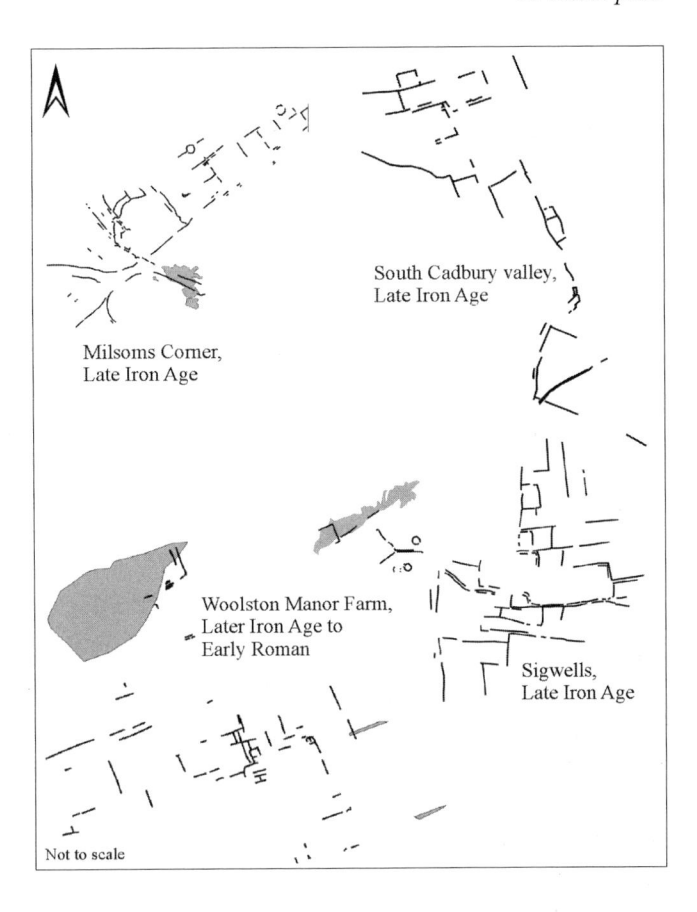

82 Ditches: re-ordering the landscape

By the second century BC, the trackway which forked and snaked from east to north-west at Sigwells had become the arterial route for smaller tracks serving arable plots to its north and more open grazing land to the south, growing out of a Bronze Age system first manifested by the metalworking enclosure. On the other hand at Woolston, where a rigorously north-south Middle Bronze alignment had given way to a Late Bronze Age system oriented with a narrow valley leading to an enclosed hilltop, a completely new pattern was established similar to that north-west of Cadbury. This went on to form the basis of the Early Romano-British scheme there.

In a few places further west, the general orientation of land division remained unchanged from the Middle Bronze Age. At Weston Bampfylde a long linear ditch and track survived on the gravelly west end of the ridge with only minor modification until it became the axis for Romano-British boundaries and there were few signs of subdivision by smaller enclosures. The surrounding heavy soils would have supported grazing and some woodland and left little room for arable expansion or population growth.

143

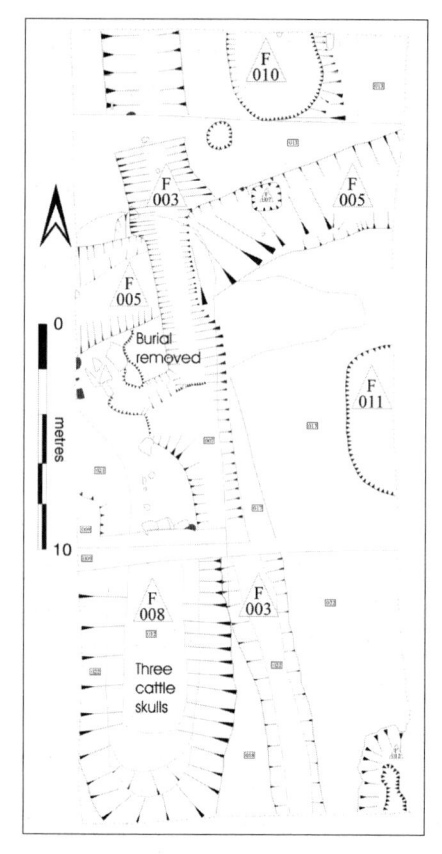

83 The Moor Trench 3: final plan, cattle skull and human burial

The character of deposits in ditches changed sharply from the Middle to the Later Iron Age. The jar inserted into the upper fills of the Milsoms Corner enclosure at the time of the shield's deposition may be an early instance of the burial of complete vessels during the closure of ditches or it may have had a more practical role during the ceremonies. SCEP's fieldwork has not identified any other instances before the later Middle Iron Age. In crude chronological terms the tradition may have been interrupted during the fourth to third century BC by the practice of placing upturned cattle skulls in ditch terminals. The example from the Middle Iron Age enclosure at Sigwells was deposited when the lower third of the south entrance's east terminal had silted up, a phase associated with Cadbury 7 pottery. The skull was sealed by large stones and a moderately humic soil followed a slow erosion silt and two more interspersed fills of rocks and silts. It was still a shallow channel when the east ditch (*72*; Trench 12, F015) was re-cut and extended during the first century AD. Of three cattle skulls in The Moor Trench 3, South Cadbury, one was close to the base of a ditch terminal under a rapid subangular limestone rubble fill, some of which was burnt, and the others were in the rubble (*83, colour plate 23*). There

A central place

were no signs of butchery but they had been exposed to the elements before and possibly after deposition. The ditch was a shallow re-cut extension of a deeper ditch. The rubble included quern fragments which might seem incidental if it were not for pieces of iron and bronze, a cattle jaw and a human femur. This one context (with a soil volume of approximately 1 cubic metre) produced 25 per cent of all the bone fragments from the trench (volume approximately 25 cubic metres).

The instances of deliberate pot deposition were far more frequent and had a later currency. Five were from long ditches and six from enclosure ditches scattered over most of the sampled areas. The earliest was a decorated later Middle Iron Age shell-tempered bowl at Worthy, Weston Bampfylde, rapidly covered by an upper middle fill of gravelly soil in the re-cut of an earlier Iron Age long linear boundary. The remainder all included a range of quartz-tempered bead rim jars or bowls, often labelled 'Durotrigan' after the tribe, although none of the so-called 'War Cemetery' style, so named after vessels found with burials at Maiden Castle. Only one other deposit had Middle Iron Age credentials, forming part of a remarkable upper middle fill comprising several shell-tempered vessels, amongst which a large jar had contained a cattle jaw before it collapsed as soil was piled on top of it. The whole deposit lay below the modern water table and included a large, fire-reddened, soft clay mass with a few charcoal sticks set in it, possibly from a wall or hearth (*colour plate 24*).

On Sigwells, single pot deposits were found in the uppermost fills of the south-west corner and east ditches of the latest phase of the Iron Age enclosure (*71*), in the middle fill of a long linear sectioned in the south of Trench 12 (not shown) and in a burnt stone scatter along the base of an internal dividing ditch of a first-century AD enclosure (see below). A vessel in Lady Field 3, Woolston, was in the rapid lower middle fills of an enclosure ditch butted with the east side of a track ditch. Vessels occurred in each of the terminals of a gully and a roughly parallel ditch forming the rear access to an enclosure in Homeground, fronting onto the Iron Age route from South Cadbury to Milsoms Corner. On the spur of the latter, a complete bowl had weathered and broken up in situ after either being left slightly exposed or being partially uncovered by water running over the middle fills of the sloping ditch. A jar was found in the east boundary ditch of the track heading south from the Crissells Green to East Field crossing of Henshall Brook, South Cadbury.

Two of the vessels were in deliberate association with human material, in both instances overlying it. The pot from the Sigwells Iron Age enclosure lay on a dump of small rubbly stones, many burnt, which partly sealed the skull of a young child. The example at Milsoms Corner was laid over a young man's pelvis, a matter of particular significance for discussion in Chapter 5. For the moment it is enough to note that the tradition of depositing bowls when infilling ditches had certainly originated by the later Middle Iron Age and that it persisted into the middle, or later, first century AD. With the exception of the Milsoms Corner

Cadbury Castle: The Hillfort and Landscapes

84 The Moor Trench 3: Late Iron Age human cyst burial 1

85 The Moor Trench 3: Late Iron Age human cyst burial 2

A central place

vessel, they were placed in the ditch immediately before an episode of partial or complete infilling. If it were not for the example from Worthy, it would be tempting to suggest that the practice had been imported with the vessels from South Dorset.

No deliberate deposits were associated with a grave cut into the backfilled conjunction where ditch F003 had cut F008 in The Moor Trench 3. A makeshift 1 x 0.6m stone cyst was built in the grave before a tall man in his fifties was concertina'd into it (*83, 84, 85*). His lower legs and one lower arm had been removed before his torso was folded at the pelvis onto the upper legs. The head was then folded back between the shoulder blades. The bone was in good condition and what remained was fully articulated but the body must have been in a fairly advanced state of decomposition to have been so flexible. Susan Jones's analysis suggested that his life had been even more eventful. Cuts into his skull show that he had survived for years after two sword slashes. He had been less fortunate with an unhealed third, acquired at around the time of his death. Most remarkably he had lived with a broken atlas (uppermost neck bone) which had never knitted back together. The whole of his spine had been slightly compressed, probably as a result of a jump or fall in which he had landed on his heels with great momentum. Clearly a warrior, it is tempting to imagine a leap from a chariot or horse in full flight going horribly wrong. His survival is truly remarkable and may in part explain his special treatment in death. The smattering of pottery suggested that this exceptionally unusual burial dated to the later first century AD.

LATE IRON AGE (*86*)

The pits and ditches have already taken the story at least as far as the Roman invasion of AD 43, possibly as far as AD 70, and it may seem artificial to identify a Late Iron Age which will go on to merge with what is treated conventionally as the Early Roman period. In parts of southern Britain there was a very real blurring of the line between indigenous communities adopting an increasingly continental material culture in the first century BC and what became the Roman occupation. Earlier, in the decades before and after 100 BC, Hengistbury Head, Dorset, was a major point of entry for goods from Europe but the balance moved emphatically after the Julian invasions of 55 and 54 BC. In the late first century BC, continental trade links with the south-east became stronger, where coins assumed the role of currency rather than gifts. The hundreds of mainly Durotrigan coins found in south Dorset suggest that they may have had the same role there, but the few Durotrigan and Dobunnic coins from Cadbury would suggest that a money-based economy would not have been sustainable in this area (*87*).

147

Cadbury Castle: The Hillfort and Landscapes

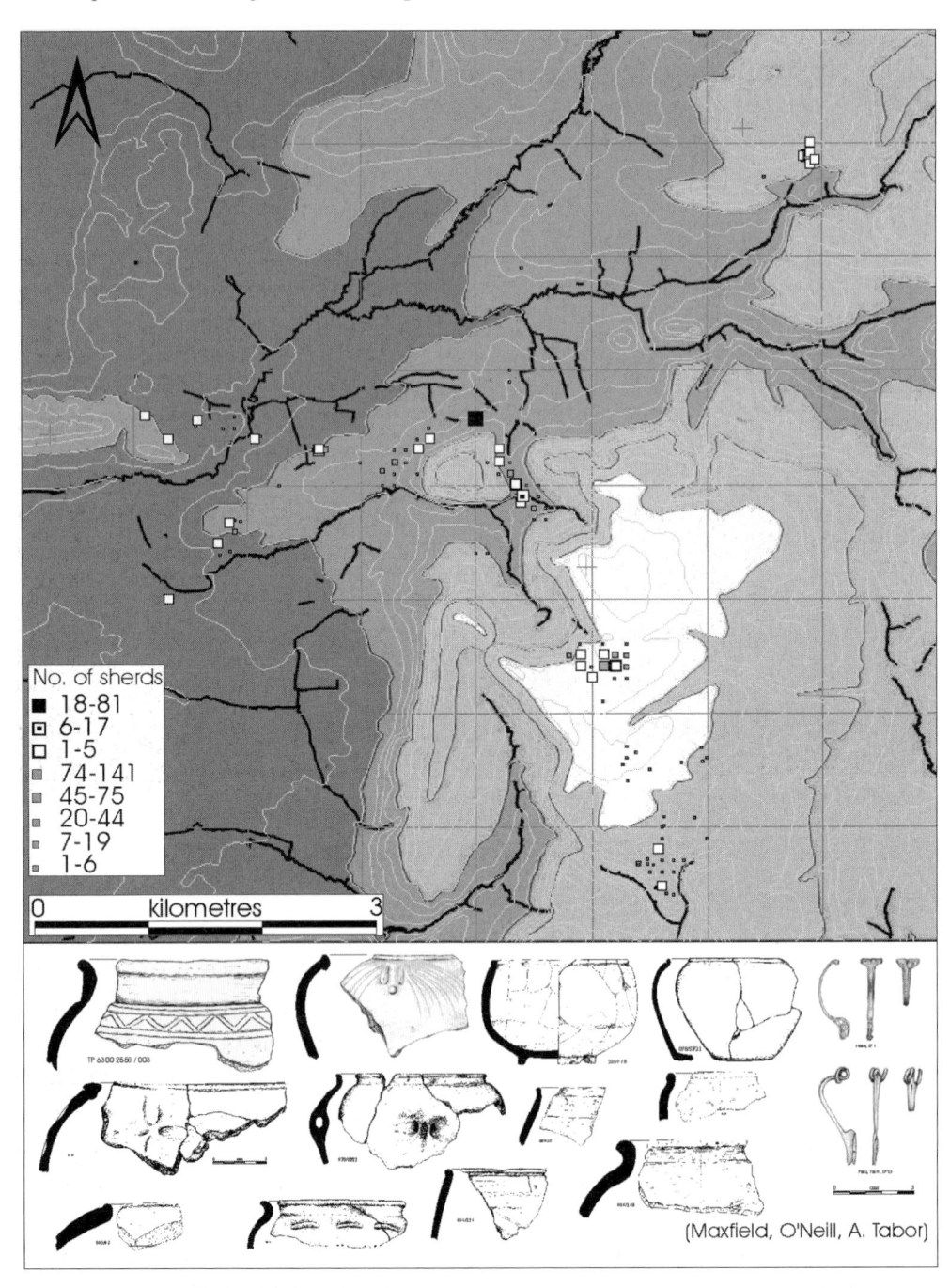

86 Late Iron Age finds and their distribution

Just as the East India Company was able to promise military support for Indian nabobs who benefited from trade with Britain in the eighteenth and nineteenth

A central place

87 Cadbury Castle: Late Iron Age Durotrigan and Dobunnic coins

centuries, so British chiefs of south-east England, seduced by access to prestigious goods, were able to threaten 'protection' from Rome. In the late first century BC, the Greek geographer Strabo listed produce and minerals obtained from Britain; tellingly, he also mentioned slaves. Once again modern parallels are provided by the way European colonisers favoured and strengthened particular groups in Africa who became the last link in a chain of middlemen which ultimately extended to groups who would raid villages and harvest a crop of human wealth which they could sell up the line. The acquisition of slaves in Britain was surely by a similar chain, breeding distrust and resentment amongst the tribes.

The Durotriges would be one of the groups most affected by the shift in trade and expansion of a centralised pottery industry in the Poole Harbour area of Dorset may have been a direct response, keeping open inland trading routes which reached as far as Danebury by the second half of the first century BC. Ann Woodward's assessment was that this very recognisable ware only occurred with more diagnostic post-invasion pottery at Cadbury. Using data from other Somerset sites, she deduced that it had not penetrated this area before the Claudian invasion of AD 43 when the future emperor, Vespasian, led the Second Legion's campaign in the south-west peninsula. The contrast with SCEP data is stark. Many contexts ranging from ditch deposits throughout the study area to the Sigwells pits included Durotrigan pottery, but none of it was diagnostically post-invasion, imported or local. Diagnostic Romano-British pottery occurred only after the abandonment of the Sigwells enclosure; there was none of it amongst the many thousands of sherds from earlier levels. Throughout the study area there are examples of pottery from Poole Harbour associated with local shell-tempered products but no 'Roman' sherds, making a strong case for Alcock's distinctive Late Iron Age Cadbury 9 assemblage.

Strabo's list included precious metals so the supply chain must have extended as far as sources in Wales. Movement was an essential part of this trading pattern. Highly nucleated settlements or *oppida* (a misleadingly narrow use. Julius Caesar used *oppidum*, the Latin word for 'town', to describe a range of settlements he encountered in Britain and Gaul; it included hillforts), many enclosed by substantial banks, were planned developments taking advantage of river crossings over an area extending from the Thames Valley in the east to the south Midlands to the north and Ilchester, Somerset, 12km (7.5 miles) west of Cadbury. It has been suggested that the latter became an urban and political centre which drew in the elites from the nearby hillforts of Cadbury and Ham Hill, but after limited excavations Peter Leach believes its low-lying situation would have allowed only seasonal use.

The Durotriges may have found themselves increasingly hemmed in. The coin evidence suggests that the Dobunni of north Somerset and Gloucestershire were influenced by the economy of the south-east, possibly gaining favour en route to Wales. Increased social division in the south-east is evident in the burials of high-status individuals with prestigious goods from the continent. In contrast there is minimal evidence for flamboyant celebration of the individual in death in west Britain. More modest flexed inhumation became a feature in Dorset and, to a lesser extent, south Somerset, although the distribution may also reflect the intensity of developer-led archaeology. In most respects social organisation was little changed since the development of the hillforts but even this limited introduction of grave goods, and the contemporaneous greater range and quantity of material in pits, may reflect an incipient consumerism.

The plotting of Late Iron Age test pit pottery is far from straight forward. Figure *86* shows material which is either diagnostically of the period or is likely to belong to it because of the lack of association with diagnostically Romano-British material. This has been superimposed on a grayscale distribution of Poole Harbour fabrics and local derivatives which might equally be Iron Age or Roman. The distribution of the latter category has the inherent disadvantage that it conceals breaks in the sequence as it is common to both periods. On Sigwells, for instance, there appears

A central place

to have been a hiatus during the mid to later first century AD, perhaps of only a few decades, before occupation resumed.

Sigwells was worked, and probably settled, much more intensively during the last decades of the Iron Age, although a great deal of effort was involved in either the storage or importing of water. Two penannular (a ring with a single gap) ditches with internal diameters of 10 and 9m encircled roundhouses belonging either to Cadbury 8 or 9, on either side of the track leading north-west from the field system to the enclosure and pits. The one to the north opens to the south-east whilst the other faces west-north-west, a very distinctive opposition suggesting cosmological significance. Arguably they occupy a liminal space between the productive, life-giving fields to the east and the space where the dead began the process of recycling in the north-west. Much of this material would eventually journey to the east again in the form of manure, the sustenance of new life. A settlement consisting of these two houses could neither have generated the volume of midden material in the pits, nor sheltered a population large enough to work Sigwell's developed field system. Were these the houses of mediators who oversaw a geographical passage between the lands of the living and the dead? Were there scrutineers here who decided when midden material was ready to return to the living and who enacted the appropriate rites? Further fieldwork might provide clues.

An entirely new farmstead was constructed over the main north to south route which connected Sigwells to the valley between it and the hillfort. Its enclosure is remarkable for showing no entrance causeway in the magnetic survey. Trapezoidal, it had maximum dimensions of 43m from west to east and 39m from north to south. A 2.5m-wide and 1m-deep ditch with an opening at its south end separated a 9.6m wide strip on the east side from the rest of the enclosure, reserving the space for a straight line of six pits. The ditch re-cut a short segment of the north to south axial boundary on the west side of the Sigwells field system and had a broken though complete Durotrigan bowl spread along its base. Excavations showed that the valley track had filled with fine wind-blown silt before a second-century AD feature cut its west edge. Highly distinctive Severn Valley pottery, rare in the study area, was found in this feature and in the upper fills of the enclosure ditch as well as in a metalled surface at the point where the track would have crossed the ditch. A very substantial dished stone base overlying rubble filling the ditch supported a gate post in the Roman phase, so clearly some or all of the enclosure survived as a boundary. Only a small trench was opened at the intersection so it is not clear whether or not the old enclosure ditch survived elsewhere. The first-phase pottery is entirely consistent with Cadbury 9, and the farm, which commanded such a strategic route, appears to have survived for only a few years.

The other major area of growth was to the west of the hillfort at Milsoms Corner and Homeground, where several enclosures followed the route of the modern Folly Lane track in South Cadbury. Excavation revealed a roundhouse in one enclosure and the magnetic signatures of two more adjoining it suggest that all were housing plots. Intensive occupation in the South Cadbury valley and at Woolston Manor Farm continued and there is a wide but thin spread of material suggesting either working of, or settlement on, low ground further west. The density at Lick Hills, Sparkford, may be understated, submerged below Mediaeval settlement earthworks. A few sherds from a test pit at Great Woolfester, 500m further west, were probably re-deposited in the quarrying debris from the hilltop enclosure immediately south and upslope from it. The apparent decline in activity at the west end of the Weston Bampfylde ridge and at Sheep Slait is matched by the lack of evidence for expansion of field systems. These areas might best have been suited to the grazing of cattle and sheep respectively. Overall the picture is of intensified land use in the decades before the Claudian invasion.

Production and anxiety

Settlement at Maiden Castle and Danebury had declined before the end of the first century BC. The destruction of the latter's gate and the rise of the neighbouring hilltop settlement at Bury Hill led Cunliffe to suggest that it fell victim to a shift in the balance of local power several decades earlier. Sharples suggests that the opposite happened in Durotrigan territory and that the move out of the hillfort reflected political stability and alliance. The evidence from Cadbury has also been interpreted as indicative of reduced settlement, yet it is a view hard to accept in the face of the structural evidence. A near sterile layer of sandy, gravelly hillwash on the east of Milsoms Corner spur securely sealed the Iron Age deposits, the highest of which included late Cadbury 8 and Cadbury 9 pottery. It formed before being cut by a ditch which included a complete Durotrigan bowl but no diagnostic post-invasion pottery. The source for a humus-free sheet of soil would have been the outer bank, probably during its construction in the early first century AD or during a phase of decay when the ramparts were no longer being maintained and material from them washed downwards.

There were no roundhouses proven of this period. A fine collection of near-complete Durotrigan and Dobunnic vessels overlay a rotary quern in a humic, charcoal-rich soil filling a depression in a layer which had formed over the natural floor of a roundhouse on Site B/W and must have arrived there as rubbish from a building upslope. There were surely some occupants on the hilltop in the earlier part of the period judging by the amount of pottery and by the continuation of metalworking on the east plateau. This craft spread further west to Site L and north-east to Site B. Soon after Alcock's excavations were completed, a paper by Mansell Spratling noted a considerable number of bronze fittings from shields, including rim bindings and four separate finds of decorated boss mounts (88), all from the east plateau. He speculated that shields were made at Cadbury and, although there is no compelling evidence that they were, there is no doubt that sheet metal was worked. The casting of horse harness was well attested on Site F by mould fragments for up to four terret rings from two pits and other

A central place

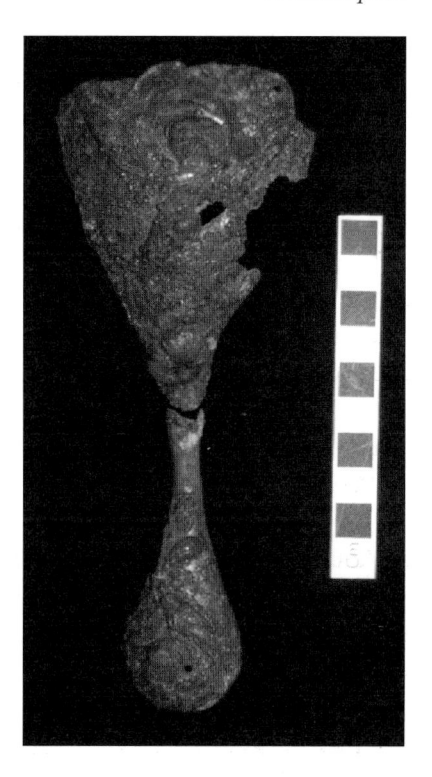

88 Cadbury Castle: shield boss, first century BC/AD

casting equipment in nearby pits. Although a paltry return compared with over 7000 mould fragments recovered from Gussage All Saints, Dorset, mould fragments are rare on hillforts, although this may reflect the limited investigation of their interiors. Three La Tène II chapes found would also have been current.

The building of the shrine, N5, after the hillfort fell to the invading Romans, represents customary use of the space privileged for religious observance. A very specific memory of the pre-invasion rites survived and probably a dilapidated or collapsed shrine as well. There is also no doubt that at around the same time, a new bank was constructed, and subsequently refurbished, on top of the earlier defences, accompanied by a typical boundary marker on Site D. The bank was built over a dish-shaped pit which contained a hoard of ironwork: a sword-shaped currency bar, an axe, one whole and one fragment of a saw, four whole or fragmentary knives, an adze, three whole and one fragment of bill or reaping hooks, and three awls. There were also bone tools, a shale plate, a fragment of wooden bowl and some clay slingshots, all representing a wide slice of community life. A more disturbing deposit was that of a young man squeezed into the rampart near the east gate; surely a deliberate, probably sacrificial, offering to protect the boundary. There were no signs of trauma on the bone but bog bodies of the period from Ireland, Britain and Denmark had been garotted. There had been no sign of sacrifice in the previous history of the hillfort, with the possible exception of the infant laid on the pebbles, so it was an unusually charged event, probably reflecting an increasingly anxious community. Given the low probability of discovering the only skeleton in one of Alcock's four trenches, it is likely that several more remain to be found.

It is difficult to reconcile the construction of one, or more probably two, outer banks less than 50 years before the invasion with the abandonment of intensive settlement and use of Cadbury Castle either as simply a religious centre or a skeleton-staffed potential place of refuge. It is possible that there was a period of near abandonment in the first century BC followed by a reinvestment in the defences which anticipated either Roman invasion or trouble with those further east who colluded with the Empire. In the event, the hillfort did indeed become a fatally flawed place of refuge.

A life of folly

During survey work a 1m² test pit in Homeground produced 80 sherds of Late Iron Age pottery, so two small trenches were dug there in 2004. The gully and ditch terminals from Trench 2 have been mention already. Trench 1 revealed 24m² (around 20 per cent) of the floor of an abandoned roundhouse in one of several enclosures following the route of the modern Folly Lane track north of Cadbury Castle. A dark soil within an arc from the south to north-west baulks was plainly visible as soon as the trench had been trowelled (*89*). The evidence showed that the building had collapsed gradually, creating an acidic broth of rotting organic material which attacked bone and the shell temper of most of the pottery, most of which comprised local coarse wares but with rare late South West decorated or Glastonbury Ware sherds. No doubt rodents would have taken advantage of the decay and only 10 per cent of the bone was identifiable, representing a characteristic range of sheep dominating cow, pig and horse. In other respects the floor was undisturbed. It sealed a human femur in the uppermost fill of an underlying ditch.

The house was built on an earthen platform over the ditch which had provided an earlier southern boundary for the Folly Lane track. There was little evidence for subsidence. It had been constructed in the long-established fashion of digging a shallow bedding trench then inserting stakes to support a wattle framework which was daubed. The hearth was off-centre, towards the north-east of the building, so that the entrance was probably from its unexcavated south.

Danielle de Carle's detailed study of the charred plant remains revealed the cereal portion of the householders' diet. Although emmer was a dominant wheat variety well into the Middle Iron Age, it was replaced increasingly by spelt and, in this instance, bread wheat. Barley is sometimes regarded as an incidental intruder, but the proportion of it in Trench 1 strongly suggests that it was cultivated. It could be used in broths, as fodder or, of course, for liquid merrymaking. Some of the weeds were directly related to disturbed ground, characteristically cultivation. They

89 Homeground Trench 1: soil stain of Late Iron Age roundhouse

included oats, bromes and vetches, all occurring in numbers which allow the possibility that they were selected for eating.

Classical literature refers to the 'Celtic' practice of plucking the heads of cereal crops rather than cutting low on the stems. Low-growing weed species suggest that the crops brought into the Homeground enclosure were cut closer to the ground or that the straw was harvested separately. The range of weeds shows nitrogen-rich and poor, dry and fairly wet, ground was cultivated consistent with emmer's preference for light soils and bread wheat's requirement for plentiful nutrients. Use of the latter suggests a high concentration of manure, possibly achieved by folding animals in small pens, although the intensive labour would be rewarded by a simpler and less-demanding threshing process. Chaff from both emmer and spelt suggest that the final stages of processing took place very nearby, probably within the enclosure, before being carried into the house on hair, clothes and footwear. The bulk of the carbonised grain was retrieved from the natural trap formed by the gully in which the wall was bedded, gradually accumulating whenever the central space was swept.

Rotary querns on the hillfort indicate that the last stage in grain processing was being carried out there in the Late Iron Age, although it has been suggested that the technology had been employed since the Middle Iron Age. The lack of an environmental sampling programme during Alcock's campaigns has deprived archaeologists of the opportunity to make comparisons with its extramural processing sequence and with the detailed narrative achieved at Danebury, but it can be asserted with confidence that the Homeground farmstead was largely self-sufficient in food and that it produced a small surplus for trade or tithe.

5

SLAUGHTER, IMPERIALISM AND RESURGENCE

No doubt the Britons knew of the military build-up in Europe through the tribes with whom they traded. Certainly, in the south-west, news of the of the Second Legion's landing and the first of 20 unprovoked, acquisitive, assaults against Dumnonian and Durotrigan *oppida* reached Cadbury within a day or two. Even without the lethal air power that precedes a modern army's advance, the population must have been in a state of terrified anticipation. Nowadays we are all too familiar with images of refugees fleeing the land they have held for generations to find a safe haven. What happened at Cadbury? Did large numbers of people pack their bags as the news got worse or did they remain to tend the land to which they were so deeply committed? We should bear in mind that whilst with hindsight we think of the invasion as inevitably successful, many of the indigenous tribes never accepted the subsequent occupation and saw no inevitability in the outcome. The following section summarises evidence from the south-west gate which continues to be the object of more detailed analysis than any other part of the Cadbury archive. It also introduces data from SCEP which has a bearing on the timing and character of events and which has been introduced above in the discussion of ditch deposits.

AD 43 TO AD 70

If Cadbury is bracketed with Arthur by the general public, the first century AD massacre deposits in the south-west gate are probably the subject most discussed by archaeologists. At the time of writing, seven years after the publication of the 'final' report, the human remains are the object of intense study again by Susan Jones, a postgraduate researcher at the University of Bournemouth. Even the experienced Alcock found the excavation of these highly complex deposits daunting and it is particularly poignant that he did not have the opportunity to present a considered report of them. More than two decades after the completion of the excavation, the production of a meaningful account from records of variable quality was even more intimidating. Ann Woodward's analysis of the stratigraphic sequence is the best available guide to the order of events but there remains ample potential for deeper understanding of the particular events through coherent closer analysis of the material archive. She identified 14 episodes, using Roman numerals, relating to structures in Site K, starting from the Neolithic. In her scheme the last episode of building associated with the gate before the massacre is VIII, dated by sherds she assigned to her ca8 (*34*), although some of the few illustrated would fit at least as well in Alcock's Cadbury 9. She argued persuasively for two major destructive episodes, the first of which, IX, is linked to a large amount of weaponry and human remains in varying states of articulation.

The intensity of the conflagration immediately outside and inside the gate was highlighted dramatically by the extent of reddened stone along the passage sides (*colour plate 25*). The fire continued to smoulder for some time so that several posts were burnt through in their sockets, leaving carbon-lined voids. A 5cm (2in) layer of charcoal and neighbouring charcoal-rich silts testify to the utter destruction of the wooden fabric as it collapsed outwards and downhill along the lower passage. Similar charcoal deposits on the base of the west guard chamber (*90*) were 5-15cm (2 to 6in) deep and included fragments of planks. Between the threshold and the guard chamber the burning was etched in red on the stone but there was a lack of in situ destruction deposits. Some human bone lay over the burnt deposits, partly sealed by rubble over and around an unburnt cut boulder (*colour plate 26*; note that the boulder can be seen under a scale at a later stage of excavation in *colour plate 27* and is the 'limestone slab' in *90*) 3m outside the gate, but the bulk of it was found inside the gate and further up the track. Some was also found in the west guard chamber. The spearheads, ballista bolt heads, shield parts, armour, scabbards and chapes were distributed over the same area in varying density, as were 115 brooches. The charcoal deposits outside the gate and in the guard chamber appear to be primary but otherwise the detritus was set into charcoal-flecked sandy silts, which appeared to be the product of downslope erosion. The material on either side of the threshold was sealed beneath gravelly burnt red stones and heavy boulders, all derived from the defensive bank but some of which showed no signs of burning (*colour plate 25*). A smaller amount of a similar range of bone and artefacts was found in the rubble.

Woodward divided the massacre deposits into five context groups: lower passage (11m^2 outside the threshold); middle passage (16m^2); upper passage (18m^2 of interior track); west guard chamber (6m^2) and rubble seal over the lower and middle passage (27m^2). The approximate surface areas are included to give a rough guide to the

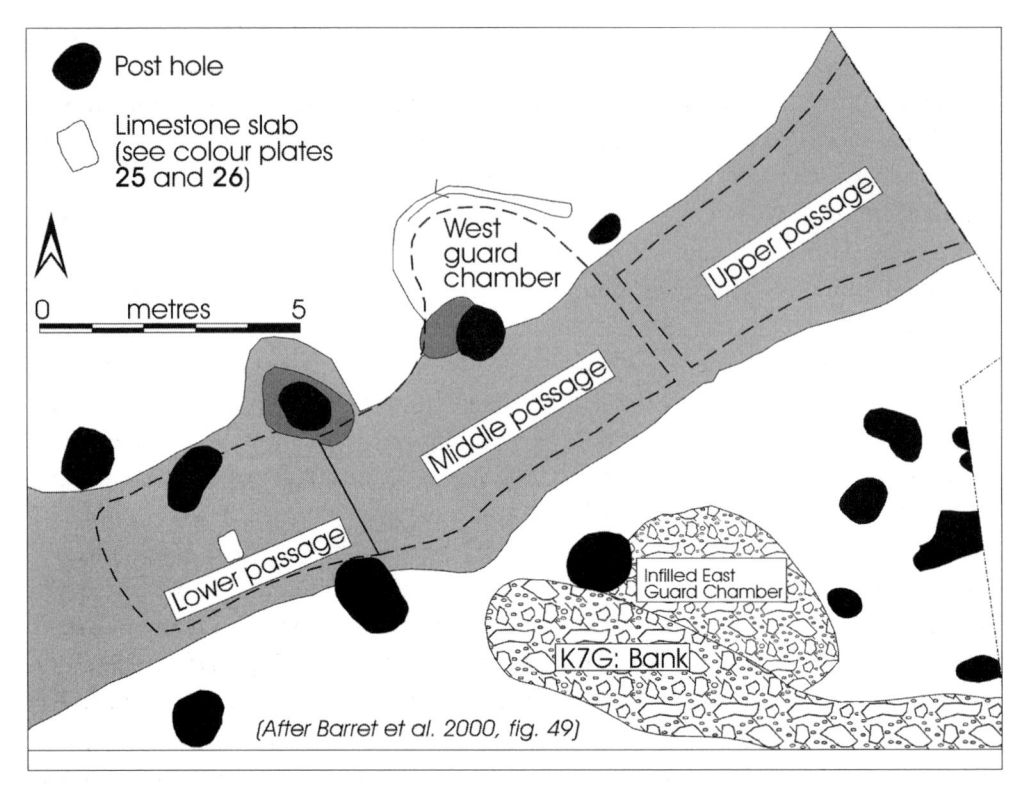

90 Cadbury Castle: south-west gate at the time of the massacre

frequency of item loss or deposition (*90*). Of a total of 58 offensive weapons, 20 came from the middle passage, 10 from the upper passage and 16 from the guard chamber, the latter obviously the highest incidence by square metre but a very cramped space in which to wield 13 spears. This might suggest that the chamber acted as a store from which weapons were issued, but three ballista bolt heads are unlikely to have been fired directly into it, implying subsequent re-deposition. Six from a total of 37 spearheads showed strong signs of deliberate folding or breaking, two from the guard chamber. Only the bolt heads were diagnostically Roman but auxiliaries were likely to have used spears similar to those of the defenders.

Between 11 and 16 of the brooches (10 and 14 per cent) were attributable to the Roman military but by far the majority (72 per cent) were identified as native. Nineteen brooches were judged to have been burnt, including five of the seven in the guard chamber. The others were from the secondary deposits in the middle and upper passage. Sixty-one of the brooches were in fresh condition, 35 were too corroded to decide, and wear was noted on 19. The bias towards fresh condition, and the sheer number, led Alcock to suggest that a trader's stall had been knocked over in the upper gate passage during the assault and re-analysis suggests that a substantial number may have derived from a trader's stock, although it should be noted that the relatively small culturally diagnostic Roman group had the highest proportion of fresh examples. All the brooches were attributable to the middle of the first century AD but, writing in the English Heritage report, Adrian Olivier perceived a slight time lapse between those in the lower passage and guard chamber and those from the secondary deposits of the middle and upper passage and the covering rubble.

During the excavations, Alcock was quick to realise that the scatter of body parts in the gate passage were not dismembered in the immediate aftermath of a battle. He suggested that they had been left exposed to carrion-eating animals. He believed the bones represented a minimum of 28 people, a figure later revised in the English Heritage report to 22, 17 per cent of whom were children aged between one and ten years. The greatest concentration of bones was in the middle passage but they occurred throughout its length, the least concentrated area being in the upper passage. Most were loose, but articulated parts included a complete leg, torso, skull, foot and hand. Some fingers showed bronze staining where rings had remained on them after the flesh had rotted and in two cases the rings remained in situ. In the threshold area and guard chamber calcined bones found in the charcoal deposits allow the possibility that a few bodies may have been burnt where they fell, but in most cases the picture is more complex. Whilst there was a very high percentage of well-roasted (but not calcined) cranial fragments and a considerable number of burnt torsos and long bones, foot and hand bones showed little, if any, burning. There were also a disproportionately small number of pelvic bones from individuals aged over 10 years.

Woodard has suggested that the discrepancies in burning might be explained by the manner in which bodies were placed on a pyre, noting that bones surrounded by fat would burn more thoroughly, hence offering a possible explanation for some of the unburnt extremities, though not the skulls. She speculated that some skulls may have been displayed on poles in the gate area and there is little doubt that body parts were treated in a discriminatory manner. Nine instances of violent injury were reported, mainly to the upper leg, but this now seems an understatement, perhaps in part due to a greatly increasing bone count. When the report was published fewer than 2000 were tabulated, but Susan Jones' work in progress has already identified more than 6000. More than 90 have cut marks to limb bones and skulls which bear signs of heavy blows to the side of the head. In one case a blade has cut into the left side neck bones. These were injuries incurred in hand-to-hand combat. A striking feature arising from the new research is the rarity of gnaw marks, in particular on the long bone ends favoured by scavenging mammals. This is unambiguous evidence for the remains being protected, perhaps by temporary burial, prior to being placed in the gate. The sinews, which would have allowed the instances of articulation, survived for variable lengths of time according to burial conditions, so it is possible that a few years elapsed before they were moved.

Both Alcock and Woodward identify evidence for refurbishment, even substantial rebuilding, of the south-west gate after the massacre. Its continuous sequence of building and use finally ended with the latter's Episode XIV, when abandonment silts including Romano-British pottery were sealed by rubble derived from another intense blaze in the gateway and guard chamber. The pottery, four brooches and a spearhead may be re-deposited relics of the massacre, but a second- to third-century AD brooch ought probably to be treated as intrusive via voids in the rubble. Jones has noted a considerable number of human bones in the rubble.

It has been noted that no diagnostically Roman pottery was associated with the enclosure at Sigwells, nor with nine deposits of Durotrigan vessels in ditches. The same is true of the house floor at Homeground. Given that diagnostically early post-invasion pottery from Somerset and Dorset (Shepton Mallet, Corfe Mullen) was in circulation on Cadbury, at Ilchester and other local sites, it would be surprising if some of it had not fallen into a few of these contexts, if they were still open in AD 50 or even three or four years earlier. All of the ditch deposits, including those of the late Sigwells enclosure, were contemporary with a phase of deliberate backfilling. Of course, ditches were by no means static features in the landscape and at Worthy there was an earlier example of the ritual. Nonetheless the sheer number of instances, the consistency of assemblages and the deposit characters offer the strong possibility that they represent a single event horizon which would best be dated to the mid first century AD. If we allow that the horizon occurred at around the time of the arrival of the invaders, a set of specific hypotheses may be formulated and then considered in the light of the evidence from the hillfort:

1) Deliberate abandonment and decommissioning of the productive landscape before the invaders arrived, both as a means of protecting the ancestors and to prevent the Roman army from using it as a resource.
2) A hurried abandonment as much of the population took to the road shortly before the invaders' arrival; final offerings were made to the gods while houses such as that at Homeground were simply left to decay.
3) A decision by the indigenous population, after the hillfort was taken, to deprive the invaders of the land's productive potential by closing ditches according to Durotrigan custom.
4) A deliberate punitive devastation of the landscape *pour encourager les autres*, executed by the indigenous population coerced by the invading troops (*colour plate 27*).

Slaughter, imperialism and resurgence

Compare these with the evidence from the latest contexts on the hillfort before the circulation of distinctively Romano-British pottery, most clearly the gate deposits:

1) An assault in which Roman military technology was employed.
2) The deliberate deposition of jewellery, weaponry and body parts, in varying states of articulation and non-articulation, of men, women and children, many with conflict trauma marks.
3) The very limited evidence for pyres and, if they were used at all, their restricted application to only a few bodies.
4) The deliberate sealing of the remains.

There were probably some casualties amongst the invaders but whether any of them were represented by the remains in the south-west gate is open to question. It can be assumed that the vast majority of the human remains belong to defenders from the local population (whilst noting that just as members of the Iraqi resistance have received outside assistance, so groups from neighbouring tribes may have fought at Cadbury in anticipation of an advance on their own territories). Mortimer Wheeler thought he had discovered a cemetery for those who died during the Roman assault on Maiden Castle. About half of the bodies displayed signs of possible battle injuries, some of which had had time to heal, but very few could be linked directly to the assault, with notable rare exceptions such as the man photographed famously with a bolt head lodged in his spine. The remains suggested a less humiliating treatment of the population there, which it was tempting to interpret as a response to different circumstances. Had the Romans 'tolerated' initial resistance and was the Cadbury community the victim of an atrocity perpetrated because they had participated in a later uprising? In fact, many of the Maiden Castle burials had characteristics making it unlikely that they had died violently and few if any showed signs of the haste and anxiety Wheeler perceived. However, even if only a few of the graves contained the battle dead, they certainly received different treatment from those beneath and in the rubble in the Cadbury's south-west gate.

In both cases the victim communities treated their own dead and the differences in fact reflect variations in local practice. Although Durotrigan crouched burials occur in Somerset and include a grave by Henshall Brook at Eastcombe Farm, the smattering of individual human bone fragments in late contexts across the study area suggests that excarnation remained the dominant rite on and around Cadbury. Burial soon after death may have allowed the people of Maiden Castle to treat their dead in the manner they preferred but at Cadbury the full due process may never have been completed, simply because the time consuming system would have been overloaded; the sheer number of bodies would have been a health hazard if left exposed. As a compromise some may have been partly dismembered, or even burnt, to accelerate the process (again, there is no compelling evidence for proper pyres, which would have reduced the bone to little more than grey and white crumbs) before being placed in the gate passage in a state of partial decay. The burial in The Moor appears to be a case where excarnation was interrupted and, in this case, the compromise was to create a cyst at the junction of two backfilled ditches.

Finally, we should consider the extent of the invaders' culpability. At first sight this appears to be a localised genocide but we should not rule out the possibility that Cadbury became a Masada where many of the community chose to die at each others' hands rather than live under the Imperial yoke. If so, then we must assume that the defenders killed those too young to fight before the assault began and went into battle with the intention of inflicting as many casualties as possible on the enemy, before succumbing. Analysis of trauma to juvenile bones in the massacre deposits ought to elucidate the issue. Students of Latin will recall the verb *vastare*, a term used specifically to describe the Roman Army's punitive devastation of an enemy's territory. It included the slaughter of animals and destruction of crops even if, as in this case, the price was a temporary inconvenience to the army's supply chain. This appears to be what happened around Cadbury Castle.

Enough locals survived, some probably enslaved, to carry out the abridged rites for the dead and, without doubt, to carry an abiding hatred of their oppressors. The partly Romanised features of a *repoussé* face on a bronze plaque (*colour plate 29*) found in the guard chamber's massacre debris suggests that feelings towards the Empire may have been ambivalent shortly before the invasion. It contrasts with an unambiguously, boldly schematic, local design of a face on a roughly contemporary bowl sherd from a Sigwells pit (*colour plate 28*). Neither represents the face of the subsequently defeated and occupied population.

By AD 47 conquest had been completed in much of the West Country, an area which included the lead mines of the Mendip Hills in the north and Dorchester to the south. It is probable that a fort and garrison were established close to a crossing of the River Yeo in Ilchester at around that time. Given the by then unquestionable supremacy of the occupation force, the post-massacre building work on the south-west gate had more to do with maintaining the dignity of the hill than refurbishment of the defences, for which there was no evidence from the other trenches cutting the inner bank. Before the work could begin a cobbled surface had to be laid over the massacre deposits, at once sealing them and making access to the interior possible. The hilltop was largely, or entirely, free of habitative settlement and the only known surviving building on the plateau was the shrine, N5 (*91*). The upper fills of its bedding trench included early post-invasion pottery which might either be infill at the end of the building's life or included in the

Slaughter, imperialism and resurgence

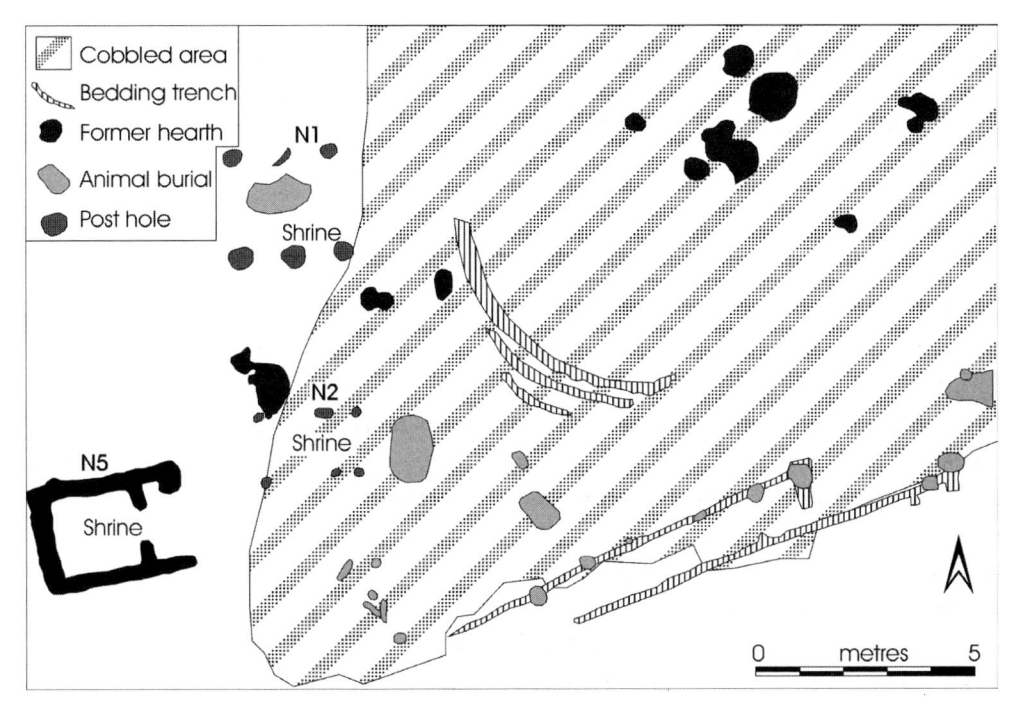

91 Cadbury Castle: shrine and earlier animal burials

packing around its posts. The small sherds would have been incidental losses, not deliberate deposits, at a time when diagnostically Roman pottery was already in fairly widespread circulation. The building may have had a role in the rites for the massacre dead and it probably retained a religious function until its abandonment or demolition between 50 and 70 BC, when barrack blocks were constructed lying over the silted-up holloway between the plateau and the north-east gate. Johnson's geophysical survey suggests there were other blocks nearby. The excavations on Site BW revealed a field oven and Roman military equipment, some showing signs of on-site repair, which could scarcely be separated in time from the gate passage material.

The brief garrisoning of the barracks surely coincided with the final demolition of the south-west gate and other areas of the inner bank, as evidence from Site D shows. Documentary evidence shows that the Second Legion was unable to assist its colleagues in South Wales at Caerleon-on-Usk during the later first century AD, presumably because the native population was still resisting the occupiers. The demolition may have been a precautionary measure in advance of the garrison's departure from an area where resentment remained strong, rather than a response to a full-blown local uprising. In the meantime, a deposit of near complete fine local Grey Ware vessels, imitating imported Samian, were found in a pit at Saxon's

Hill, the bungalow neighbouring South Cadbury Church. The excavator John Laidlaw thought this represented the foundation of the modern village, but it is hard to explain the throwing away of the best china. Was the man who aspired to Roman materialism a collaborator imposed as a leader on the surviving local population, who feared for his life in the face of its contempt and fled?

AD 70 TO AD 450 (92)

From its outset SCEP's principal objective was to set Cadbury Castle in its prehistoric environs. The first two years of excavations targeting Romano-British remains on Sigwells should be regarded as a necessary aberration to accommodate the training needs of Birmingham University students. Although excavations at Castle Farm in 1996 were conducted under the project's auspices, they were development led. All large- and most small-scale excavations since then have successfully avoided substantial Roman remains and the concomitant welter of finds.

Rumours of large numbers of Roman coins being found on the hillfort go back several centuries, but Alcock failed to find them and concluded that after the barracks ceased to be used the hill was returned to agriculture. Philip Freeman was not entirely convinced. Noting the presence of Roman masonry in the post-Roman bank, he has suggested that a cruciform ditch on the plateau was the robbed foundation of a temple, similar to a second-century example at Vienne in France. Alcock found no stone chippings or mortar and believed that the trench was intended to support a Late Saxon church which was never erected.

As we have seen, large portions of the landscape were taken out of commission at around the time of the massacre. During the third quarter of the first century AD the population had been reduced by the slaughter of many of the young generation who would have inherited the land, and by forced movement of the population. Whilst it seems likely that agriculture never ceased entirely, there would have been a spread of scrubby growth in many fields. By the end of the first century or in the early second, some ditches were re-cut or dug along the line of old ditches, notably throughout the South Cadbury valley and at Woolston. Curiously, the reinvestment in the north-west of Sigwells appears to have been determined by the orientation of one of the Bronze Age long linears. The Severn Valley pottery within the enclosure across the north to south track shows that the farmstead was resurrected there.

By the later second century a brick production site (and possibly other industries) at Nine Acres took advantage of the clays along the Weston Bampfylde ridge track, which headed towards Ilchester (Roman Lindinis) and a wider market for its

Slaughter, imperialism and resurgence

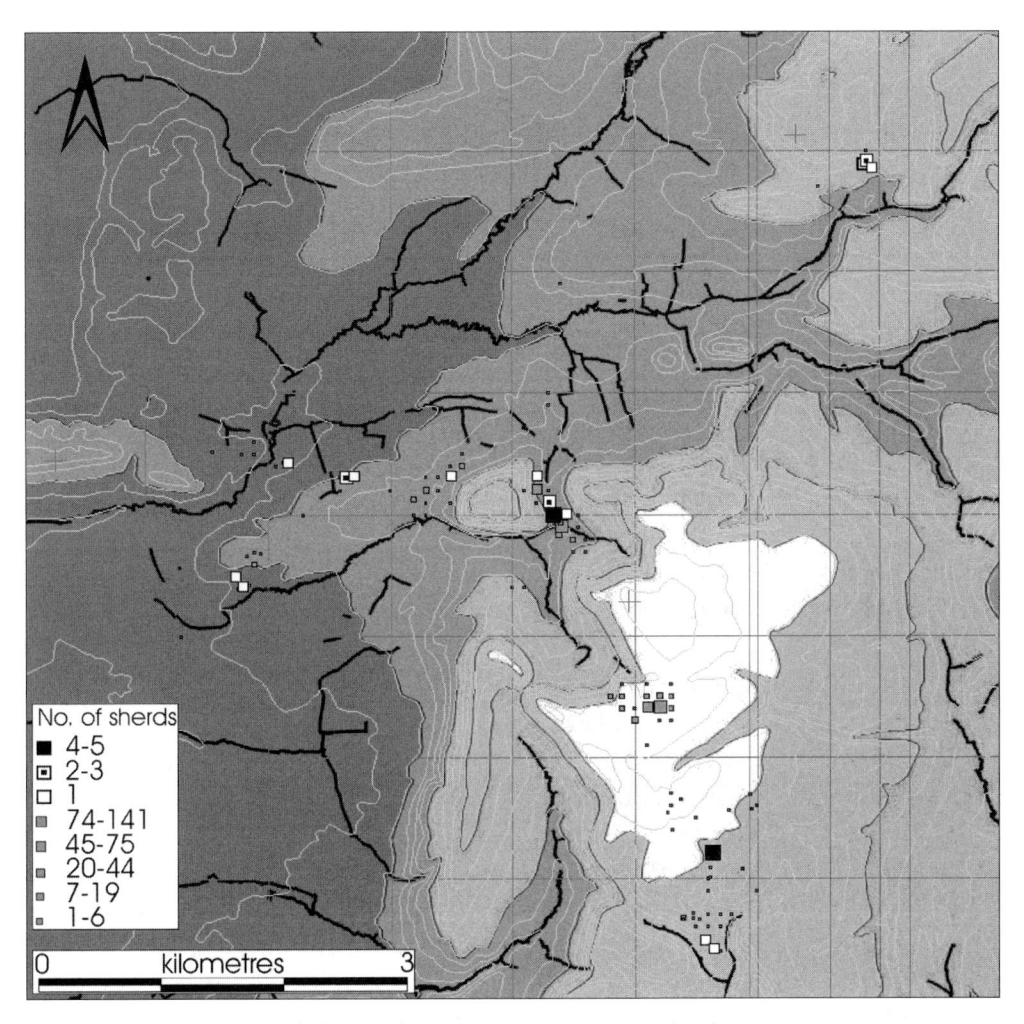

92 Early Romano-British finds distribution

products beyond the crossing of the River Cam, at Sparkford. South Cadbury was busy enough for a large midden to have formed in the area below the hillfort's east gate. It continued to grow until at least the end of the fourth century and cobbles laid on top of it may date to decades beyond that. A single hypocaust flue tile offers thin evidence for a villa in the south area of the modern village but the nearest known examples are at Bratton Seymour 4km (2.5 miles) to the north-east and possibly at Queen Camel, a similar distance to the north-west. Such a pattern would contrast with the much greater density around Somerton and what had become the regional administrative centre or *civitas* at Ilchester by the later third century AD, but it probably reflects earlier research agendas more than the actual distribution of rural settlement. Two large heavily truncated ovens or furnaces cut into the fourth-century layers of the midden may be contemporary with, or pre-date, the cobbles and are a testament to local economic growth. The wealth of pottery of this phase at Castle Farm and Saxon's Hill massively outweighs the assemblage from the hillfort, which represents little more than a manuring scatter on land already rich in nutrients from centuries of intense settlement. There was also marked change in the butchery which seems to have become industrialised judging by the amount of material, the use of a much heavier knife and a standardisation of the cuts.

At Woolston the old Iron Age field system and settlement was restored and grew, after a short hiccup, in a sequence of habitation and farming of the same plot which appears to have started in the Middle Iron Age and continues today. In contrast, the widely spaced stone-founded rectangular buildings, set in a newly created field system on Sigwells, eventually went into decay and were never replaced.

Being Romano-British

It is no coincidence that in the eighteenth and nineteenth centuries the British aristocracy and educated classes developed a passion for all things Roman. Despite the example of Gibbons landmark history, Rome was perceived as an ultimately benign Empire which brought good to the western world, a model and vindication for British expansionism of the time. No doubt there were great rewards to be had for those locals of high status who ensured that the community provided a trading surplus which was converted to personal wealth along the famous network of well-built roads. For others there were important losses. Seasonal fairs of craft and exchange ceased at places like Meare, in the Somerset Levels, and with them important meetings with people from different communities. By the mid fourth century the effects of the loss of such traditions was registered in an unequal access to goods, variations in health and even in parts of the rural gene pool. A general measure of this is the longer life expectancy for women and, especially, men living in towns such as Lindinis compared with those in the rural settlements whose bones often displayed signs of repetitive strain and osteoarthritis. Generally, women tended not to survive beyond 30 years, mainly due, no doubt, to childbirth. The mortality rate amongst infants seems very high in the rural areas, although it has to be acknowledged that variations in burial practice may have inflated the figure as the very young were often buried within or at the threshold of a building. This continuation of an Iron Age practice would not have contravened Roman law if the infant was less than 30 days old.

A small farming community at Bradley Hill, near Somerton, epitomises the rural plight. In the 1970s Roger Leech excavated three buildings which had housed people and wintered animals over a period estimated at between 50 and 100 years.

The range of bone reflected the characteristic mix of food animals, with sheep dominating the assemblage. However, the higher meat-bearing bones were notably absent. This was emphatically a producer and supplier farm, in thrall to a local villa owner who either consumed the valuable meat or sold it to support a lavish lifestyle. Roman law requiring burial of the dead outside the settlement boundary was ignored entirely as there is every reason to believe that 55 individual graves represented all those who made their home there. Thirty-seven of the dead were infants. All but two of the skeletons displayed common anomalies; reproduction was clearly a family affair. In the farmstead's last years people were living and working in buildings which had begun to collapse around them.

Bradley Hill represents an economic, social and physical impoverishment deeply rooted in the imposition of a legalistic, hierarchical and urbanised society created by Roman imperialism, a process which was already evident in Rome itself, where massive unemployment had resulted in the need for welfare laws as early as the second and first centuries BC. Despite this, the survival of ancient beliefs throughout the period is observable in the traces of local rites which extended back at least to the Middle Bronze Age. A scrap of fresh Samian was the only dating evidence for a targeted test pit context which included the deliberate deposit of a cow's lower jaw under two large stones in a stream at Middle Mead, Weston Bampfylde. John Davey found more in third or fourth century AD ditch terminals in a small trench at Castle Farm in 2003. A different ritual, but similarly centred on a cattle skull, was observed during the 1996 excavations there: a complete skull was set into the upper fills of a pit, which cut through the cobbles sealing the midden. Votive pots had their rims and shoulders removed and were placed upside down on either side of it. The pots were similar to those found at the Late and Post-Roman Lamyatt Beacon temple site 12km (7.5 miles) north of Cadbury.

AD 450 TO AD 900

Using early British and Anglo-Saxon documentary resources alongside the archaeological evidence, Leslie Alcock mapped a Britain of competing kingdoms with a marked material cultural divide between east/central Britain and the west. The south-west peninsula had the two most significant known landings for late fifth- to sixth-century east Mediterranean Fine Ware bowls and amphorae, imported for their wines and pastes, at Bantham, south Devon, and Tintagel, north Cornwall. Sherds from these vessels are rarely found but were fairly frequent at Cadbury Congresbury, close to north Somerset's Bristol Channel, and sparse at Glastonbury, Cannington and Cadbury Castle (*colour plate 30*). The Byzantine Christianity of one source is illustrated by the occasional presence of *chi rho* stamps on the bowls, including one from Cadbury, but, bearing in mind the apparent persistence of pre-Roman ritual behaviour in the study area, there is no strong evidence that the local population were devout. Gildas, a monk writing in the mid sixth century AD, was scathing about the moral turpitude of contemporary British leaders and there can be little doubt that this imperial religion foisted on the people was more often a matter for the local hierarchy of political affiliation with the Mediterranean world rather than conviction.

The period between the collapse of the Romanised economy and introduction of distinctive Late Saxon pottery is notoriously difficult to recognise in the field. The archaeological method of research favoured by John Davey was to explore Late Romano-British and Early Mediaeval sites in the hope of finding either continuing or preceding settlement. He targeted geophysical survey and keyhole excavation at areas in, and on the periphery of, the study area identified by Giles Cooper. In addition to fieldwalking and pottery analysis, Cooper collected the tithe map fieldnames from every parish impinging on SCEP study areas and applied limited etymological analysis of archaeological indicator names. Based on a surfeit of negative evidence from fieldwork for the target period, Davey speculated that many of the field systems which flourished in the late third and first half of the fourth centuries remained in use, but that habitative space within them was relatively ephemeral. Each generation would have created new dwellings near the old ones which rotted down with their associated middens to provide a valuable fertility resource but leaving no visible and datable remains, a model previously offered for Early to Middle Bronze Age semi-arable economies.

The problem with this view lies in the fact that whilst SCEP has on many occasions identified organically rich, charcoal-flecked soils with few or no finds which are demonstrably pre-Roman, there has been a distinct lack of comparable layers above the Roman levels, other than those associated with very rare Saxon, rare post-Norman Conquest and prolific later finds. There would appear to be a marked down-turn in the rural economy when compared with any other pre-Norman period since the Late Neolithic, with little sign of recovery until the late ninth or tenth century. It is equally true of data from Davey's small-scale excavations of later Romano-British sites and SCEP's regular and targeted test pits and excavations that ditches appear to fill, and structures to collapse without replacement, during the fifth century AD. By the early to mid sixth century AD Cadbury Castle stood out in a sparsely occupied buffer zone over which quarrelsome factions competed.

Davey made much more effective use of regressive map analysis linking Cooper's fieldnames and other textural evidence with modern ordnance survey and older estate maps. Wisely he expanded his documentary study area to encompass parts of north Dorset and the Ilchester area, convincingly showing continuity of estate holdings. SCEP's fieldwork results provide support for the general apportionment of land originating in the Iron Age or earlier, surviving into the later Mediaeval period, although there is some disagreement over the particular territories. Otherwise the evidence for a living population within a span of at least 350 years can be summarised very briefly.

At Castle Farm in 1998 Paul Johnson excavated several cut features in an area very disturbed by animal burrows with little dating evidence, apart from a Saxon silver coin from the first half of the eighth century in a possible timber slot. At Henehill geophysical survey revealed a large, roughly oval, anomaly slighted by a track to a ford across Henshall Brook, immediately below the south-east of Cadbury Castle. A rectangular feature respected the track. Both were of a scale and magnetic signature consistent with timber building bedding trenches. Sherds of Late Saxon and Saxo-Norman pottery were found between 40 and 200m south of them. Intersecting with, or more probably slighted by, the track, the oval anomaly is the earlier of the two but the close proximity of the structures in an area with no other signs of habitation for several hundred metres suggest that one was the direct successor of the other. Immediately north of the hillfort an aerial photograph taken in 1947 shows an earthwork from the Romano-British field system revealed by magnetic survey. Its survival in a busy area of productive arable soils shows that it remained a useful component in successive agricultural reorganisations of the landscape well into the twentieth century.

The most tantalising evidence was from Great Cowleaze, Woolston Manor Farm. A test pit exploring a broad linear anomaly south-east of the building platforms which were first constructed in the late Middle Iron Age and were expanded and modified until their abandonment in the fourteenth century (58) revealed deep deposits between a Roman layer and one including a Late Saxon pot rim. The result of an application for radiocarbon dating will determine whether or not we have uncovered extremely rare direct evidence for cereal cultivation during this period. The deposits appear to offer an exceptional opportunity for Early Mediaeval field-based research.

A stronghold of late antiquity
The reconstruction of Cadbury's defences in the second half of the fifth century AD was the largest engineering project of the period in Britain, with the possible exception of long 'dykes', although these may be later. It would have required ample natural resources (wood and stone) and manpower, as well as capable planning and administration, although none of these on the scale necessary for the original Iron Age defences. Alcock suggested that the motivation was to create a secure administrative centre to replace Lindinis, probably at the instigation of

a 'king' who had the charisma to unite the local or even the regional population. There is ample documentary evidence for mortal rivalry amongst British leaders as well as the external threat of Saxon raiding parties which were within a few days' striking distance from their advanced settlements in the upper Thames Valley.

The new defences were equipped with a stone breastwork and rear revetment laced with vertical and horizontal timbers. Presumably close to the end of construction, a bow or frame saw blade used on the timbers was folded and placed in the bank on Site D as mark of completion. Some of the stone was reused from earlier from earlier banks, some from Romano-British buildings which had stood either in an unexcavated part of the interior or somewhere further afield, but much of it was freshly quarried. Four large posts were set into the metre-deep silts which covered the cobbles sealing the massacre deposits in a rough square in the south-west gate, with timber sills between the front and back pairs to support twinned-leaved gates. Cobbles metalling the gate passage had been well worn before a build-up of silt and debris necessitated the laying of a new surface sealing the deliberate deposit of an axe hammer and a pendant, subsequently transformed into a buckle (*colour plate 30*). The former has Romano-British antecedents but the decoration of the latter is analogous to Saxon brooches from the upper Thames Valley, dating from the mid to later sixth century AD, providing the earliest date after which the road was resurfaced and abandoned following a short period of use. Alcock makes the reasonable suggestion that they provided 'supernatural' security for the gate.

The pendant was by no means the only Saxon find. A design in relief of a warrior's helmeted head on a button brooch (*colour plate 30*) is of a distinctive type dated to the two decades either side of AD 500. Glass from beads, bowls and beakers had manufacture dates ranging over the fourth to sixth, possibly even seventh centuries AD but whilst a significant number of sherds were typical of imports from mainland Europe found in west Britain, there was an equally significant assemblage of contemporary Saxon material. Alcock speculated that these items might have been symptomatic of exchange, even of war booty, preferring to determine cultural affiliation with reference to the ceramics.

There can be no doubt that Alcock was immensely excited when Paul Kent, a local teenager, found an unworn piece of amphora in a timber bedding trench on Site L during the 1968 excavations. He wanted to find a 'feasting hall'. By opening a much larger area around it in 1969 he was able to identify the ground plan of postholes making up a 19 x 10m rectangular aisled building with bowed gables, the bedding trench supporting a screen dividing the east third from the main body of a hall. Since Alcock built the hall critics have tried to demolish it. As a boy working on Site L, I was well aware that one or two of the postholes in the original

93 Cadbury Castle: the sixth-century hall. Cadbury Castle archive

outline (*93*) had been filled with red soil and must have been pre Iron Age. In his 1995 report, Alcock explained away an analysis by David Fraser which found no consistent volumetric or depth relationships between the post settings by noting the uneven scouring of the plateau by ploughing, as well as the problems of defining settings cutting earlier features. His tentative attributions of a small rectangular building comprising two bedding parallel trenches and a porched roundhouse (the latter would pre-date the hall) to this phase are possible but a further muted roundhouse bisecting the north-east corner of the hall lay directly over a much re-used Iron Age building sequence, to which it surely belongs. Despite this, I have no doubt that in broad terms Alcock was correct in his judgement of the hall, supported by the compelling distribution of imported pottery (*94*).

There were surely other buildings enclosed by the new bank, both outside the excavated areas and lacking diagnostic finds within them, but despite the thin scatter of imported sherds over most of the plateau, the particular function of the hilltop may have required only occasional large-scale provision of shelter. At the very least, any building intended to stand in the long term would have needed occupation to avoid deterioration. The massive investment in the defences indicates that even if the people living there regularly were not of the highest status, they had important day-to-day roles, probably in the general running of the surrounding territory. They would have been directly accountable to a more powerful person who either lived there or visited frequently. His arrival would have coincided with a muster of

Cadbury Castle: The Hillfort and Landscapes

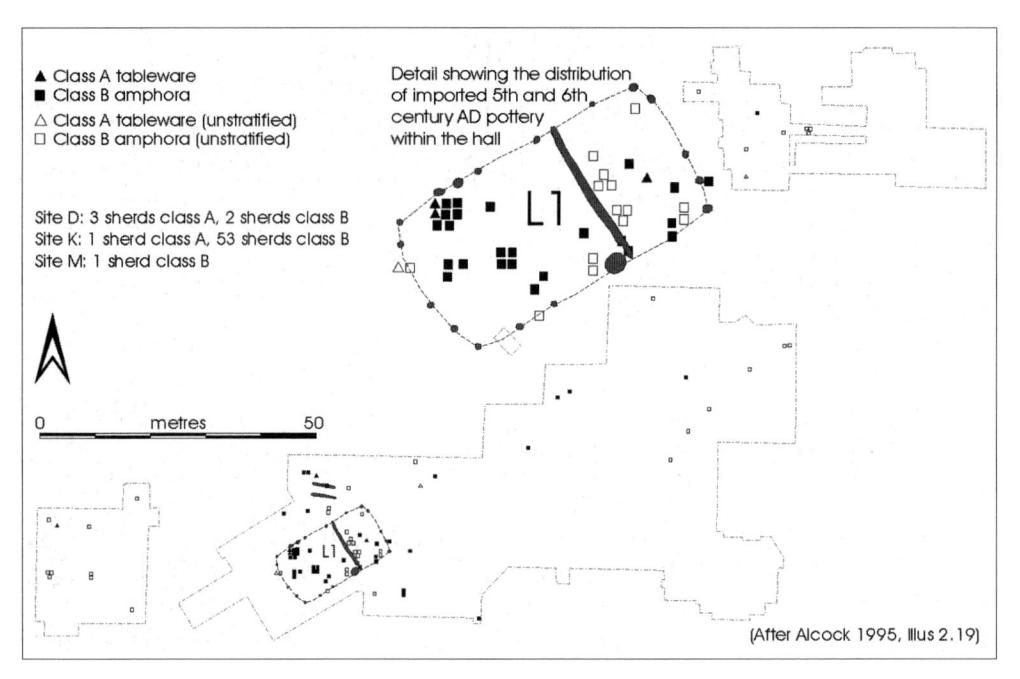

94 Cadbury Castle: plateau distribution of imported fifth- to sixth-century pottery

able-bodied men who were given battle training. They may have gone on raiding parties into neighbouring British territory or further afield, into Saxon lands, but the mere existence of a trained body would have deterred some incursions from outside.

A system based on the regular contribution of service can be sustained during periods of perceived threat but not indefinitely. There is no evidence for violent assault against the Dumnonian strongholds but the repeated high investment to maintain them would have caused resentment and the eventual disintegration of the system. The lack of imported pottery of the late sixth and seventh centuries AD on any of the south-west peninsula's settlements suggests either that the infrastructure which attracted the Mediterranean suppliers had collapsed, or that withdrawal of supply brought on the collapse. Alcock speculated that it was precisely this atomisation of society in the later sixth century which emboldened Wessex to drive a wedge between Welsh and peninsula Britons by defeating them at the Battle of Deorham, thought to be at Dyrham, 10km (6.2 miles) north of Bath.

After the hillfort

John Davey resisted the temptation to describe as 'Saxon' a seventh-century AD cemetery at Hicknoll Slait, 1km (0.6 mile) due east of Cadbury Castle, although

95 Hicknoll Slait: seventh-century burial. Cadbury Castle is in the background. Mary Claridge

his suggestion that the dead were former occupants of the hillfort is flawed by a misreading of Alcock, who insisted that its occupation ceased 'in the decades before AD 600'. The cemetery was discovered in January 1966 when workmen building a reservoir disturbed four graves. Only one skeleton remained in situ by the time L.C. Hayward, a reputable local amateur archaeologist, arrived to retrieve what he could from the spoil heap. Of a spearhead, punched decorated metalwork and a 'sugar-loaf' shield boss, the latter was distinctively Saxon in style and attributed to the seventh century AD. In 2001 two further graves were found during excavations by Davey. An approximately north to south oriented man was accompanied by a diagnostically Saxon knife and a lump of flint lay between his palate and lower jaw (*95*). The east to west oriented grave of a girl in her mid teens was robbed soon after burial, leaving only half a blue glass bead and some flecks of bronze in the area around her neck. Stable isotope analysis of teeth from the skeletons showed that both individuals were more likely to have been reared fairly locally rather than on the chalklands to the east.

Leaving aside arguments over whether the orientations of the graves or presence of grave goods should determine if these burials were Christian, pagan or both, Davey has used the data to imply that the people were most probably Britons acculturated by Wessex, or of mixed ethnicity 'who used a direct path from the east or north-east entrance of the hillfort to the top of Hicknoll Slait'. My own view remains that the founding graves in the cemetery were for recent Saxon arrivals who appreciated the political importance of Cadbury to the British population and symbolised their dominion over it by choosing the only hill offering an expansive view of the interior (*95, colour plate 2*), as well as a panorama of west Wiltshire, the notional homeland of the new group. The pattern of inhumation in Late and Early Post-Roman local rural sites was of cemeteries close to or within their settlements or, in the case of Lamyatt Beacon, with a shrine. The choice of an isolated hilltop was entirely new to the area. Whilst accepting the view that grave assemblages may include exotic goods acquired through exchange or theft, it seems perverse to argue that the bodies were Britons when all the diagnostic items were Saxon and the less distinctive objects were probably so as well. The nearest neighbouring cemetery of this period is at Camel Hill, 4km (2.5 miles) west of Cadbury where distinctively Saxon weaponry was found in burials discovered during quarrying in the 1920s. There are no traces of contemporary settlement in the immediate vicinities of the cemeteries or on the hillfort.

It was an apt spot on which to found a cemetery, the burial place of one or more of the armed men who gained control of the area by force or the threat of it. The cemetery may have served a population in South Cadbury but access would have been a great deal easier from the Compton Pauncefoot direction, 1km to the east. An entry in the *Anglo-Saxon Chronicle* for AD 658 (dates can only be treated as reliable to within three decades; the chronicles were compiled in the later ninth century in Alfred's reign, retrospectively integrating oral traditions already filtered through seventh-century AD *Easter Annals*) states that the Britons were pursued to west Somerset's River Parrett, after a defeat by a Wessex army at Peonnum, generally thought to be Penselwood, 14km (8.7 miles) to the east of Cadbury Castle. This would fit well with the Hicknoll Slait evidence, although W.G. Hoskins has offered as an alternative battle site Pinhoe near Exeter, Devon, which on geography alone would pose problems for this interpretation.

With the exception of the silver coin, the Cadbury area fades from the documentary and archaeological record, although we can assume that it was within the See of Sherborne, newly created by King Ine in AD 705, following Wessex's expansion across most of the South West.

FROM ETHELRED TO ARTHUR

The SCEP test and shovel pits have produced a smattering of tenth- or more probably earlier eleventh-century AD pottery from Sparkford, Weston Bampfylde, Woolston and Henehill, all areas where slightly later, post-Norman Conquest

96 Cadbury Castle: the Late Saxon south west gate

sherds have also been found. Their scarcity probably has more to do with the preferred technology than the population size at that time. Cadbury Castle itself was to undergo one last phase of occupation in the early eleventh century AD for a very specific purpose. In either AD 1009 or 1010, Ethelred II moved the mint at Ilchester to Cadbury and instigated a rebuilding of the defences (*96*). It has been assumed that this was a temporary security measure but Alcock is surely right to recognise that the massive bank (it would have been nearly 6m wide from breastwork to rear revetment judging by the evidence from Site D) of imported lias slabs indicates the intention to establish a permanent settlement or *burh*. Coins minted at Cadbury have been found as far afield as Scandinavia but neither they nor the buildings in which they were made, or the moneyers housed, have been found on Cadbury itself. A few of their tools were found on Site BW, as well as two padlock and two mounted (door) keys, one of the latter in a pit along with decorated bone plaques for a casket (*colour plate 32*). A third padlock key was an unstratified find on Site D.

The only possible building was the cruciform foundation trench on the plateau which Freeman has suggested might be a second-century AD temple. I see no reason to doubt Alcock's view that it was for a church which was never built. This is consistent with his belief that the wall of the new *burh* was never completed as circumstance prevented Ethelred from doing so. Two moneyers left for other mints after his death in AD 1016 but one remained and was joined by another shortly afterwards, when they produced Cnut's distinctive coins to fulfil the harsh financial terms exacted by the new king upon Ethelred's defeated son, Edmund. Once that task had been completed, a tidying up operation preceded the resumption of an agricultural tradition which continues today.

Mediaeval ditches scoring the plateau were the boundaries of ploughed plots which started the destruction and smudging of the archaeological deposits that was to continue into the early 1960s when, paradoxically, cereal cultivation allowed Mary Harfield to pick up the finds which led to Alcock's excavations. In the interim a charter may have given permission for a castle to be built in John's reign. The castle was not built and it may be a different Cadbury! In the sixteenth century John Leland, a friend of the Hastings family who held the manor at North Cadbury during Henry VIII's reign, promoted Cadbury's connection with the legendary King Arthur. Massive boulders found on top of the defences in the south-west gate may have been a fraudulent attempt a couple of centuries later to show evidence that the hill was Camelot, but a more generous view is that they were the foundation for a chivalric folly. Subsequently mixed woodland was planted over the ramparts, providing cover for game birds tended by a keeper whose cottage was set on a levelled area on top of the third bank, close to King Arthur's Well. English Heritage has encouraged the removal of the woodland which contributes so much to the atmosphere of this remarkable hill and part of the outline of the cottage is now distinctly visible.

For a few summer months each year cattle are a reassuringly mundane presence on the slopes and plateau which they have to share with an increasing number of visitors drawn by the advertising of Somerset's Arthur-driven tourist industry. For me it will always be my place of refuge and recreation as a child, an inspiration in my teenage years and the playground for my own and other local children.

6

CONTINUITY, RUPTURE AND THE FUTURE

Cadbury Castle has been a conceptual core of the landscape for communities in the study area since the Early Neolithic without a discernible break. Even in the Early and Middle Bronze Age, for which there are few or no signs of settlement in it, the distribution of surrounding activity reveals it as a primary focus. During that period the twin barrow on Sigwells formed a platform from which a person could look at Cadbury then turn through 180 degrees and see Hambledon Hill, Dorset. Similarly, the first Saxon settlers buried on Hicknoll Slait were able to 'view' Cadbury and the Wiltshire hills to the east. Nowadays Cadbury's centrality is expressed in the number of houses and businesses called 'Camelot', 'Avalon' or, most bizarrely, 'Saxon's Hill'.

On the practical level SCEP has been able to show the long-term significance of particular boundaries. The most intriguing case is surely Sigwells, where the influence of one of the earliest long linear boundary systems known in Britain is clear cut until the later Middle Bronze Age. Subsequently many of its components fell out of use, superseded by an entirely new orientation, originating in the Late Bronze Age and persisting until the Roman period. In an unexpected twist the earlier system determined the layout of a later Roman scheme which survives in a modern farm track. In contrast, a Bronze Age scheme at Weston Bampfylde has structured the landscape without interruption up to the present.

It is probably true that certain estate boundaries pre-date the Roman occupation but the much smaller holding at Woolston Manor Farm is the best example of continuous core settlement with associated fields. In their 2000 years or more of existence, the larger units will have survived not only changes of the families controlling them but changes in the character of hierarchical control itself. Similarly the fields within the larger structures have frequently changed shape and size as they have accommodated differing agricultural regimes, levels of technological development and patterns of small-scale tenure. Progress has not been linear, rather it has been a pulse of varying intensity, of repeated expansion and contraction depending on the circumstances of the time, of lessons learned in the Bronze Age or at the end of the Iron Age being re-learned in the twentieth century, as cultivation causes soil depletion or new empires make the same mistakes as old ones.

We cannot fully comprehend the nature or significance of the rites associated with structured deposits but the repetition of particular patterns over time gives clues to issues of self-conception and identity. In a case such as the deliberate deposition of querns, we witness a procedure which extended far outside the study area. On the other hand the depositing of lower cattle jaws in ditches is a peculiarly local tradition with a duration comparable to that of receiving Christian communion. It is a practice which allowed a subversive expression of affiliation throughout the period of Roman occupation and may have contributed to a sense of communal unity when the Imperial system went into decline. As an aside it is noteworthy that the Romano-British example of the practice found in a natural stream (*97*, *53*) may have had a more authentic relationship with its origin. Ditches may have been surrogate natural water courses when the first mandibles were placed in them.

97 Middle Mead: deliberate deposit of a cattle jaw in a stream

Continuity, rupture and the future

Other rites seem almost a matter of fashion by comparison. During the three to four centuries spanning the period between the Sigwells metalworking enclosure and the Sheep Slait ringwork it became important to close dismantled structures or backfilled ditches with burnt stones, particularly those with a bluish colour from a lack of oxidisation. During the same period the red burnt stones lining the base of a shallow scoop at Milsoms Corner (*colour plate 11*) and the green and red querns from the metalworking enclosure are different facets of the same ritual scheme. Cold venous blue was surely death to arterial red's life and green's growth and regeneration. There are also hints of a more complex paradoxical symbolism in the way that red stones created by open fire were placed on the bases of the scoop and those of the metalworking enclosure's postholes (*colour plates 9 & 10*), deprived of air whilst the blue closure stones created in a closed environment weathered on the exposed surface. A change in practice appears to represent a change of affiliation in the case of Late Iron Age bowl deposits in ditches. The replacement of lower ditch-fill upturned cattle skulls (*colour plate 23*) as a closure practice by the deposition of bead rim pots (*colour plate 24*) marks a decisive shift towards the Dorset Durotrigan culture, further marked by inhumation of the dead.

SCEP has been fortunate to witness critical changes in production and the availability of technology. Early Neolithic hazel shells denote a continued reliance on sustainable natural resources, though as at places such as Yarnton, Oxfordshire, there was little sign of wild animal exploitation. On the other hand, stone axes and querns imply the generation of an imperceptible surplus for exchange, possibly in the form of labour (we should note the extraordinary workers' settlement found only months before the time of writing at Durrington Walls). In the Early Bronze Age the long linear bounding of large tracts of land began a process which would lead to a sense of property, ostentatious production and consumption, and depletion of the means, the soil. The Wiltshire middens are at once an expression of the problem and possibly an attempt to redress the balance, assuming that some of the material within them was returned to the land. In the Iron Age the pattern of naked exploitation changes, a sign of rising consciousness that resources needed to be managed with care if they were to be sufficient. The pits which in so many ways symbolise the subtexts of Iron Age life also had a fundamental practical role in the mediation of regeneration through death.

The discovery of the most complete Bronze Age metalworking layout in Britain has supported the hypothesis that it was the province of peripatetic craftsmen. This particular skill was one pretext for the gathering of diverse local communities which would enable the exchange of ideas, products, matable livestock and people in a society which might otherwise be unhealthily atomised. As such it gave the craftsmen great economic and ultimately, perhaps, political influence.

During the Middle Iron Age the once secret processes of metalworking were widely known and locally practiced, yet fairs with a much greater range of goods brought together people on marginal land, close to tribal boundaries, as at the seasonally busy Meare on the Somerset Levels. Within these communities some people would have had more access to prestigious goods or the best food, indeed it may have been members of the elite or their intermediaries who attended the fairs. However, the much-vaunted improved communications of the Roman occupation not only increased the divide between rich and poor, facilitated by the abstraction of wealth in coinage, but created discrete rich and poor communities, as surplus was commoditised for individual gain. Access to members of other communities and goods may have become more restricted for some poorer people, as town-based markets replaced seasonal craft centres. When fairs were resurrected in Mediaeval times they were controlled by the monarch's charter.

DIRECTIONS FOR HILLFORT AND LANDSCAPE STUDIES

The first objective of SCEP's methodology was to identify traces of Middle Iron Age activity around the hillfort, so notably absent from the surveys at Maiden Castle and, subsequently, Danebury. Extensive geophysical survey provided base maps for discrete landscape systems which were occasionally dated by regularly spaced test pits that, in themselves, provided ample evidence of surrounding Middle Iron Age occupation. Surface collection techniques performed poorly for this period and despite the application of geophysical survey, regular test pitting, shovel pitting and fieldwalking, the first published chronology of the pilot study on Sigwells proved substantially wrong when tested by excavations. The replacement of surface techniques by test pits targeting key geophysical anomalies made a huge positive impact on our ability to phase the development of the bounded landscape.

The regular test pits remain valuable as general indicators of activity for most periods, whilst simultaneously providing data about soil formation through time. In this way they have demonstrated that surface techniques are an entirely unreliable means for generating a representative landscape narrative. It is important to be aware that the build-up of soils in the valleys is not only a problem because it obscures the archaeological record beyond surface recovery, but because it is a symptom of intensive ploughing on hilltops which has already degraded friable pottery beyond visibility and is well on the way to doing the same to more durable pottery and lithics. It is this process which offers the best explanation for the project's failure to identify the Iron Age and Middle Bronze Age activity on Sigwells with regular test pits. Quite simply the plough had cut into natural paleosols or solid geology with sufficient frequency to remove all stratigraphy. In its early stages this process increased the visibility of the archaeology, but after years of ploughing

Continuity, rupture and the future

the finds 'disappear'. By then regular test pits were successful only if they dug into a cut feature but the problem is obviated by the introduction of targeted test pits. At face value the project's methodology has been unsuccessful in identifying Early Mediaeval archaeology. The currently received opinion is that there was little disruption to the productive landscape during that period. I would argue that, in fact, SCEP methodology has revealed a genuine down-turn in the rural economy but that nonetheless we are beginning to discern data from that phase.

There are current techniques which have only been used in a limited way, or not at all, which would increase our understanding of landscape economy, notably geochemistry and plant macrofossil analysis. The original research plan envisaged the incorporation of both but they were excluded from applications for funding because of concerns about cost. In anticipation of changing circumstances, soil samples have been retained from most test pit and excavation contexts since 2003 and a smaller number from excavations dating back to 1995. They have already been the object of magnetic susceptibility testing and analysis of the results will appear in future formal academic publications.

One aim of this book is to provide an example of what can be achieved by a group of amateur enthusiasts who, with training and experience, can become skilled practitioners in tasks ranging across geophysical survey, test pit and trench excavation

98 Cadbury Castle: Ralegh Radford and Leslie Alcock (right). *SCEP archive*

and recording, to finds analysis. Had I realised at the outset the degree of self-sufficiency the project required I would scarcely have believed it possible to achieve. Fortunately, after a gestation period of several years culminating in the basic methodological design first implemented in 1998, it grew organically, attracting people of intelligence and commitment who appreciated the need to carry out hard, physical, work or dull, repetitive, tasks to gain an overall view. Their achievement has been to demonstrate that there is a labour-intensive, but cost effective, means for generating a narrative for previously concealed aspects of the prehistoric landscape in a rural environment applicable to all periods. They have forced a re-conception of the relationship between hillforts and their landscapes and almost as an aside have made a major contribution to the study of prehistoric metalworking. Sadly, some of the first volunteers have not lived to see the results and it is my particular regret that the project's mentor and patron, Leslie Alcock (*98*), died in 2006.

The project's results reveal a methodological benchmark which many field researchers would prefer to ignore because of its labour intensity but which should be invoked as the scale against which to measure negative or thin evidence from other archaeological survey programmes.

APPENDIX: MAPS

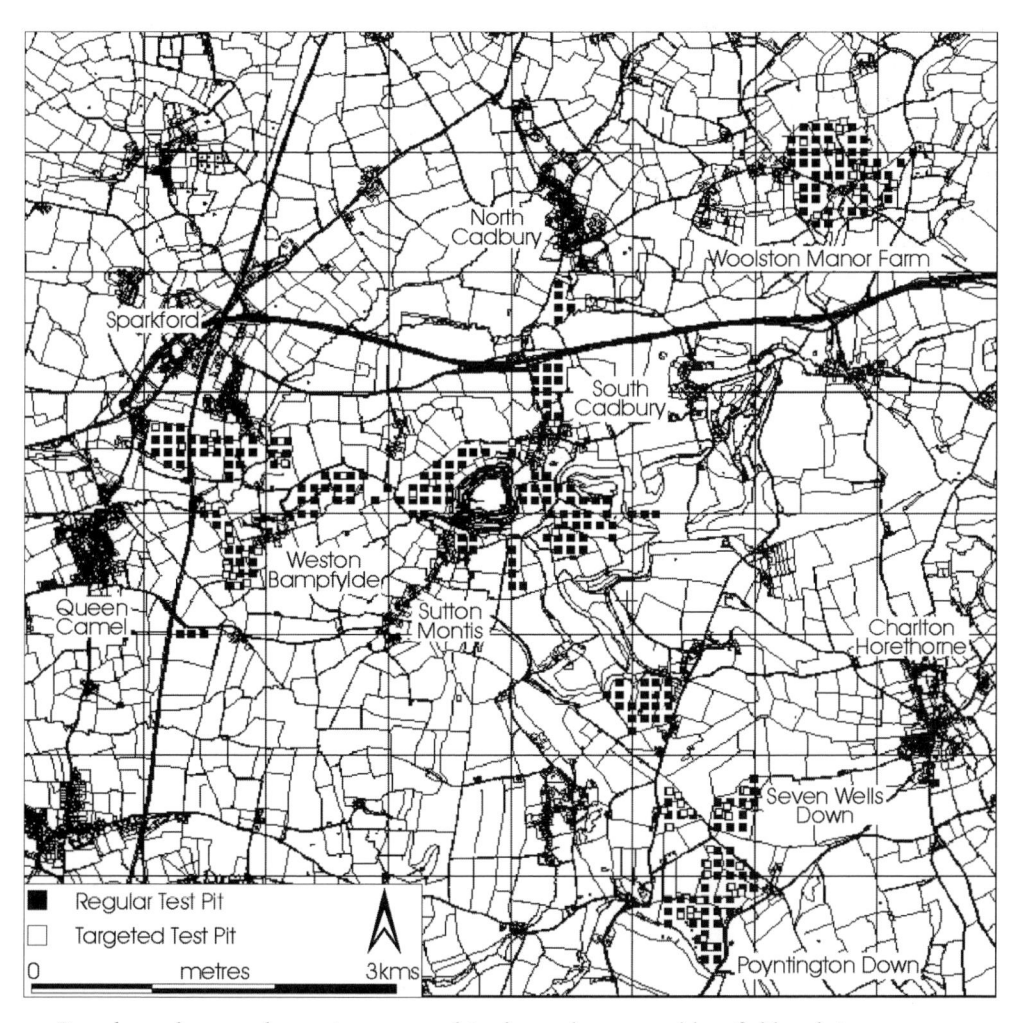

99 Regular and targeted test pits excavated in the study area, and key field and site names

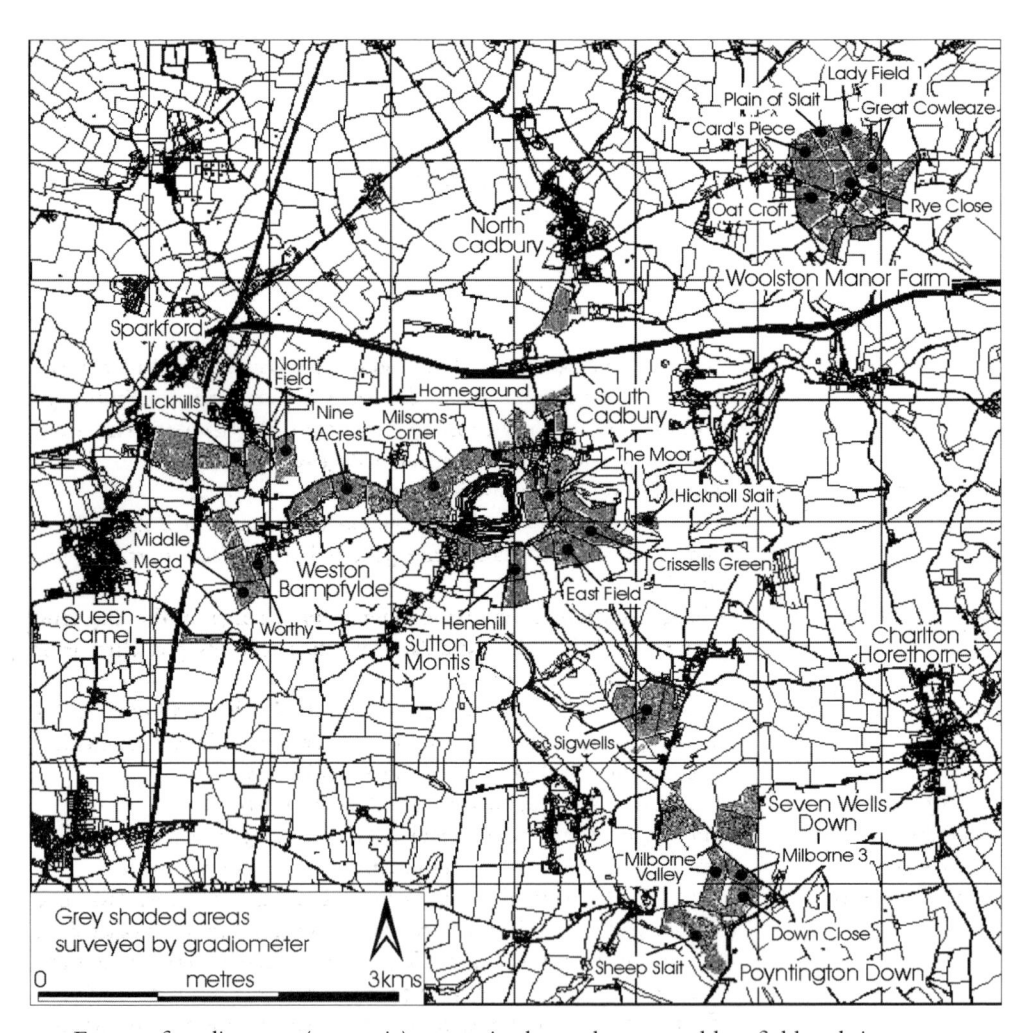

Cadbury Castle: The Hillfort and Landscapes

100 Extent of gradiometer (magnetic) survey in the study area, and key field and site names

GLOSSARY

barrow, round	An upturned basin-shaped mound usually associated with the burial of human remains either in the form of inhumation, primary (in situ) or secondary (redeposited) cremation. They range in date from the Late Neolithic to the Middle Bronze Age.
Bronze Age	The period from approximately 2300 BC to 750 BC.
flotation	The method for separating low-density (charcoal, snail shells) from higher-density materials (stone, pottery, bone) in environmental soil samples.
gradiometry	The geophysical technique for identifying changes in the magnetic properties of the soil, particularly effective at locating ditches, areas of burning and large pits.
hillwash (colluvium)	Soils on lower slopes, valley bottoms and sides derived from hilltops and upper slopes by natural hillslope recession or by a combination of cultivation and erosion by water and wind.
Iron Age	The period from approximately 800 BC to AD 50.
Mesolithic	The period from approximately 8000 BC to 3800 BC.
multivallate	An enclosure defined by more than one concentric bank.
negative evidence	The lack of a particular range of data in a particular area. This may be due either to a lack of activity during the period associated in the area, to total subsequent destruction of the material or the use of a research methodology inappropriate to the ground conditions (for instance, fieldwalking on an area covered by a deep hillwash)
Neolithic	The period from approximately 4000 BC to 2200 BC.
shovel pitting	The collection of finds through the sieving of a fixed amount of top- or ploughsoil at regular intervals.
sampling	The intermittent collection of data using a predetermined or random system.
test pitting, regular	Excavation over a given surface area to geological or other targeted deposits at predetermined intervals.
test pitting, targeted	Excavation of a restricted surface area determined by information from geophysical survey, fieldwalking, earthworks survey etc. from the surface to the geological or other targeted deposits.

FURTHER READING

HILLFORTS IN BRITAIN
Cunliffe, B. *Danebury: An Iron Age Hillfort in Hampshire: Vol. 6. A hillfort Iron Age hillfort in perspective* (Council for British Archaeology 1995)
Cunliffe, B. *Danebury Hillfort* (Tempus 2003 revised edition)
Sharples, N. *Maiden Castle: Excavations and field survey 1985-86* (English Heritage 1991)

CADBURY CASTLE AND ITS LANDSCAPE
Alcock, L. *'By South Cadbury, is that Camelot...' Excavations at Cadbury Castle 1966-70* (Thames & Hudson 1972)
Alcock, L. *Cadbury Castle, Somerset: The Early Mediaeval Archaeology* (University of Wales Press 1995)
Barrett, J., Freeman, P., & Woodward, A. *Cadbury Castle Somerset: The later prehistoric and early historic archaeology* (English Heritage 2000)
Cunliffe, B. *The Danebury Environs Programme: The prehistory of a Wessex landscape. Volume 1: Introduction* (English Heritage and Oxford Committee for Archaeology 2000)
Davey, J. *The Roman to Mediaeval Transition in the Region of South Cadbury Castle, Somerset* (British Archaeological Reports 2005)
Leach, P. *Roman Somerset* (Dovecote Press 2001) Archaeological survey
Tabor, R. *Regional perspectives in archaeology: from strategy to narrative* (British Archaeological Reports 2004)

PREHISTORIC BOUNDARIES AND FARMING
Fowler, P. *The farming of Prehistoric Britain* (Cambridge University Press 1983)
Reynolds, P. *Ancient Farming* (Shire Books 1987)
Yates, D. *Land Power and Prestige: Bronze Age field systems in southern England* (Oxbow 2007)

THE MILSOMS CORNER SHIELD
Coles, J., Minnitt, S. & Wilson, A. *Ceremony and Display: The South Cadbury Bronze Age Shield* (Somerset County Council)

INDEX

Numbers in **bold** are page numbers for relevant images

agriculture 19, 41, 46, 49, 54, 69, 99, 106, 114, 143, 154, 155, 176, 179, 181
Alcock, L. 10, 20-23, 39, 43, 53, 56, 69, 74-77, 82, 106, 107, 124, 150, 154, 156, 158, 159, 164, 167, 169-71, **181**, 182
Alfred, King 174
ammonite 133, **134**
Anglo-Saxon Chronicles 174
Arthur, King 19, 20, 174, 176
Arts and Humanities Research Council 11, 26
Ashe, G. 21
Avebury 107
Aveline's Hole 40
axes, bronze 47, 104, 105
axes, iron 107
axes, stone (*colour plate 3*), 40, 44

ballista bolts 158
Bantham 167
Barrett, J. 28
barrows, round 49, **50-52** , 54, 56
Belgae 114
belief 178-79
Bell, M. 32
Bennett, Revd J. 10, 15, 20, 56
Black, D. 38
Blenman, K. 141
bone, animal 67, 90, 96, 98, 122, 127, 134, 154, 166
bone, human – see human remains
bone, singular deposits 60, 86, 178

bracelets, gold 73, 83
Bradley Hill 166, 167
Bratton Seymour 22, 165
Brean Down (*colour plate 1*), 18, 50, 73, 83
Breiddin, The 66, 107
Brent Knoll (*colour plate 1*) 19, 50
brooches
    first century AD **131**, **132**, 135
    Iron Age **131**, **132**
    'massacre' 158, 159
    Roman 158, 159
    Saxon (*colour plate 30*), 170, 179
Bulleid, A. 20
burial
    cow 123
    dog **131**, **132**, 134, 136, **137**, 138
    human 22, 49, **50**, 59, 85, 91, 112, 118, **131**, **132**, 134, 135, 138, 139, 141, **146**, 147, 153, 154, 161, 162, 167, 172-74
    raven **131**, 139, **140**
    sheep **131**, **132**, 135, **141**
burnt mounds 57, 70
Bury Hill, Hampshire 152

Cadbury Castle (*colour plate 2*), 13, 43, 46, 69, 73, 74
    banks (*colour plate 16*), 21, 22, 44, 75, 81, 107-10, 116, 117, 153, 154, 162, 169, 170, **175**
    barracks 163
    burh 175
    gates 20, 44, 83, 84, 111, 117, 156-62, **175**
    geophysical survey 21, 121
    guard chambers 118, 157, **158**, 159, 162

187

hall 170, **171**
'massacre' (*colour plates 25, 26, 29*), 156-64
mint 175
physical setting (*colour plates 1, 2, 13, 17, 27*), 17-19,
pits 121, 122
rectangular structures 44, **82**, 83, **104**
roundhouses 82, 85, **104**, 108, 118, **119-21**
shrines 104, 139, 162, **163**
water sources 18
Cadbury Congresbury 167
Caerleon-on-Usk 163
Caesar, J. 150
Camden, W 20
Camelot 20, 176, 177
Camelot Reseach Committee 21
Cannington 167
Castle Farm, South Cadbury 164-67
clearance 41, 44, 49, 69
Cnut, King 175
cobbles 83, **104**, 126, 134, **135**, 162, 165, 170
coins
    Danegeld 175
    Iron Age 114, 147, **149**
    Roman 164
    Saxon 174
Coles, J. 88
Cooper, G. 11, 24, 168
Cranborne Chase 15, 43
cremation (sheep) 133, 134
Crissells Green, South Cadbury **52**-54
crucibles 106
crystal, quartz (*colour plate 14*), 98
Cunliffe, B. 10, 16, 17, 73, 75, 83, 105, 138, 139
Cunnington, M. 14
currency bars 153

dagger, rivetted 49
Danebury 16, 17, 30, 33, 75, 83, 105, 114, 118, 121, 124, 128, 138, 139, 142, 149, 152, 155
Danebury Environs Project 10, 33, 100, 114
Dartmoor Reeves 47
Davey, J. 26, 167, 168
de Carle, D. 154
diet 41, 45, 46, 67, 154, 155
ditches 142-47
    linear 16, 17, 47, 49, 54, 54-62, 79, 94, 102, 143, 164, 177
Dobunni 114

documentary 24, 34, 35, 168
Down Close, Seven Wells Down 51, 54
Dumnonii 114
Dundon Hill 19
Durotriges 114, 149, 161, 179

earthworks 115, **116**
Easter Annals 174
East Chisenbury 80
economy 45, 46, 70, 71, 98, 99, 147, 179, 180
    village 103
enclosures, circular 46
enclosures, rectangular **53**, 57, **58**, **59**, 69, 130-41, 145, 151
environment 38-40, 43, 67, 141
erosion 32, 46, 92, 93, 178, 180
Ethelred II, King 174, 175
excarnation 138
exchange 17, 65, 70, 179, 180
    marine 167

Fens, The 89
fieldnames 12, 24
field systems 11, 17, 47, 56, 71, 93, 94, **99**, 115, 151, 169
fieldwalking 23, 29, 31-33, **35**, 37, 168, 180
flint distribution
    Bronze Age **48**
    Bronze Age **55**
    Neolithic **17**
floors 41, 44, 45, 61, 69, 70, 84, 92, 98, 118, **125**, 126, **127**, 154, **155**, 160
flotation 38
Fraser, D. 171
Freeman, P. 11, 23, 164
furnace 65, 106, 165, 166

geology 19, **25**, 40, 54
geophysical survey 17, 21, 23, **24**, 33-37, 43, 49, **52**, **53**, 56, 83, 93, 121, 124, **129**, **130**, **184**
Gildas 168
glass
    beads 170, 173
    vessels 170
Glastonbury 167
    Lake Village 20
    Tor (*colour plate 1*), 18, 50, 51
Gosden, C. 17
Great Cowleaze, Woolston **116**, 169
Gussage All Saints 153

Index

Ham Hill 19, 150
Hambledon Hill 13, 43, 50
Harfield, M. 20, 176
Hawkes, C. 15-16
Hayward, L. 173
hazelnut shells (*colour plate 3*), 41, 44-45, 179
hearths (*colour plate 19*), 44, 45, 60, 112, 127
Henehill, Sutton Montis 169
Hengistbury Head 75, 147
Hicknoll Slait, Compton Pauncefoot 21, 22, **129**, 130, 174
hillforts 13-17, 77, 78
 decline 152
Hodson, F. 16
Homeground, South Cadbury 57, 58, 142, 151, 154, 155
horse harness **131**, **132**, 152
Hoskins, W. 174
human remains 53, 69, 85, 91, 122, 145, 156

Ilchester (*Lindinis*) 150, 162, 164-66, 169
 civitas 165
imperialism 148, 149
industry 128, 143
 textile 110, 111
Ine, King 174
Invasion
 Claudian 147, 156
 hypothesis 15
 Julian 113, 147, 150

John, King 176
Johnson, P. 23, 24, 43, 50, 83, 121, 124, 169
Jones, S. 147, 156, 159

labour
 professional 114
 student 164
 volunteer 26, 34, 114, 181, 182
Lamyatt Beacon 19, 167, 174
Leach, P. 25, 150
Leech, R. 166
Leland, J. 15, 19, 20, 176
Leverhulme Trust 11, 24, 114
Lock, G. 17
loomweights 57, 69, 106

Maddle Farm Project 30, 32
magnetic susceptibility 38
Maiden Castle 15, 43, 114, 129, 145, 152, 161
 landscape survey 33

marriage 67
Meare 20, 166, 180
Mendip Hills (*colour plate 1*), 18, 40, 43, 50, 162
metal sources 66, 162
metalworking 57, 63-69, 106, 123, 152, 153
 peripatetic (*colour plate 8*), 66, 70, 71, 99, 103, 179
metal work styles
 Arreton 47, 104
 La Tène 113, 122, 148, 154
 Hallstatt 74, 104, 105
 Ornament 56
 Taunton 56, 104, 105
 Wilburton (*colour plate 6*), 67
 Yetholm (shield) 89
middens 41, 80, 82, 83, 96, 106, 122, 151, 166
Milsoms Corner, South Cadbury 44, 49, 54, 58-60, 77, 120, 142, 144, 145, 151, 152
Moor, The, South Cadbury 144, 145
Morgan Evans, D. 20
moulds, clay casting (*colour plate 6*), 63, 66, 67, 79, **81**, 152, 153
Musson, C. 107

Nine Acres, Weston Bampfylde 164, 165
North Cadbury 21, 22
North Field, Weston Bampfylde 54
Northover, P. 89

oppida 150, 156
ovens 82, 111, 165, 166
 furniture 57, 69, 106

Palmer, R. 16
Penselwood 174
pilot study 34
pits
 Bronze Age 82
 cooking (*colour plates 4, 5*), 61, 67, 90, 120
 geophysical survey 128-30
 groups 128-42
 Iron Age (*colour plates 20-22*), 15, 83, 118, 121-25, 126, 127-33, 134-37, 138, 139-41
 Neolithic (*colour plate 3*), 44, 45
Pitt Rivers, A. 15, 21, 49
Poole, C. 75, 139
Potterne 80, 96
pottery
 Beaker **48**, 51, 52, 59

189

Corfe Mullen 160
Durotrigan (*colour plate 28*), 76, **148**, 151, 157, 160
Globular Urn 61, **66**
Grey Ware 163
Hembury/Carn Brea (*colour plate 3*), **42**, 44
Post Deveril Rimbury (Plain Ware) 77, **78**, 92
Potterne **78**, **97**
Samian 163, 167
Severn Valley
South West Decorated (Glastonbury) 76, **148**
Tintagel (*colour plate 30*), 167, 168, 170-**72**
Trevisker **55**, 60
pottery, phased distribution
   Early Bronze Age **48**
   Early Iron Age 100, **101**, 102, 117
   Early Neolithic **42**
   Early Romano-British **165**
   Late Bronze Age **78**
   Late Iron Age **148**, 157
   Middle Bronze Age **55**
   Middle Iron Age **113**, 116
   Post Roman 167-**72**
   Saxon 169
Poyntington Down 21
Ptolemy 113

Queen Camel 21, 165, 174
querns
   Bronze Age (*colour plate 7*), 65-68, 98
   Iron Age 110, 123, **131**, **132**, 145, 152, 155
   Neolithic 44, **45**
   sources 43, 65

Radford, R. 20, 21, **181**
Randall, C. 11, 26, 39, 67, 74, 124, 138
Richards, J. 31
ridge and furrow 92
ringworks, Late Bronze Age
   Mucking North Ring, Essex 97
   Sheep Slait, Dorset 80, 92-99, 125, 179
   South Hornchurch, Essex 97
Thwing, Yorkshire 98

sampling **25**, 27-31, 34, 35
scanning 31, 32
scoops (*colour plate 6, 11*), 57, 58, 64, 67, 84, 90, 118

Second Legion 156, 163
Seven Wells Down 46, 93
Shapwick 24, 31, 33
Sharples, N. 129, 152
Sheep Slait, Poyntington Down
   barrows **51**
   field system **94**, 97, 98
   finds **97**
   geophysics **93**
   Iron Age **125-27**, 128
   linear ditches **51**
   palisade **94**, 95, 96
   ringwork 80, 92-99, 125, 179
shields (*colour plates 12, 13*), 84, **85-88**, **89-91**, 92, 112, 152, **153**, 173
shovel pitting 24, 34-**36**, 180
shrines 83, 104, 105, 139, 153, 162
Sigwells, Charlton Horethorne 23, 33, **34**, 49, 50, 57, 129-41, 150, 151
   Bronze Age enclosure (*colour plates 4-10*), 61, **62-65**, 66-69
   finds **66**
   geophysics 34
   Iron Age enclosures **131-33**
   Iron Age pits **131**, **132**, **134-37**, 138, **139-41**
   linear ditches 49, **50**
Skowranek, C. 66, 67
soil chemistry
Somerset Levels 18, 33, 89
South Dorset Ridgeway 43
South East Somerset Archaeological and Historical Society 23, 24
Spears 158, 173
special deposits 135
   animal skulls (*colour plates 20, 23*), 122, **131**, **132**, 135-138, 144, 167
   associated bone groups **131**, **132**
   cattle jaw **60**, 68, 84, 90, 167, **178**
   closure (*colour plates 7, 9, 10*), 68, 69, 90, 96, 133, 179
   ditches 60, 98
   hazelnut shells 41, 44, 45
   postholes (*colour plates 9, 10*), 68, 85
   pots 44, 61, **85**, 92, **131**, **132**, 133, **134-37**, 145, 151, 160, 167, 179
   quern (*colour plate 7*), 44, 45, 68, 179
   scoops (*colour plates 6, 11*), 69, 84, 90
   single bone 60, 84-86, 91, 167
   stones, burnt 68, 69, 84, **85**, 90, 91, 96, 133, 179

Spratling, M 152
St George Gray, H 10, 20
Stanford, S. 15, 16
Stevens Cox, J. 20
Stonehenge Environs Project 31
Strabo 114, 149
structures
    rectangular 44-46, 96. 105, 106, 133, 153
    round **59**, 64, **65**, 89, 90, 92, 105, 108, 110, **111**, 117-22, 132, 142, 152-**55**
    villas 165
Stukeley, W. 20
Suddern Farm 112
survey techniques – see fieldwalking; geophysics; scanning; shovel pitting; test pitting
swords (*colour plate 6*), 67, 122, 174

Tacitus 113
territory 43, 49, 71, 180
test pits 11, 39, 43, 100
    regular 34, 36, 57, 114, **183**
    targeted 93, 115, 154, **183**
Thames Valley 89, 96, 97, 150
tin 66
Tintagel 20, 167
tools
    agricultural 56, **57**, 153
    metalworking 64, **66**
    textile (*colour plate 18*), 123

tracks 43, 44, **45**, **46**, 47, 49, 54, **58**, 61, 69, 72, 83, 97, 98, 102, 105, 108, 109, 112, 114, 115, 117, 118, 131, 134, 142, **143**, 151, 164

Vespasian 150

Warre, Revd F. 15
water courses
    Axe, river 73
    Cam, river 19, 56, 102, 114, 165
    Henshall, brook 54, 145, 161, 169
    Parrett, river 19, 174
    Yeo, river 19, 93, 162
water sources 67, 68
Wessex Hillforts Survey Project 17
Weston Bampfylde 43, 54, 57, 102, 106, 114, 143, 145, 152, 167
Wheeler, M. 15, 21, 161
Whitesheet Hill 43
Wilson, A. 87
Wiltshire Conservation Centre 87
Woodward, A. 75, 76, 81, 118, 149, 157, 159, 160
Woodward, P. 43
Woolston Manor Farm 54, 61, 77, **80**, 102, 128-130, 152, 164, 166
Worlebury 15

Yates, D. 47, 71, 80, 98
Yeovil Archaeology and Local History Society 23